"In a world of a wrongly supposed benign globalization on the one hand, and various forms of militant reactionary movements on the other, millions of people are on the move looking for a new homeland. But everywhere the politics of fear and exclusion seem to predominate. In a thoughtful, yet critical engagement with the philosophies of Levinas and Derrida, Andrew Shepherd argues that the fundamental human reality need not be an inevitable violence between the self and the other leading to a proliferation of 'gated' communities. Instead, a redeemed relationality expressed in 'communion' and radical hospitality is a normative possibility. This is so, because in the embrace of the radical Other, the Messiah, all social, ethnic, economic, and ideological differences have been absorbed and transcended to make way for the 'community of the Beloved.' This passionate book makes philosophical and theological discourse prophetic. May we all come under its spell!"

—CHARLES RINGMA

Regent College, Vancouver;
Asian Theological Seminary, Manila;
The University of Queensland, Brisbane

The Gift of the Other

Princeton Theological Monograph Series

K. C. Hanson, Charles M. Collier, D. Christopher Spinks,
and Robin Parry, Series Editors

The Gift of the Other

Levinas, Derrida, and a Theology of Hospitality

Andrew Shepherd

With a Foreword by Steven Bouma-Prediger

PICKWICK *Publications* · Eugene, Oregon

THE GIFT OF THE OTHER
Levinas, Derrida, and a Theology of Hospitality

Princeton Theological Monograph Series 207

Pickwick Publications
An Imprint of Wipf and Stock Publishers
199 W. 8th Ave., Suite 3
Eugene, OR 97401

www.wipfandstock.com

ISBN 13: 978-1-62032-766-1

Cataloguing-in-Publication data:

Shepherd, Andrew.

    The gift of the other : Levinas, Derrida, and a theology of hospitality / Andrew Shepherd ; foreword by Steven Bouma-Prediger.

    xii + 264 pp. ; 23 cm. Includes bibliographical references.

    Princeton Theological Monograph Series 207

    ISBN 13: 978-1-62032-766-1

    1. Hospitality—Religious aspects—Christianity. 2. Lévinas, Emmanuel. 3. Derrida, Jacques. I. Bouma-Prediger, Steven. II. Title. III. Series.

BV4647.H67 S47 2014

Manufactured in the U.S.A.

Contents

Foreword

Few today would doubt the claim that violence seems pervasive in contemporary society. Whether reading the local newspaper or the global online news, whether watching the latest film or listening to the newest music, violence of one sort or another seems omnipresent. The violence of our late-modern age, furthermore, seems embedded in competing claims about boundaries and identities and what some philosophers call our relationship to "The Other." Some people cheerily claim that boundaries are (or soon will be) no more, since modern technologies are shrinking the walls and distances that separate us. Such shrinkage will, these optimists argue, render violence a thing of the past. Others claim that the promise of such technological mastery is illusory. These cultural observers worry that the next technology is just domination by another name. Meanwhile an all too precious few worry about the plight of refugees and strangers in our midst and strive to offer hospitality to those who are homeless in an increasing number of ways.

In his fine book *The Gift of the Other*, Andrew Shepherd dives into these deep waters and presents a timely and powerful argument for why we Christians ought to resist the multiple forms of violence that tempt us and why we ought to offer hospitality to the homeless in this age of multiple displacements. In the first half of the book Andrew explains and critiques the views of postmodern thinkers Emmanuel Levinas and Jacques Derrida. While finding much of merit in Levinas and Derrida, Andrew also identifies how they view alienation and hostility as intrinsic to human being-in-the-world. Despite their best intentions these thinkers conceive of human existence as inevitably adversarial and thus they cannot construe the world in terms of an ontology of peace and communion. For Derrida especially, violence is inescapable, since intersubjectivity itself is always already violent, and hence there is no credible hope that hostility can be overcome.

In the second half of the book Andrew cogently argues that the Christian doctrines of the Trinity, creation, sin, and redemption—properly understood—provide robust resources for a theology and practice of genuine homemaking and homecoming. Violence need not be, since we humans are persons gifted, called, and named by the triune God of love. In essence, Andrew presents a careful case for a theological rehabilitation of the concept of hospitality. By attentively reading Scripture, mining the riches of the Christian theological tradition, and engaging contemporary thinkers, Andrew roots the practice of hospitality to the stranger in rich theological soil. This soil includes some of the wisest of aged saints, such as Irenaeus, Athanasius, and Gregory of Nyssa, along with more recent voices such as Barth, Bonhoeffer, Moltmann, and Zizioulas.

As Andrew insists, pace many of the postmodern philosophers, violence is not woven into the warp and weft of creation but a distortion of the shalom-filled way of being God intended for all creation. Difference does not necessarily mean conflict. Mutuality and reciprocity are potentially achievable and real—both the work of human hands and the gift of divine grace. Self and Other are not necessarily engaged in a Hobbesian war of all against all, but capable of authentic communion. What Andrew in *The Gift of the Other* calls ecclesial hospitality reminds me of what Brian Walsh and I, in our book *Beyond Homelessness: Christian Faith in a Culture of Displacement*, call sojourning community. We are neither well-ensconced home-dwellers, safe and secure in our fortresses of sameness, nor are we nomads perpetually peripatetic, on the road, heading nowhere. We are neither eternal dwellers nor eternal wanderers, but Christ-following sojourners at home on the way, traveling with others as people of memory, community, and hospitality.

God's blessings to you as take up and read this stimulating work of timely scholarship. May you in reading it be inspired to engage in the practice of ecclesial hospitality—the disciplined habit of offering a gracious and joyous welcome to the strangers at your door. In so doing, you bear witness to God's great good future of shalom.

Steven Bouma-Prediger

Preface

ALL THEOLOGY TAKES PLACE IN THE CONTEXT OF A COMMUNITY OF FAITH and there are numerous others whose gifts—time, wisdom, and other resources—have enabled and enriched this project. My thanks, firstly, to Mark Forman for the discussions around New Zealand songwriter Dave Dobbyn's anthem to hospitality, "Welcome Home," which gave renewed impetus to my long-time theological reflections upon the importance of the practice of "hospitality." Kodesh Christian community in Auckland, New Zealand, was our home during the early stages of research and their provision of emotional and practical support demonstrated the very ethos I sought to write about. I am grateful too for our next-door-neighbors and friends, Marcel and Daphne, who provided me with both office space and rich fellowship.

This book has its origins in a doctoral thesis undertaken through the University of Otago, New Zealand. I acknowledge with gratitude my supervisor Murray Rae, whose patience, theological astuteness and erudition ensured that the quality of work was of a far higher standard than would have been achieved without his input and guidance. Likewise, I am grateful to fellow postgraduate students who offered comments and reflections on draft sections of the work and to Ingrid, Mark, and Jono for their painstakingly proofreading. Suffice to say, any mistakes contained within stem therefore from my own oversights or omissions.

The axiomatic nature of the saying "hospitality begins at home" is one that I can testify to. Without the support, aroha, and patience of my wife Ingrid and daughters Julia, Kristin and Natalie this project would never have been possible. It is a gift and joy to practice "hospitality" with them to the many family, friends, and strangers who pass through our home and lives. Finally, but most significantly, I acknowledge my father's English foster parents, without whose profound act of radical hospitality during the Second World War—the welcoming of a sick, orphaned infant into their home and loving of him as their own—neither my father, and therefore nor I, would be here today. Accordingly, this work is dedicated to the memory of Ted and Florence Kennell.

Introduction

A World for All?

WE LIVE IN AN INTRIGUING PERIOD OF HUMAN HISTORY. THE LAST CENtury has seen the exponential growth of the human population—from 1.5 billion in 1900, to 2.5 billion in 1950, to over 7 billion today. Yet, with this burgeoning growth in the human population, there is also perhaps a greater awareness than at any stage of human history of our essential interconnectivity and inter-relatedness. The collapse of both ideological and physical barriers erected during the Cold War, and the technological and economic "developments" of the last two decades mean that, notwithstanding the differences and diversity of "human civilizations" spread across the globe, there is a growing realization of our existence as inhabitants of a single "global village."

This sentiment, that at the beginning of the twenty-first century contemporary human civilization is characterized by a new reality of "connectedness" and "openness" is conveyed in the script of an advertisement screened on New Zealand television for tertiary education institution, *The Open Polytechnic of NZ-Kuratini Tuwhera.* Accompanied by the image of a developing baby in a placenta, the advert begins, "Your world, was once a small one. As you grew, it did too. But now your world is bigger than it's ever been before and it has no boundaries." To a montage of digitally-animated images—the word *boundaries* disintegrating into butterflies, closed circles being burst open, and climaxing with the distinctly iconic New Zealand image of new life, a koru—the advert continues its acclamation of this new "open" world, proclaiming:

> We are no longer limited by tradition, language or distance.
> What once was fixed is fluid and there's no one path.
> We work more jobs, learn more skills and share more ideas than
> ever before.

And, we don't have to stop our lives to start new ones.
When we understand this: Our world is infinite.
Everything is possible. Everything is open.

Evangelists for this social phenomenon of globalization and for the new "open" world with no boundaries it gives rise to, are not hard to find.[1] Commentators such as Thomas Friedman point to the enormous economic growth and the associated increase in quality of life that has stemmed from the implementation of neo-liberal economic theories and an adherence to free-market doctrine. The globalised market, free of the limiting boundaries of economic regulation, such proponents argue, is one in which all have equal access to the market-place, and thus to greater wealth and happiness. Similarly, American computer scientist Vint Cerf, the so-called "Father of the internet," in an article in *The Observer*, speaks glowingly of the way in which the world-wide-web has the capacity to expand and improve people's world. Echoing the laudatory tone of the Open Polytechnic's advertisement agency, Cerf asserts that, the "social repercussions" of the internet "will take decades to be fully understood, but it has already done much to *benefit the world*. It has provided access to information on a scale never before imaginable, lowered the barriers to creative expression, challenged old business models and enabled new ones."[2] Cerf states: "After working on the internet for more than three decades, I'm more optimistic about its *promise* than ever. It has the potential to change unexpected parts of our lives: from surfboards that let you surf the web while you wait for the next wave to refrigerators that can email you suggested recipes based on the food you already have."[3]

Cerf concludes his ode to the promise of the internet declaring: "We're at the cusp of a truly global internet that will *bring people closer together* and democratize access to information. *We are all free* to innovate

1. To speak of the social phenomenon of "globalization" is itself rendered problematic by both the complexity and the apparent contradictions contained within the phenomenon. A description offered by the United Nations Development Programme in its *Human Development Report 1999* recognizes these competing characteristics of "globalization" and provides a useful working definition: "Globalization, a dominant force in the twentieth century's last decade, is shaping a new era of interaction among nations, economies and people. It is increasing the contacts between people across national boundaries—in economy, in technology, in culture and in governance. But it is also fragmenting production processes, labour markets, political entities and societies. So, while globalization has positive, innovative, dynamic aspects—it also has negative, disruptive and marginalizing aspects."

2. Cerf, "If You Thought the Internet Was Cool," 35. Emphasis added.

3. Ibid. Emphasis added.

on the net every day and *we should look forward to more people around the world enjoying that freedom*."[4]

But does the process of "globalization" really offer a new world of unfettered promise, a new reality of unlimited opportunities and *freedom* where "everything is possible, everything is open"? While living in a world celebratory of *difference*, is it really true that in such a world "all voices are heard"? Is the "global village" of the twenty-first century really the land of *promise* that many suggest?

While acknowledging that a percentage of the 7 billion village inhabitants do now have a higher "quality of life" in terms of basic material needs—food, water, shelter and health—than at any other time in human history, there is also no denying that such advances in standards of living, the benefits accrued from participation in the global free-market, are by no means equally, nor universally, shared. Indeed, while Cerf speaks of the promise of refrigerators offering gastronomic inspiration to the culinary-challenged, a large percent of the globe's population are still not connected to the world-wide-web and, at least 1.4 billion citizens of the village living in *extreme poverty* will go to bed each night with neither food in their non-existent refrigerators nor, more significantly, with sufficient food in their stomachs.[5] While the minority of individuals living in "developed" Western countries may indeed feel as though life offers an infinite smorgasbord of new opportunities and that their existence is characterized by a multiplicity of "open" paths they can choose to travel down, for a significant number of twenty-first century global village inhabitants life consists of an endless struggle for survival.

For, despite the rhetoric of "freedom" and "openness," what is increasingly apparent is that in the global village, free and equal access to the market-place where goods are bought and sold is an illusion. Far from the well-lit and palatial architecture of the village centre, down murky and hidden lanes, one can discover inhabitants with terrible tales of the dark side of village life. In the global village of the twenty-first century, "the undeniable progress of inclusion" is, as Croation theologian Miroslav Volf suggests, built upon "the persistent practice of exclusion."[6] Volf believes there are three modes of exclusion that feature in the contemporary world: (1) exclusion as *elimination* or in its more benign form as *assimilation*;

---

4. Ibid. Emphasis added.

5. Statistics on the percentage of the global population who are connected to the internet vary between 34–75 percent.

6. Volf, *Exclusion and Embrace*, 60.

(2) exclusion as *domination*; and, (3) exclusion as *abandonment*. Volf's classification of "exclusion" provides a useful framework which we will employ to reflect further upon the current global reality, and specifically, to understand the plight of those who, rather than enjoying the so-called benefits of the new "open world" are, to use a biblical motif, contemporary "aliens and strangers," existing on the margins of global civil society.

Elimination and Assimilation, Domination and Demonization

The first mode of exclusion, *elimination*, is undoubtedly the most brutal, and due to its lack of subtlety and sophistication, when exposed, is also widely condemned. From the haphazard clearing of squatter camps and slums on the periphery of the major metropolitan cities of the "developing" world—where millions seek to eke out an existence for themselves from the drips that "trickle-down" from the economic fountain-head higher up—through to the "death squads" that roam the streets of major cities in Guatemala, Brazil, Honduras, Argentina, Colombia and Philippines, engaging in "social cleansing," *elimination* is the macabre, vicious and socially-unacceptable mode of exclusion.[7]

In contrast to the silenced voices of these "undesirable" squatters or street children are another stratum of *aliens and strangers* and new breed of "global traveler": the international migrant worker. Unlike *undesirables*, who with no access to capital therefore have no role either as *producers* or *consumers* in the global village, international migrant workers find themselves playing a lowly, but critical role in the functioning of the global economy.[8] Attracted to industrialized/developed countries with greater economic rewards than their own countries of origin, these migrant workers provide the cheap and unskilled labor required in industrialized economies—engaging in work that inhabitants of these countries no longer wish to do—and simultaneously assist their home economies through the sending back of remittances. Often having little or no legal rights,

7. For an account of the existence of "death squads" that *eliminate* social *undesirables*, see MoLoney, "Vigilante Heaven," 22–24.

8. In 2008, the United Nations estimated that there were over 200 million migrants worldwide (up from 180 million in 2000), 2.9 percent of the total global population. Of this figure less than 10 percent are regarded as refugees, the rest are part of the growing phenomenon of migrant workers, leaving their "homelands" in search of lives of greater economic prosperity elsewhere. United Nations, *Trends in International Migrant Stock*.

international migrant workers find themselves subsumed and *assimilated* into the global world market, their employers ensuring that the slave-wage they receive is earned through their blood, sweat, tears, and often their lives.[9]

And what of those countries, regions, or people who, too visible to be *eliminated* nor easily *assimilated*, find themselves living an uneasy existence on the margins of the global system? Such is the hegemonic logic of the ideology of "social inclusion" that those outside the global market, construed as threats, must be, for the security of the system, brought back into the fold. Alistair Kee provocatively concludes:

> Any group that is described as "excluded" cannot be allowed to get away. They must be brought into the body of mainline society. Attention is focussed on their plight and their problems. Ideology chuckles behind its hand. No evaluation is required of mainline society. Its essential health and virtue are simply assumed. Its part in exclusion is never examined. The possible and potential role of the excluded in the regeneration of society is not even envisaged. The fact of their exclusion is not seen as a symptom of disorder, neither as a witness to corruption. . . . Blessed are those who exclude. And twice blessed are the excluders who graciously attempt to draw the victims into the kingdom of this world.[10]

With the defeat of the old enemy of communism, global capitalism is now the only economic "game in town." Yet, despite the celebration of *difference* and *otherness*, such is the assimilative and totalizing dynamic at work that ultimately capitalism, in a twist of irony, subsumes, conflates and *consumes* these differences. In a bid to ensure its own perpetuity, those unenthusiastic about this new game must be, either by "carrot" or "stick," cajoled or coerced into participation in the global market. Such re-inclusion of the unfortunate "excluded" occurs in a number of ways. While new legislative bodies such as the World Trade Organization (WTO) penalize nations who are averse or unwilling to abide according to the rules of global capitalism, another mechanism employed is that of military intervention.

9. Multiple reports from the International Labour Organisation, Human Rights Watch, and other agencies draw attention to the ongoing abuse that characterize the lives of "international migrant workers" in various global contexts. For one example of the plight of such migrant workers, literally engaged in the construction of "islands of happiness" while living lives of exploitation and abuse see Human Rights Watch, "Island of Happiness."

10. Kee, "Blessed Are the Excluded," 352.

Countries who refuse to participate in the new "open" market, whose resources remain locked up unable to be accessed, are perceived as a risk to the stability and security of the global market, and find themselves termed as "threats to civilization," "haters of freedom,"[11] and demonized as "terrorists." Such "rogue states," potential participants in the "axis of evil" are accordingly brought, through the process of *liberation*—i.e., Volf's second mode of exclusion: *domination*—out of international exile and into the global economy, their oil, gas, and other natural resources now made available to trans-national corporations (TNCs). In a seldom noticed irony therefore, despite their supposed differences, both neo-liberal markets (*assimilation*) and neo-conservative foreign policy *(domination)* achieve the same result: *enforced inclusivism.*

Indeed, this close collaboration between the economic interests of TNCs and US foreign policy, far from being conspiratorial, is rather a frank admission made by ardent advocates of globalization. Thomas Friedman, in his influential book *The Lexus and the Olive Tree*, stresses that the benefits of capitalism and democracy will not be brought about automatically through the dynamic of the free market. Rather, Friedman sees America as "the ultimate benign hegemon and reluctant enforcer" and contends that "the hidden hand of the market will never work without a hidden fist. . . . And the hidden fist that keeps the world safe for Silicon Valley's technologies to flourish is called the U.S. Army, Air Force, Navy and Marine Corps."[12] Whether those who have been on the receiving end of this *unveiled* fist are fully aware of the benefits of capitalism and democracy they have received, is, of course, at least to Friedman, a moot point.

The nonsensical, absurd-like nature of this ideology, in which one is either within the system or demonized as the "Other," a "terrorist" who threatens the established status quo, is observed by British journalist, Robert Fisk. In a striking passage, Fisk notes how the face of evil changes depending on one's perceived enemy at the time and also how "us–them" logic commits one to an endless cycle of conflict.

> "Terrorism" is a word that has become a plague on our vocabulary, the excuse and reason and moral permit for state-sponsored violence—*our* violence—which is now used on the innocent of the Middle East ever more outrageously and

---

11. "They hate us and they hate freedom and they hate people who embrace freedom." United States President, George W. Bush's dictum explaining the motivation for terrorism, given during an interview on Al Arabiya television, 6 May 2004.

12. Friedman, *Lexus and the Olive Tree*, 466.

promiscuously. Terrorism, terrorism, terrorism. It has become a full-stop, a punctuation mark, a phrase, a speech, a sermon, the be-all and end-all of everything that we must hate in order to ignore injustice and occupation and murder on a mass scale. Terror, terror, terror, terror. It is a sonata, a symphony, an orchestra tuned to every television and radio station and news agency report, the soap-opera of the Devil, served up on prime-time or distilled in wearingly dull and mendacious form by the right-wing "commentators" of the American east coast or the *Jerusalem Post* or the intellectuals of Europe. Strike against Terror. Victory over Terror. War on Terror. Everlasting War on Terror. Rarely in history have soldiers and journalists and presidents and kings aligned themselves in such thoughtless, unquestioning ranks. In August 1914, the soldiers thought they would be home by Christmas. *Today, we are fighting for ever. The war is eternal. The enemy is eternal, his face changing on our screens.* Once he lived in Cairo and sported a moustache and nationalized the Suez Canal. Then he lived in Tripoli and wore a ridiculous military uniform and helped the IRA and bombed American bars in Berlin. Then he wore a Muslim Imam's gown and ate yoghurt and planned Islamic revolution. Then he wore a white gown and lived in a cave in Afghanistan and then he wore another silly moustache and resided in a series of palaces around Baghdad. Terror, terror, terror. Finally he wore a kuffiah headdress and outdated Soviet-style military fatigues, his name was Yassir Arafat, and he was the master of world terror and then a super statesmen and then, again, a master of terror, linked by his Israeli enemies to the terror-*Meister* of them all, the one who lived in the Afghan cave.[13]

So, what of those who have nothing to contribute to this all-inclusive global system? What becomes of the *Others* who cannot, either through *elimination/assimilation* or *co-option/domination*, be brought to participate as *consumers* or *producers* in this new world order? Speaking of this third mode, exclusion as *abandonment*, Volf adeptly observes that: "If others neither have the goods we want nor can perform the services we need, we make sure that they are at a *safe distance* and close ourselves off from them so that their emaciated and tortured bodies can make no inordinate claim on us."[14]

---

13. Fisk, *Great War for Civilization*, 464–65. Emphasis added.
14. Volf, *Exclusion and Embrace*, 75. Emphasis added.

Such is the plight of the Palestinians. Living for sixty years as refugees, without an officially recognized home, crammed into small tracts of inhospitable land, the Palestinians find themselves *abandoned*, their predicament only gaining international attention when politicians—whether US, European, Palestinian or Israeli—reinitiate the peace process arguably for their own electoral purposes, or, when the volatile powder keg erupts into a new round of tit-for-tat violence and thus offers news-worthy scenes for public titillation. Likewise, Africa remains the "forgotten continent." While TNCs tap natural resources such as oil in Nigeria and diamonds in the Democratic Republic of Congo and local power-brokers use the revenue from such deals to maintain their control, the vast majority of the population continues to live in dire poverty, wracked by the catastrophic effects of global climate change, natural disasters, civil war, and AIDS.[15]

While international worker-migrants are *assimilated* and "rogue states" *dominated*, millions of others find themselves *abandoned*, as they flee from the violence, oppression, and starvation that often wrack their countries. These conditions frequently stem either directly from the intervention of their *liberators-dominators* or begin to emerge as their nation suffers the negative consequences of a forced *assimilation* into the new free-market economy.[16] While those seen to pose a risk to the security of the system are demonized, becoming larger-than-life figures, the *abandoned others* are for all intents and purposes, invisible. A UNICEF report, reflecting on the "disturbing muted response" to the fact that 25,000 children die each day in the global village, comments:

> They die quietly in some of the poorest villages on earth, far removed from the scrutiny and the conscience of the world. Being

15. The Democratic Republic of Congo is one example of this structural dynamic in which TNC's profit from their access to natural resources, Western *consumers* therefore receive new products, and local militia are thus provided with funds for armaments to assert their control, all-the-time while the local population remains empty-handed, doomed to lives of ongoing poverty and misery. See Hari, "How We Fuelled the Deadliest War."

16. Important to note is the increasing number of a new category of refugees, that of the Internally-Displaced Peoples (IDP's). In Sudan, Colombia, and as already mentioned, Congo, the forced relocation of population as well as brought about by violence, human rights abuses, or natural disasters, is also often the result of so-called "development displacement." For example, rural poor in Colombia displaced from their land for the "development" of palm-oil plantations—an ingredient in many luxury items found on the shopping list of the world's richer countries.

meek and weak in life makes these dying multitudes even more
invisible in death.[17]

Keeping the Other Distant

If however, we live in a new "open" and "fluid" global village, one with
"no boundaries," how is the Other actually held at a *safe distance?* There
is a chilling poignancy in a passage written by French economist Jacques
Attali, who in the early 1990s predicted:

> By 2050, 8 billion people will populate the earth. More than
> two-thirds will live in the poorest countries. Seeking to escape
> their desperate fate, millions will attempt to leave behind their
> misery to seek a decent life elsewhere. But neither the Pacific
> nor the European spheres will accept the majority of poor no-
> mads. They will close their borders to immigrants. Quotas will
> be erected and restrictions imposed. (Renewed) social norms
> will ostracize foreigners. Like the fortified cities of the Middle
> Ages, the centres of privilege will construct barriers of all kinds,
> trying to protect their wealth.[18]

Twenty years after being penned, Attali's frightening vision of the
future is already coming to pass. In a disturbing trend, as the "war on
terror"[19] being waged by "free" countries exacerbates violence and in-
stability in certain regions, thus contributing to the diasporas of global
refugees, concurrently the domestic immigration policies of these same
countries become more restrictive. In response to the threat of "global terror," border security of these "open countries" is beefed up and legislative
bodies pass stringent new immigration policies making access to "lands of
freedom" for would-be asylum seekers and refugees increasingly difficult.
In spite of the rhetoric of freedom, the open boundaries constitutive of the
globalised village, in reality, is largely limited to the flow of bits and bytes
on the world wide web, or to capital transferred in international financial
markets.

The incongruous nature of this emerging global village is perhaps
most clearly demonstrated in the construction of the "US$1 million-
per-mile border security fence" on the US-Mexico border, a fence that

---

17. UNICEF, *Progress of Nations 2000*, 20. Emphasis added.

18. Attali, *Millennium*, 74–78.

19. Re-branded during the later years of the presidency of George W. Bush to:
"struggle against violent extremism."

"delineates, for the first time, a frontier that was previously just a four-strand cattle fence at best."[20] Caroline Moorehead, in her deeply moving book, *Human Cargo*, reflects on this inconsistency in which wealthy nations desire cheap migrant labor while simultaneously seeking to ensure that the unwanted masses do not pose a threat to their lives of privilege and wealth. Referring to the already existing portion of this fence in California as part of the American's "myths of arrival," Moorehead writes:

> The fence is part of the myth. It is about a poor country looking across the border and seeing money and opportunities, all the lures that enticed the first settlers, and wanting to have a share in them. It is about the way that, ever since anyone can remember, poor Mexicans have migrated north in search of the American dream, which for them has meant jobs in agriculture, factories, the building and service industries, and the way they have been welcomed and discouraged by turn, and have simply kept on coming, even during times of determined and brutal rejection, and the way that the Americans have feared being swamped and losing their own identities and livelihoods. It is the old and simple story of exclusion.[21]

The actions of tightening restrictions on refugees and asylum-seekers and the construction of literal fences to prevent the "poor nomads" from entering are not, however, unique to the United States but are, as Attali predicted, a growing global phenomenon. Citizens of such far-flung countries as Australia and New Zealand have watched—with either disgust or delight dependent on one's political persuasions and ethical convictions—as asylum-seekers and refugees arriving to their distant shores have experienced similar hostile receptions. In many cases, refugees have been met with imprisonment in solitary confinement—due to the suspected "security threat" they pose—internment in processing camps in the inhospitable environment of the Australian outback or on remote South Pacific islands, or, relocation to their troubled "homeland" of origin. The words of Hannah Arendt, written to describe her own sense of statelessness and exile in the turmoil of World War Two, ring as true in the supposedly new reality of the "global village" today as the day they were written. "Contemporary history," Arendt wrote, "has created a new kind of human being—the kind that are put in concentration camps by their

---

20. Von Drehle, "New Line in the Sand," 28.
21. Moorehead, *Human Cargo*, 72.

foes and internment camps by their friends."[22] Fellow Jewish writer, Elie Wiesel, succinctly summarizes the lot of contemporary *aliens and strangers*: "Refugees live in a divided world, between the countries in which they cannot live, and countries which they may not enter."[23]

This fear of the unknown Other and the desire to keep at a distance those seen as a threat to "centers of privilege" and "wealth" is not simply the domain of national governments, outworked in immigration policy and the construction of border barriers. Indeed, the very popularity of such political decisions is indicative of the extent to which an atmosphere of fear has become prevalent in many affluent Western nations. The breakdown of community in contemporary Western societies, which sociologists refer to as a loss of "social capital" or the decline of "neighborliness," is evidenced in the increasing popularity of exclusive "gated communities" and the growing fascination with fence-building within suburbia.[24] Despite the statistics showing that physical and sexual abuse is far more likely to be perpetrated by those known by or related to the victim, the myth of "stranger-danger" continues to be expounded by concerned parents to their children. No longer allowed to walk to school, children arrive daily at the school gate, disembarking from the "safe" cocoons of family vehicles.

But if such is the state of our contemporary world, how are we to respond to the plight of the "poor nomads," to those who seem to bear the burden of the benefits that others reap from the new "openness" and "freedom" of global consumer capitalism? What individual and communal practices and virtues are required to respond to the immediate plight of the excluded Other and to provide an alternative way of peace for societies and countries?

The Philosophy and Practice of Hospitality

Seeking to respond to such questions, in recent years the concept of *hospitality* has gained eminence in philosophical and religious writings, with the work of philosophers Emmanuel Levinas and Jacques Derrida being

22. Arendt, *Jew as Pariah*, 56, 60.

23. Source unknown. Quoted in Moorehead, *Human Cargo*, 1.

24. The classic text on this phenomenon is Putnam, *Bowling Alone*. While Putnam sees the decline in volunteerism as evidence of the loss of "social capital," another indicator of such a shift in societal dynamics is the physical composition of our built environments. "Gated-communities" and the building of fences are simply physical embodiments of the desire to protect one's own wealth from the threat of others, a desire grounded in a paranoia about the Other, which is nourished by the discourse of fear perpetuated by contemporary media.

heralded as of particular merit. In contrast to the conflictual and competitive logic of both capitalism and the discourses of "terror," in which it is the unknown nature of the Other which provides the fertile soil for seeds of fear, Levinas and Derrida affirm and celebrate both the *difference* and the incomprehensibility of the Other. The Other, they argue, is not first and foremost one to be understood, but rather one whose ethical plight we are called to respond to. Drawing upon the Abrahamic religions which shape their own intellectual and cultural identity, Levinas and Derrida point to the practice of hospitality, the *welcoming of the stranger*, as the constitutive element of what it means to be human.

But does a philosophy and the practice of hospitality have the capacity to overcome the totalizing discourses of global capitalism and the "war on terror" which are relentlessly reinforced by the media of our technological societies? Christine Pohl, in her book *Making Room: Recovering Hospitality as a Christian Tradition*, notes the way the rich Christian tradition of hospitality has, over the centuries, gradually been eroded by other social and economic discourses and dynamics. Early Christianity was a social movement known for its care of the sick and poor and its attention to the needs of the stranger. However, with the development of commercial inns during the sixteenth century, the growing secularization of civic institutions such as hospitals and "poor relief houses"—originally established by the Church in Europe in the seventeenth and eighteenth century—and with the State taking on welfare in the twentieth century, the practice of hospitality, Pohl contends, has largely been forgotten by the Ecclesia. This ancient ethical practice has now become the domain of secularized commercial and professional institutions and become increasingly depersonalized and institutionalized.[25]

Consequently, for the vast majority of those in Western societies, the concept of "hospitality" is immediately associated with the—arguably oxymoronic—term: "hospitality industry." Accordingly, the Other is, at best, construed as simply another *producer/service provider*, one with whom, in our patronage of bars, restaurants, or accommodation providers we enter into contractual agreements to give or receive *hospitality* services. Alternatively, with the contraction of the welfare state, and the accompanying emergence of specialized and "professionalized" caring agencies the Other is conceived as a *consumer/client*, to whom professional carers, are *duty-bound* to provide quality care and service.

25. See Pohl, *Making Room*, 7, 53.

On the other hand, at worst, the Other, is conceived according to the dictates of the respective discourses of paranoia and the market. The Other is thus the dangerous stranger, a potential terrorist or criminal who has come to harm, and thus not to be granted welcome, but best kept at a *safe distance*. Or, following the atomized logic of the "free-market"[26]—the Other is construed as a competitor for the limited resources available for consumption, one with whom we may collaborate for mutual advantage but who, once no longer useful for our advancement, we discard.[27]

The Project in Brief ·

This work contends that the practice of hospitality, offered as a corrective to the exclusions which blight our global village, is itself only possible if one first responds to the distortion of the notion of hospitality itself brought about by the ideologies of the contemporary world. That is, the recovery of the life-giving and redemptive practice of hospitality depends upon the concept of hospitality first being freed from its cultural captivity to the dual discourses of the market and fear, and also from the assumptions which underlie many postmodern philosophies offered in the name of "hospitality." Such a freedom is only conceivable if the concept of hospitality is reestablished upon theological foundations.

To undertake this rehabilitation of the term *hospitality*, this work is split into two sections. In section one we begin by considering the philosophies of Emmanuel Levinas (chapter 1) and Jacques Derrida (chapter 2). Such has been the significance of their work in drawing Western thought back to questions of ethics, and the plight of the Other, that it would be remiss to ignore their valuable contribution. Levinas' belief in the "infinite responsibility" that the subject has before the "transcendence of the Other" and Derrida's advocating of a radical "unconditional hospitality," offer powerful reinterpretations of the nature of human ethics. In engaging with their respective thought, two questions will be addressed: (1) The extent to which their philosophical work is able to respond to the particular problems of the contemporary predicament outlined above, and therefore, (2)

---

26. Perhaps expressed must concisely in former British Prime Minister Margaret Thatcher's famous quip: "Society? There is no such thing! There are individual men and women and there are families . . ."

27. Television programs such as the reality-show *Survivor* vividly portray such an approach to human relationships in which "alliances" are made and broken depending on whether they best serve one's own interests.

the extent to which their philosophical projects offer resources for the development of a more explicit Christian theology of hospitality.

While sympathetic towards the Levinasian-Derridean project, there are particular aspects of their thought which are troubling. Chapter 3 offers a summary of both the strengths and deficits of the work of Levinas and Derrida and highlights the major areas of concern. Ultimately, it is noted that our unease regarding Levinasian-Derridean notions of self-hood, inter-human relationality, eschatology and teleology, stems from a deeper concern regarding the *differential* ontology upon which their ethical account is grounded.

In section two drawing upon the rich imagery that saturates Levinas' and Derrida's philosophies of hospitality, while simultaneously responding to potential conceptual weaknesses within their thought, we seek to offer a constructive theological account of the ethic of hospitality. The question of ontology is the focus of chapter 4. In contrast to the differential ontology offered by Levinas and Derrida, the Christian Doctrines of Trinity and Creation, we argue, offer an alternative and distinctive ontological account. With particular engagement with the thought of Orthodox theologian John Zizioulas, we contend that hostility and violence, far from being woven into the fabric of *being*, exist due to the failure of humanity to accept the *free* gift of the Trinitarian God and live in God's all-encompassing love and grace. It is communion and hospitality, not conflict and hostility, which are primordial.

In chapter 5 we argue that it is the gift of Christ which overcomes this *hostility* brought about by humanity. In contrast to moral and exemplarist Christologies, we claim that the life and death of Jesus only has salvific merit if understood ontologically as a gift-giving event of the Triune God. Responding to accusations of *violence* proffered by our philosophical interlocutors and also by atonement critics, we posit that God's salvific action of overcoming this *hostility*, and the responsive action of speaking about this—that is, "doing theology"—are both non-violent, non-coercive activities.

Having outlined an alternative ontology and given an account of how, in Christ, the *hostility* that exists in the world has been overcome, chapters 6 and 7 extrapolate the nature of human personhood and ethics that flow from this. In chapter 6 in contrast to the "fractured" and "divided" self offered in Levinasian-Derridean thought, we suggest that authentic personhood is discovered as the self, through the "disturbing" and renovating work of the Spirit, is brought into an ecclesial existence. Our account both affirms the concept of a self-identity while recognizing that this identity is shaped by a relation with *otherness* and, due to its eschatological nature, still awaits a final revealing. Chapter 7 then gives an account of the shape that human relations, reconfigured according to this ontology of *communion*, take. We suggest that lives undergoing the transforming work of the Spirit and incorporated into the Ecclesia are re-narrated and thus drawn into a different script, one in which genuine gift-giving and the welcome of the stranger once again becomes possible. Such gift-giving/hospitality rather than stemming from duty, becomes a free outward expression of the love that the self, dwelling in Christ, is experiencing.

A Final Preface

Finally, before commencing further, it is important also to explicate clearly what this work is, and what it is not. While offering a close reading of Levinas and Derrida, by no means should the work be conceived of as primarily one of "pure" philosophical theology. Neither though, does it fit neatly into the various categories subscribed to by some, whether that be systematic theology, political theology, public theology, biblical theology, historical theology, contextual theology, or Christian ethics![28] Rather, the work itself, one could suggest, is consciously "hospitable." Seeking to respond to the themes outlined above—the issue of hostility and exclusionary violence in the world—the work draws widely upon different theologies and traditions—Catholic, Orthodox and Protestant—to develop its case.

To employ a metaphor from the realm of hospitality, the work could therefore perhaps be best construed as a dinner party. As with all good parties, there are a number of notable—one could almost say distinguished guests—who through sheer force of personality and insight, provide a focal point to the conversations that ensue. As well as Levinas and Derrida, other significant contributors to our conversation include John Zizioulas, John D. Caputo, Kathryn Tanner, Miroslav Volf, Karl Barth, Dietrich Bonhoeffer and John Milbank. None of those assembled dominate the conversation, but rather the collective pooling of their wisdom and reflections hopefully lead to a greater clarity and coherence. Such, at least, is the hope of the host of this conversation and author of what follows.

28. As such, if a category is required, then the work could be regarded as an example of constructive theological ethics.

Also, akin to good parties, sometimes the intensity of conversation with multiple voices can—particularly if one is an introvert—become a little overwhelming. On such occasions it is often the retreat from the hubbub of the party and a secluded one-on-one conversation which often proves to be the most stimulating, provoking and enriching. Accordingly, in the second section of this work between each chapter, we change pace and tone and accompany *side by side* a number of Biblical characters, entering, as it were, into a *tête à tête*. It is our hope that the "deconstructive" and imaginative rereadings of the well-known biblical narratives offered in these interludes will reiterate and reinforce themes already raised and thus further develop the case we seek to put forth.

With such prefatory remarks now made, it is time to swing open the doors, for the guests to arrive, and for the conversation to begin.

1

The Transcendence of the Other and Infinite Responsibility

The Philosophy of Emmanuel Levinas

A Brief Biography

BORN IN LITHUANIA IN 1906, WHERE HE RECEIVED A TRADITIONAL JEW-ish education, Emmanuel Levinas began his philosophical studies at the University of Strasbourg in 1923. It was in Strasbourg that Levinas also met and began a lifelong friendship with Maurice Blanchot. In 1928, Levinas moved to Freiburg University to continue his studies in the emerging field of phenomenology being pioneered by Edmund Husserl. Here at Freibrug, Levinas also met and sat under the teaching of Martin Heidegger, whose work *Sein und Zeit (Being and Time)* (1927) had recently been published. In 1930, Levinas became a naturalised French citizen and with the outbreak of World War Two was ordered to report for military duty. Captured by the German Army, Levinas spent the duration of the war as a prisoner of war, living in separate barracks with other Jewish prisoners. While his wife and daughter, with the assistance of Blanchot, found safe refuge in a French monastery, all of Levinas' extended family, including his mother-in-law, father and brothers, were victims of the holocaust. That such experiences of hostility and hospitality clearly shape Levinas' own philosophical thought, is made overt in his second major work *Autrement qu'être ou au-delà de l'essence—Otherwise than Being or Beyond Essence* (1974) which Levinas dedicates: "To the memory of those who were clos-est among the six million assassinated by the National Socialists, and of the millions on millions of all confessions and all nations, victims of the same hatred of the other man, the same anti-semitism."[1]

After the war Levinas became a teacher at, and then later director of, a private Jewish High School in Paris, but it was not until 1961 that he gained a tertiary academic position, teaching philosophy at the University of Poitiers. Nevertheless, his work was already having a major influence on the thought of other French thinkers such as Jean-Paul Satre, Jean Wahl and Jacques Derrida. An essay on Levinas' thought by Derrida—"Violence and Metaphysics" (1965)—along with the translation into English of his major works *Totalité et infini: essai sur l'extériorité* (*Totality and Infinity*) (1961) and *Autrement qu'être ou au-delà de l'essence* (*Otherwise than Being or Beyond Essence*) (1974), led to a growing awareness of Levinas' philosophy amongst a broader audience.[2] In recent decades numerous philosophers, religious thinkers and Christian theologians—including notably Pope John Paul II—have shown a keen interest in his thought.[3] Levinas died in Paris on December 25th, 1995.

Totality, Infinity, and the "Other"

At the heart of Levinas' philosophy is an attempt to change the nature of the Western philosophical tradition. According to Levinas, the Western philosophical tradition since the time of Plato has been obsessed with questions of ontology. This has resulted in philosophies in which the ethical relations between particular beings is subservient to universal mediators such as the Form/*eidos* in Plato, *Spirit* in Hegel or Being/*Dasein* in Heidegger.[4] For Levinas, the problem is that in attempting to ground meaning in *being-ontology*, these philosophies have failed to give an account of the relationship between ethical beings. While showing the influence of Husserl and Heidegger, Levinas rejects philosophy's traditional preoccupation with metaphysical questions about being and epistemological concerns giving instead priority to ethics. In contrast to traditional philosophy—*the love of wisdom*—Levinas seeks through his work to articulate a *wisdom of love*.

For Levinas, "totalizing" philosophies, in their quest to find meaning in ontological questions, are indifferent to the "Other" and exhibit anti-humanist tendencies which lead ultimately to the horrors of the

---

1. Levinas, *Otherwise than Being*.
2. Derrida, "Violence and Metaphysics"; Levinas, *Totality and Infinity*.
3. See, e.g., Zimmermann, "Karol Wojtyla and Emmanuel Levinas."
4. Critchley, introduction to *Cambridge Companion*, 11.

Holocaust.[5] Such philosophy, Levinas believes, is not merely incapable of responding to the ethical challenges posed by the post-holocaust world, but is, itself, partly to blame for a world of inhumanity.[6] In contrast to these philosophies of *Totality*, Levinas articulates a philosophy of *Infinity*, encountered through the transcendence of the Other.

Levinas' philosophical project centers around his use of Descartes' idea of *Infinity*. In his *Third Meditation* Descartes argues that when we think of and conceive of infinity, infinity itself exceeds the idea one can have of it. While for Descartes this structure of infinity was applied to the divine—God always exceeds the concept of God that we as subject think— Levinas takes this Cartesian concept and applies this formal structure of thought, which emphasizes inequality, non-reciprocity and asymmetry, to the relationship of the subject to the human Other. For Levinas, the absolute exteriority of the other person means that the Other can never be assimilated or incorporated into a totality. The Other is infinite. This idea of infinity, this pre-ontological alterity, is the core principle around which Levinas' philosophy is gathered. This pre-ontological alterity is *beyond essence* and *being* but its formal structure can be seen in the concrete phenomenon of our ethical interaction with the Other. For Levinas, "the ethical relation with the face of the other person is the *social* expression of this formal structure."[7]

Ethics as First Philosophy

Levinas shares the concern of other French post-structuralist writers that in seeking to express an understanding of God through the language of ontology, God ceases to be transcendent. Within this perspective Western metaphysical philosophy is constantly in danger of lapsing into forms of

---

5. Levinas contends that the history of Western philosophy from Plato to Heidegger "can be interpreted as an attempt at universal synthesis, a reduction of all experience, of all that is reasonable, to a totality wherein consciousness embraces the world, leaves nothing outside of itself, and thus becomes absolute thought." Levinas, *Ethics and Infinity*, 75.

6. While rarely mentioned by name in his writings, many commentators see Levinas' work as an extended polemic against his former teacher Martin Heidegger. Initially attracted to the ontological philosophy of Heidegger with its search for meaning in Being (*Dasein*), Levinas saw Heidegger's support of National Socialism during the Second World War as the inevitable socio-political-ethico corollary of the totalizing and thematizing nature of such philosophical enquiry.

7. Critchley, introduction to *Cambridge Companion*, 15.

idolatry.[8] Further, his concern is that such metaphysical thinking draws attention away from the plight of the Other and fails to lead people into ethical action. A long passage from *Totality and Infinity* illustrates Levinas' concern towards these twin problems of potential idolatry and ethical inaction which he sees as inherent in Western philosophy, and articulates his response to these problems. He writes:

> To posit the transcendent as stranger and poor one is to prohibit the metaphysical relation with God from being accomplished in the ignorance of men and things. The dimension of the divine opens forth from the human face. A relation with the Transcendent free from all captivation by the Transcendent is a social relation. It is here that the Transcendent, infinitely other, solicits us and appeals to us. The proximity of the Other, the proximity of the neighbor, is in being an ineluctable moment of the revelation of an absolute presence (that is, disengaged from every relation), which expresses itself. His very epiphany consists in soliciting us by his destitution in the face of the Stranger, the widow, and the orphan. The atheism of the metaphysician means, positively, that our relation with the metaphysical is an ethical behaviour and not theology, not a thematization, be it a knowledge by analogy, of the attributes of God. God rises to his supreme and ultimate presence as correlated to the justice rendered unto men. The direct comprehension of God is impossible for a look directed upon him, not because our intelligence is limited, but because the relation with infinity respects the total Transcendence of the other without being bewitched by it, and because our possibility of welcoming him in man goes further than the comprehension that thematizes and encompasses its object. It goes further, for precisely it thus goes into Infinity. The comprehension of God taken as a participation in his sacred life, an allegedly direct comprehension, is impossible, because participation is a denial of the divine, and because nothing is more direct than the face to face, which is straightforwardness itself. A God invisible means not only a God unimaginable, but a God accessible in justice. Ethics is the spiritual optics. ... metaphysics is enacted where the social relation is enacted- in our relations with men. There can be no "knowledge" of God separated from the relationship with men. The Other is the very

---

8. Bruce Ellis Benson argues that the work of phenomenologists such as Levinas, Derrida and Marion is an attempt to speak of the Transcendent without lapsing into conceptual idolatry. Benson, *Graven Ideologies*.

locus of metaphysical truth, and is indispensable for my relationship with God.[9]

Levinas' response to the perceived problems of idolatry and ethical inaction in Western philosophy is thus structured around twin moves—an advancing of a form of metaphysical atheism, and the elevation of the Other to a quasi-transcendental position.[10] For Levinas, "intelligibility of transcendence is not ontological. The transcendence of God can neither be said nor thought in terms of being."[11] In place of transcendental ontological philosophy Levinas postulates a form of transcendental-subjectivity in which we encounter the Infinite-the Transcendent in our ethical encounter with the Other. Levinas proposes not only that "ethics is the spiritual optics" but asserts that "metaphysics is enacted in ethical relations"[12] and states that "Morality is not a branch of philosophy, but first philosophy."[13] According to Levinas, such a philosophy based in transcendental-subjectivity, overcomes the totalizing and idolatrous nature of ontological philosophy and leads to ethical obedience. Hence he states: "ethical signification signifies not *for* a consciousness that thematizes, but *to* a subjectivity that is all obedience, obeying with an obedience preceding understanding."[14]

Thus, Levinas seeks to replace a metaphysic of transcendental ontology with a metaphysic of ethical response. His philosophy is, as termed by one of his commentators Edith Wyschogrod, a form of "ethical metaphysics."[15]

Heteronomy and Alterity as Irreducible Structure

In his first major and critically acclaimed work, *Totality and Infinity*, Levinas posits that the priority of the ethical, "an irreducible structure upon

9. Levinas, *Totality and Infinity*, 78–79.

10. Note the use of the word "quasi-transcendental." While it is clear that Levinas believes knowledge and experience of transcendence takes place in the ethical encounter with the Other, it is less clear whether he actually sees the Other as the Divine itself. The blurring of lines between the "Other" that is encountered and a possible Divine Other, beyond essence, is a puzzling aspect of Levinas' philosophy still debated by scholars.

11. Levinas, *Of God Who Comes to Mind*, 77.

12. Levinas, *Totality and Infinity*, 79.

13. Ibid., 304.

14. Levinas, *Of God Who Comes to Mind*, 77.

15. Wyschogrod, *Emmanuel Levinas*.

which all other structures rest," is demonstrated in the Transcendence of the Other.[16] According to Levinas' account, human subjectivity itself is evidence of the heteronomous and asymmetrical relationship between the subject and the Other, of the pre-ontological relation to and structure of alterity. While post-Enlightenment Western philosophical thought emphasized that subjectivity is based on autonomy, Levinas argues that human subjectivity is based on heteronomy. Human subjectivity is grounded not in consciousness—*I think therefore I am*—but in our "infinite responsibility" to the Other—*Here I am!* It is this basic structure of alterity and heteronomy that is the basis for human subjectivity and ethics. Levinas states: "My ethical relation of love for the other stems from the fact that the self cannot survive by itself alone, cannot find meaning within its own being-in-the-world, within the ontology of sameness."[17]

If one conceives that one understands or comprehends the Other, and if the relationship with them is based on correlation, reciprocity and equality, then one has actually totalized the Other. Instead, according to Levinas our relationship with the Other is based on the absolute priority of the Other and therefore is non-reciprocal and asymmetrical by nature. This transcendence of the Other, the formal structure of the priority of ethics over ontology, is conveyed succinctly when Levinas writes:

> The transcendence of the Other, which is his eminence, his height, his lordship, in its concrete meaning includes his destitution, his exile [*depaysement*], and his rights as a stranger. I can recognize the gaze of the stranger, the widow, and the orphan only in giving or in refusing; I am free to go or to refuse, but my recognition passes necessarily through the interposition of things. Things are not, as in Heidegger, the foundation of the site, the quintessence of all the relations that constitute our presence on the earth (and "under the humans, in company with men, and in the expectation of the gods"). The relationship between the same and the other, *my welcoming of the other, is the ultimate fact*, and in it the things figure not as what one builds but as what one gives.[18]

That the "welcoming of the other, is the ultimate fact" is expressed in *Totality and Infinity* by Levinas' assertion that "the subject is a host."[19]

16. Levinas, *Totality and Infinity*, 79.
17. Levinas, "Ethics of the Infinite" 60.
18. Levinas, *Totality and Infinity*, 76–77. Emphasis added.
19. Ibid., 299.

The Face

In *Totality and Infinity*, Levinas attempts to speak of this transcendence of the Other made manifest to the subject, through the complex concept of the Face. According to Levinas, the face of the Other appears to us and demands our response, but its appearance is not a phenomenon as one would normally understand it. "The face" Levinas writes, "is present in its refusal to be contained. In this sense it cannot be comprehended, that is encompassed. It is neither seen nor touched—for in visual or tactile sensation the identity of the I envelops the alterity of the object, which becomes precisely a content."[20] Concerned with the way in which human perception and consciousness seeks to control and "totalize" phenomenon, Levinas' concept of the face epitomizes the broader tendencies of Levinas' philosophy—an emphasis on the flesh and blood of physical reality, but a desire to avoid any system of totality. The face operates, therefore, as an epiphany, an element which is not captured through consciousness, but rather which captures the subject with its ethical demands. For Levinas, the "gaze" of this face "supplicates and demands."[21] Elsewhere he states: "the relation with the Other, discourse, is not only the putting in question of my freedom, the appeal coming from the other to call me to responsibility, is not only the speech by which I divest myself of the possession that encircles me by setting forth an objective and common world, but is also sermon, exhortation, the prophetic word."[22] For Levinas:

> The face with which the other turns to me is not reabsorbed in the representation of the face. To hear his destitution which cries out for justice is not to represent an image to oneself, but is to posit oneself as responsible, both as more and as less than that being that represents itself in the face. Less, for the face summons me to my obligation and judges me. The being that presents himself in the face comes from a dimension of height, a dimension of transcendence whereby he can present himself as a stranger without opposing me as obstacle or enemy. More, for my position as *I* consists in being able to respond to this essential destitution of the Other, finding resources for myself.

---

20. Ibid., 194.

21. Ibid., 75. Levinas' concept of the gaze of the Face is more apparent and striking in French—where the word *visage* means both "to gaze" and "face."

22. Ibid., 213.

The Other who dominates me in his transcendence is thus the stranger, the widow, and the orphan, to whom I am obligated.[23]

Infinite Responsibility and Hospitality

The theme of human obligation to the Other, predicated on the theory that human subjectivity is grounded in alterity, that is, the "welcoming of the other," is developed and intensified in Levinas' ongoing philosophical work. In *Totality and Infinity* the response of the subject to the Other appears at times dependent on cognition: "To recognize the Other is to recognize a hunger. To recognize the Other is to give."[24] However, in his later work, *Otherwise than Being or Beyond Essence* Levinas develops the concept of "infinite responsibility" and argues that the subject is responsible to the Other prior to any consciousness or action. Levinas writes: "Responsibility for the Other is not an accident that happens to a subject, but precedes essence in it, has not awaited freedom, in which a commitment to another would have been made. I have not done anything and I have always been under accusation—persecuted. The ipseity, in the passivity without arche characteristic of identity, is hostage. The word *I* means *here I am*, answering for everything and for everyone."[25]

This emphasis is apparent too in, *Humansime de l'autre home—Humanism of the Other* (1972). "Infinite responsibility" of the subject to the Other here is predicated on the theory that "responsibility" to/for the Other exists in a pre-ontological, pre-original structure of alterity. Levinas asserts that the "infinite responsibility" of the subject is "responsibility prior to freedom . . . prior to all free engagement. . . . It is a responsibility before being intentionality."[26] Later, in the same work, Levinas writes:

> No one can stay in himself; the humanity of man, subjectivity, is a responsibility for others, an extreme vulnerability. The return to self becomes interminable detour. Prior to consciousness and choice, before the creature collects himself in present and representation to make himself essence, man approaches man. He is stitched of responsibilities. Through them, he lacerates essence. It is not a matter of the subject assuming responsibilities or avoiding responsibilities, not a subject constituted, posed in itself and for itself like a free identity. It is a matter of

23. Ibid., 215.
24. Ibid., 75.
25. Levinas, *Otherwise than Being*, 114.
26. Levinas, *Humanism of the Other*, 52.

the subjectivity of the subject, as non-indifference to others in limitless responsibility, limitless because it is not measured by commitments going back to assumption and refusal of responsibilities. It is about responsibility for others, where the movement of recurrence is diverted to others in the "moved entrails" of the subjectivity it tears apart. Foreign to self, obsessed by others, un-quiet, the Ego is hostage, hostage in its very recurrence of an ego endlessly failing to itself.[27]

This movement in Levinas' thought, in which "infinite responsibility" shifts from the ontic world of language and intention to the pre-ontic ultimate transcendence of subjectivity, is summarized well by Robert Bernasconi, who writes: "I am radically responsible for the other prior to any contract, prior to having chosen or acted, indeed prior to my taking up a subject position in relation to an other. In *Otherwise than Being* the responsibility inherent in subjectivity is prior to my encounter with an other, whereas *Totality and Infinity* had located the possibility of ethics in the concrete encounter that realized the formal structure of transcendence."[28]

The development of Levinas' ethical metaphysics and the absolute uncompromising nature of his understanding of the "infinite responsibility" of the subject for the Other are evidenced by the increasingly powerful, emphatic—and arguably, violent—nature of Levinas' rhetoric. Just as the subject as "host" gives way to the subject as "hostage," so the epiphany of the face of *Totality and Infinity* that "supplicates and demands" and that presents itself in discourse as "sermon, exhortation, the prophetic word" is now replaced by more extreme terms such as "substitution," "persecution," "expiation" and "obsession." Levinas now describes the "infinite responsibility" that one has for the Other, thus:

> Vulnerability is obsession by others or approach to others. It is *for others*, from behind the *other* of the stimulus. An approach reduced neither to representation of others nor to consciousness of proximity. To suffer by the other is to take care of him, bear him, be in his place, consume oneself by him. All our love or hatred of one's fellow man as a thoughtful attitude supposes this prior vulnerability this "moaning of the entrails" mercy. From the moment of sensibility, the subject is *for the other*: substitution, responsibility, expiation. But a responsibility that I did not assume at any moment, in any present. Nothing is more passive

---

27. Ibid., 67.
28. Bernasconi, "What Is the Question," 242.

than this challenge prior to my freedom, this pre-original challenge, this sincerity.[29]

The corporeal nature of Levinas' language is not purely figurative or metaphorical. In Levinas' thought, the ethical demand of the transcendent Other, the "infinite responsibility" of the subject to the Other, works itself out in the physical world which we inhabit and his "ethics," as Bernhard Waldenfels suggests, "are rooted in a phenomenology of the body."[30] The transcendence of the Other is not a mystical transcendence, but rather is a transcendence that calls the subject to "infinite responsibility" and ethical action in the physical world of being. Levinas writes:

> *But the transcendence of the face is not enacted outside of the world,* as though the economy by which separation is produced remained beneath the sort of beatific contemplation of the other (which would thereby turn into the idolatry that brews in all contemplation). The "vision" of the face as face is a certain mode of sojourning in the home, or—to speak in a less singular fashion—a certain form of economic life. *No human or interhuman relationship can be enacted outside of economy; no face can be approached with empty hands and closed home.* Recollection in a home open to the Other—hospitality—is the concrete and initial fact of human recollection and separation; it coincides with the Desire for the Other absolutely transcendent.[31]

The fact that hospitality is seen as the archetypal response to the "infinite responsibility" borne by the subject beneath the transcendence of the Other should not be surprising. For Levinas, the enacted and economic action of hospitality in the world of being is the direct consequence of the "irreducible structure"[32] in which "my welcoming of the other, is the ultimate fact."[33] The fact that "intentionality, consciousness . . . is attention to speech or welcome of the face, hospitality and not thematization"[34] means that: "Metaphysics, or the relation with the other, is accomplished as service and as hospitality."[35]

---

29. Levinas, *Humanism of the Other*, 64.

30. Waldenfels, "Levinas and the Face of the Other," 65.

31. Levinas, *Totality and Infinity*, 172. Emphasis added.

32. Ibid., 79.

33. Ibid., 77.

34. Ibid., 299.

35. Ibid., 300.

It is this irreducible structure of ethical transcendence which expresses itself in the "infinite responsibility" of the subject as both "host" and "hostage" for the Other that, according to Levinas, keeps the world from descending into complete barbarity. He writes:

> It is through the condition of being hostage that there can be in the world pity, compassion, pardon and proximity—even the little there is, even the simply "After you, sir." The unconditionality of being hostage is not the limit case of solidarity, but the condition for all solidarity. Every accusation and persecution, as all interpersonal praise, recompense, and punishment presuppose the subjectivity of the ego, substitution, the possibility of putting oneself in the place of the other, which refers to the transference from the "by the other" into a "for the other," and in persecution from the outrage inflicted by the other to the expiation for his fault by me. But the absolute accusation, prior to freedom, constitutes freedom which, allied to the Good, situates beyond and outside of all essence.[36]

Fellow French philosopher, Jacques Derrida, whose thought we will engage with in more depth later, is heavily influenced by Levinas' understanding of "infinite responsibility" and sees Levinas' work as a giant treatise on hospitality. In a paper to honor Levinas on the first anniversary of his death, Derrida states: "Intentionality opens, from its own threshold, in its most general structure, as hospitality, as welcoming of the face, as an ethics of hospitality, and, thus, as ethics in general. For hospitality is not simply some region of ethics, let alone, and we will return to this, the name of a problem in law or politics: it is ethicity itself, the whole and the principle of ethics."[37]

Derrida concurs with Levinas that the underlying structure of human consciousness and subjectivity is alterity expressed in the act of welcome. Accordingly ethics, which is "first philosophy," is in its nature "hospitable." As this work continues we will reflect further on this claim that hospitality is the basis of human subjectivity and ethics, but firstly we will turn our attention to the style of Levinas' expression—noting how the very manner of Levinas' writing reflects his attempt to offer a new form of philosophy.

---

36. Levinas, *Otherwise than Being*, 117–18.
37. Derrida, *Adieu to Emmanuel Levinas*, 50.

The Saying and the Said: Emphasis and Excessive Ethics

While Levinas' basic premise—of the irreducible structure of hospitable-ness which constitutes human nature—in one sense, is relatively simple, his attempt to communicate this thesis is anything but straightforward. In attempting to articulate the *wisdom of love*, in writing about the pre-onto-logical structure, the welcoming of the other present in human subjectivi-ty, Levinas recognizes that he falls prey to his own critique of the totalizing tendencies of discourse. The central problem that Levinas' philosophy faces is the age-old philosophical quandary of language itself. It is Levinas' awareness of this dilemma—the necessity of putting into language and therefore bringing into *being* that which is *beyond being*—which explains the complex, and for first-time readers, often convoluted and enigmatic nature of Levinas' prose. Seeking to articulate that which he believes is beyond words involves a stretching of language almost to breaking point. Thus Levinas invents neologisms and employs excessive hyperbole; his writing characterized by recurring phrases, and reiterated sentences, each offering a different nuance, as he seeks to expound his point. The difficult yet nonetheless compelling style of Levinas' prose, which Michael Purcell suggests "verges on a philosophical Midrash," is eloquently expressed by Derrida. Referring to *Totality and Infinity*, Derrida declares: "The thematic development is neither purely descriptive nor purely deductive. It proceeds with the infinite insistence of waves on a beach: return and repetition, al-ways of the same wave against the same shore, in which, however, as each recapitulates itself, it also infinitely renews and enriches itself. Because of all these challenges to the commentator and the critic, *Totality and Infinity* is a work of art and not a treatise."[38]

Levinas' own awareness of the dilemma that his philosophy encoun-ters is conveyed in his notion of the *Saying* and the *Said*. "The responsibil-ity for another," Levinas writes, "is precisely a saying prior to anything said."[39] For Levinas, the pre-ontological condition of infinite responsibil-ity, the welcome of the Other, the *saying*, cannot be named clearly, defined, or communicated in language, and yet, the *saying* however must be made "incarnate" and manifest in language, and thus become the *said*. For Levi-nas, however, this manifestation of the saying into the said, and into the condition of ethics, comes at a cost.

---

38. Derrida, "Violence and Metaphysics," 103n7. Purcell, *Levinas and Theology*, 29.
39. Levinas, *Otherwise than Being*, 43.

> This pre-original saying does move into a language, in which saying and said are correlative of one another, and the saying is subordinated to its theme. . . . The correlation of the saying and the said, that is, the subordination of the saying to the said, to the linguistic system and to ontology, is the price that manifestation demands. In language qua said everything is conveyed before us, be it at the price of a betrayal. . . . Language permits us to utter, be it by betrayal, this *outside of being*, this *ex-ception* to being, as though being's other were an event of being.[40]

Levinas' complex writing style stems therefore from the desire to offer a new way of doing philosophy. With human subjectivity as his starting point Levinas seeks not to ground his ethics in a "foundation" but rather proposes an alternative philosophical method in which "there is another sort of justification of one idea by the other: to pass from one idea to its superlative, to the point of its emphasis. . . . The new idea finds itself justified not on the *basis* of the first, but by its sublimation."[41] In Levinas' poststructuralist account, "the real world is the world that is posited, its manner of being is the thesis."[42] This understanding that the world is constructed by our language-discourse thus leads to Levinas employing hyperbolic-excessive language in positing the world he is advocating. Levinas writes of this philosophical methodology of "emphasis" as the "*via eminentiae*" and states: "*Emphasis* signifies at the same time a figure of rhetoric, an excess of expression, a manner of overstating oneself, and a manner of showing oneself. The word is very good, like the word "hyperbole": there are hyperboles whereby notions are transmuted. To describe this mutation is also to do phenomenology. Exasperation as a method of philosophy!"[43]

The move beyond foundationalism and the philosophical method of *emphasis*—visible in the excessive and hyperbolic language employed—gives an excessive quality to Levinas' ethical demands. Simon Critchley, commenting on this, writes:

> Levinas describes this demand, like other moral perfectionists,[44] in exorbitant terms: infinite responsibility, trauma, persecution,

---

40. Ibid., 6.

41. Levinas, *Of God Who Comes to Mind*, 88–89.

42. Ibid., 89.

43. Ibid.

44. Critchley, using Stanley Cavell's schema, suggests that there are two sorts of moral philosophers: legislators and moral perfectionists. While "legislators" such as Rawls and Habermas "provide detailed precepts, rules and principles" to guide our ethical behavior, Levinas, Critchley contends, belongs to the species of "moral

hostage, obsession. The ethical demand is impossibly demanding. It has to be. If it were not so demanding then it would let us
off the moral hook, as it were, and ethics would be reduced to
a procedural programming where we justified moral norms by
either universalizing them, assessing them in the light of their
consequences, or referring them to some already given notion
of custom, convention or contract.[45]

The excessive and hyperbolic nature of Levinasian ethics is compel-
lingly provocative and deeply unsettling. As many commentators suggest,
there is a deeply "prophetic" edge to Levinas' ethical demands. It is this
"prophetic" tendency which provides an immediate point of contact with
a more explicitly Christian approach to ethics. The refusal to allow ethics
to be reduced to a "procedural program" and instead the pronouncement
of excessive demands is, after all, a hallmark of the biblical prophets.

Levinas' Ethical Source: The Torah

That there seems to be more than a passing similarity between the excessive
ethical demands of the biblical prophets and those of Levinas should not
surprise us. While Critchley points out that it would be a misnomer to call
Levinas a Jewish philosopher, it is clear that Levinas' ethical philosophy is
"inconceivable without its Judaic inspiration,"[46] and in particular Levinas'
reading of the Torah. While Levinas seeks to keep a clear demarcation
between his philosophical writings and his explicitly religious Talmudic
writings, he openly admits the extent to which his reading of the Hebrew
Scriptures shapes his philosophical thought.[47] While maintaining that he

---

perfectionists" who seek "to give an account of a basic existential demand, a lived fundamental obligation that should be at the basis of all moral theory and moral action."
Critchley, introduction to *Cambridge Companion*, 27–28. Colin Davis agrees, stating:
"Levinas offers an ethics without rules, imperatives, maxims or clear objectives other
than a passionate moral conviction that the other should be heard." Davis, *Levinas*,
144.

45. Critchley, introduction to *Cambridge Companion*, 28.

46. Ibid., 22.

47. In an interview, Levinas states, "I always make a clear distinction, in what I
write, between philosophical and confessional texts. I do not deny that they may ultimately have a common source of inspiration. I simply state that it is necessary to
draw a line of demarcation between them as distinct methods of exegesis, as separate
languages. I would never, for example, introduce a Talmudic or biblical verse into one
of my philosophical texts to try to prove or justify a phenomenological argument."
Levinas, "Ethics of the Infinite," 54.

has "never aimed explicitly to 'harmonise' or 'conciliate' both traditions'" Levinas suggests that "one could say that biblical thought has, to some extent, influenced my ethical reading of the interhuman, whereas Greek thought has largely determined its philosophical expression in language."[48] The extent to which his project is an attempt to render the ethics of Judaism into the language of philosophy is stated explicitly in *Of God Who Comes to Mind*, where Levinas states: "My concern everywhere is precisely to translate this non-Hellenism of the Bible into Hellenic terms and not to repeat the biblical formulas in their obvious sense, isolated from the context that, at the level of such a text, is *all* the Bible."[49]

For Levinas, the ethics of Judaism revealed in the Torah is the priority of the Other. It is Levinas' belief that

> in the entirety of the book, there is always a priority of the other in relation to me. This is the biblical contribution in its entirety. . . . The Bible is the priority of the other [*l'autre*] in relation to me. It is in another [*autrui*] that I always see the widow and the orphan. The other [*autrui*] always comes first. This is what I've called, in Greek language, the dissymmetry of the interpersonal relationship. If there is not this dissymmetry, then no line of what I've written can hold. And this is vulnerability. Only a vulnerable I can love his neighbor.[50]

Elsewhere he asserts: "The Torah is transcendent and from heaven by its demands that clash, in the final analysis, with the pure ontology of the world. The Torah demands, in opposition to the natural perseverance of each being in his or her own being (a fundamental ontological law), care for the stranger, the widow and the orphan, a preoccupation with the other person."[51]

Indeed, for Levinas, the Torah provides abundant evidence of his claim that our encounter with the Other is a subjective experience, beyond comprehension and totalization, with its numerous accounts of characters, who, encountered by the infinite call of the Other, can only respond with the "prophetic signification" 'Here I am!'"[52] For Levinas, the utterance of the Hebrew phrase *hineni*—"Here I am!" by characters such as

---

48. Levinas, *Ethics and Infinity*, 24. See also Levinas, "Ethics of the Infinite," 57.

49. Levinas, *Of God Who Comes to Mind*, 85.

50. Ibid., 91.

51. Levinas, *In the Time of Nations*, 61.

52. Levinas, *Of God Who Comes to Mind*, 75.

Abraham, Moses and Isaiah,[53] this preconsciousness response before the Other, "*testifies* to the Infinite."[54]

Thus far we have offered a brief sketch of Levinas' ethical philosophy. How Levinas' ethical metaphysics differs from ethics as traditionally construed within the Western philosophical tradition is given greater clarity when his thought is compared and contrasted with that of Immanuel Kant.

Kant and Levinas: Affection and Reason and the Move Beyond Ontology

Historically, Western philosophy has conceived of ethics as a subset within the broader scope of philosophy. Within this schema, ethics and ethical behavior is deduced from broader universal maxims grounded in natural moral law—as in the case of Kant—or derived from a transcendental theory of God, or the divine. Levinas' philosophical project turns this traditional structure upside down. For Levinas, ethics is not a conception known *a priori*, grounded in ontological or metaphysical theories. Indeed, for Levinas, this attempt to ground ethics in a foundation is an act of totalizing violence. [55]

In contrast to this "foundationalist" approach, in which ethics is founded upon *being*, Levinas' conceives of ethics as an adjective that describes *a posteriori* an event of being in relationship with the Other that is irreducible to comprehension or explanation. Levinas' post-structuralist approach "starts from the human, and from the approach of the human who is not simply that which *inhabits* the world, but which *ages* in the world."[56] Ethics for Levinas is not an obligation based on universal laws, maxims or appeal to metaphysical theories. While post-Kant, Western philosophy has seen ethics as taking place at the level of consciousness— that as rational, autonomous beings we use practical reason to calculate and determine the appropriate ethical action, based on universal laws and appeals to moral theories—for Levinas, ethics is rooted in the subject's sensibility. Simon Critchley concisely captures this distinction, stating: "Ethics does not take place at the level of consciousness or reflection; it rather takes place at the level of sensibility or preconscious sentience. The

53. See Gen 22:1, Exod 3:4, and Isa 6:8.

54. Levinas, *Ethics and Infinity*, 106.

55. Levinas, *Of God Who Comes to Mind*, 88.

56. Ibid.

Levinasian ethical subject is a sentient self *(un soi sentant)* before being a thinking ego *(un moi pensant)*. The bond with the other is affective."[57]

Despite these differences, there is a clear parallel between Kant's moral imperative and Levinas' ethical imperative.[58] Kantian ethics sought a basis for morality separate from religion, custom or other social pressures. Moving beyond ontological or metaphysical groundings for ethics, Kant proposed that morality is grounded in "objective principles"—akin to scientific laws and principles—that are self-evident, universal by nature and discernible by reason. Morality could distinguish between two kinds of imperatives: the *hypothetical* and the *categorical*. *Hypothetical imperatives* characteristically did not concern all people and thus took on the form of a recommendation. *Categorical imperatives* embodied rational moral principles which were always valid and universally binding, and were encapsulated in the following rule, expressed in two ways:

> Act only according to that maxim by which you can at the same time will that it should become a universal law . . .

> Act as though the maxim of your action were by your will to become a universal law of nature.[59]

Kant believed that as autonomous rational beings the highest state of humanity is the freedom and ability to act autonomously and to follow these *categorical imperatives*—that is, to live in accord with the ostensibly self-evident rational moral principles. Levinas' philosophical project, while vastly different from Kant's, shares a key resemblance in the attempt to see ethics as separate from any theological or metaphysical theories.[60] While for Kant morality is rooted in the notion of "the autonomy of the will as the supreme principle of morality"[61] and the universal laws of morality are discernible through reason, Levinas locates morality in heteronomy and sensibility. Where Kant's theory of ethics has the subject at the centre of the ethical event and gives primacy to reason, Levinas inverts this by placing the Other at the centre and giving primacy to affection. For Kant, morality is a simple given—in the same way that gravity is simply a scientific law—and thus ethics is an *obligation*, a *duty* which autonomous

---

57. Critchley, "Original Traumatism," 239.

58. Bernstein, "Evil and the Temptation of Theodicy," 264.

59. Kant, *Foundations of the Metaphysics of Morals*, 39.

60. Despite the major differences in their respective philosophies Levinas clearly regards Kant's separation of morality from ontology as a defining moment and positive movement in philosophy. See Levinas, *Otherwise than Being*, 129.

61. Kant, *Foundations of the Metaphysics of Morals*, 59.

rational beings *ought* to obey. For Levinas, morality flowing from the alterity of the Other is again simply a given, and is expressed in the concept of "infinite responsibility"—that is, the *duty* we have to the Other. Levinas describes the inescapable quality of this duty as:

> the impossibility of cancelling responsibility for the other, impossibility more impossible than jumping out of one's skin, the imprescriptible duty in surpassing the *forces of being*. A duty that did not ask the consent, that came into me traumatically, from beneath all rememberable present, anarchically, without beginning. That came without being offered as a choice, came as election where my contingent humanity becomes identity and unicity, through the impossibility of escaping from election. Duty imposed beyond the limits of being and its annihilation, beyond death, putting being in its resources and deficit.[62]

Accordingly, for Levinas, it is the sheer facticity of the Other, the transcendence of the ethical encounter, "face to face" with the Other, that is the compulsion and motivation for ethicity. The question for Levinas is not "Why should we respond to the Other?" but rather, "How can we not respond to the Other?" Like Kant, and unlike other ethical theories, Levinas' philosophy is not a justified reasoning of how one should act ethically, but rather an assertion of the basic fact of ethicity—a commendation of our basic humanity. Indeed, for Levinas, any attempt to give a justification for one's ethical actions is in fact, inconceivable. This experience of the transcendence and infinity of the Other—of our infinite responsibility before the "gaze of the face" is not something that we can give a rational account of, but rather is an inexpressible subjective experience. In the same way that one cannot describe one's experience of "love" or give an account for our unusual behavior when "in love," the encounter with the Other—the givenness of ethicity—is what it means to be human, and is ultimately beyond the capacity of language to explain.

Unlike other ethical accounts where the subject employs practical reason and deliberation to determine one's ethical response in a given situation, Levinas' assertion is that the subject does not choose to be ethical through an act of consciousness, but rather is, prior to consciousness, already "elected." According to Levinas' account, we are, by our very nature as humans, ethical beings with an infinite responsibility for the Other. This responsibility for the Other, prior to ontology or being, is "irreducible."

---

62. Levinas, *Humanism of the Other*, 7.

Yet, such an assertion raises an obvious question. If at the most el-
emental and inexpressible level humanity is composed by its relation of responsibility to the Other, if humans, by their very nature are constitutively
"hospitable," then why is that some people act ethically—hospitably—and
others do not? According to Kant, while as autonomous rational beings
we can recognize the existence of the moral law, this does not mean we
always follow it. For Kant, *ought* implies *can*, but in his theory he does not
ask why some do not follow the *categorical imperative*. Similarly, Levinas'
postulating of an *ethical imperative* recognizes that we can respond ethically towards the Other, but gives no account of why some do not.

This question points to the first and most obvious distinction between Levinas' or Kant's philosophical accounts of hospitality and a theological account. In both Kantian and Levinasian thought, hospitality is
understood as originating in human subjectivity, and is conceived of as
a response to *duty*. Kant understands hospitality as a reasonable and rational act of an autonomous will, while Levinas explains hospitality as an
act of human inclination. In Kant, the idea of the *categorical imperative*
appears to be a philosophical form of the Golden Rule: "Do unto others
as you would have them do unto you" and thus the motivation for acting
hospitably to another ultimately stems from self-interest; the desire that
likewise one will receive hospitality in return. Levinas' placement of the
Other at the centre of ethics and his understanding of hospitality as the
base structure of inter-human relationships overcomes the self-interest
and contractual nature of a Kantian hospitality, but he is still unwilling
and/or unable to give an account for why such ethical and hospitable behavior is not always present in inter-human relations.

In contrast, as we will explore in more detail later, a theological
understanding of the human practice of hospitality finds the source and
impulse for this ethical action in the ontological and performative drama
of the Triune God, and conceives of hospitality not as a *duty* or *obligation*
but rather as a free response, as an expression of love in response to this
prior divine hospitality. Conversely, while the theological doctrine of sin
is able to account for why often human action is anything but ethical/
hospitable, Levinas' belief in hospitality as the "irreducible" structure of
inter-human relationships, embedded in human inclination, appears, at
times, to be less a description of reality than a form of utopian idealism. As
Andrius Valevicius suggests: "It would be wonderful to be able to believe
that all men carry within themselves a feeling of responsibility for others,
but there is too much evidence to the contrary. We could pour through

phenomenological or psychological investigations for reassurance, but more than likely we have already seen in others if not within ourselves, that egoism, oppression and abuse are just as abundant as goodness."[63]

An Evaluation

So what of Levinas' philosophy? Chapter 3 offers a more detailed critique, but here we will outline some initial strengths, weaknesses and questions that emerge from our overview of Levinas' thought. While there are aspects of Levinas' work which show considerable resemblance to Christian thought and therefore can potentially be integrated into an explicit Christian understanding of hospitality, there are also substantial differences.

The Torah and the Excessive, Affective Nature of Ethics

That Levinas' ethical account is inextricably shaped by his reading of the Torah, provides an immediate correlation with the Christian ethical tradition grounded in the same texts. The potential affinities between Christian and Levinasian ethics, however, do not merely reside in the common source of the Torah. Though in the Christian ethical tradition the Deuteronomic Law and the prophets of the Torah are reinterpreted in the light of the person of Jesus, nevertheless, there are clear parallels between the excessive nature of Levinas' "infinite responsibility" and the ethics espoused and practiced by Jesus.

The ethical project proclaimed and enacted by Jesus as the fulfillment of the Torah[64] is itself a response to the procedural program of laws and regulations as set down by the Pharisees and other religious leaders of his time. Jesus' ethical manifesto expressed in the Sermon on the Mount is loaded with excessive and hyperbolic statements: "If you say 'You fool!,' you will be liable to the *Gehenna* of fire"; "If your right eye causes you to sin, tear it out and throw it away . . . if your right hand causes you to sin, cut if off and throw it away"; "Do not resist an evildoer"; "If anyone wants to sue you and take your coat, give your cloak as well"; "Love your enemies and pray for those who persecute you." Jesus' excessive ethical demands refuse to be reduced to a procedural system and in doing so challenge the

---

63. Valevicius, *From the Other to the Totally Other*, 89–90.

64. Matt 5:17–20.

motivating factor behind ethical behavior, and draw attention to the way in which ethical systems create injustices and abuses of their own.[65]

Likewise, Levinas' emphasis on the corporeal-affective and active nature of ethics has particular resonance with language employed in the Synoptic Gospels. The Greek word *splanchnizomai*—verb of *splancha*—which expresses the way in which one's innards-entrails, the seat of emotions, are moved by the plight of others, appears a number of times in the Synoptic Gospels both to express the emotion and accompanying action of Jesus[66] and to describe the actions of the key characters at critical turning points within three parables.[67] Levinas' understanding of ethics not as a set of codified principles, but as a concrete action rooted in human affection and sensibility, unable to be reduced to formulaic maxims or principles, bears strong resemblance to the ethics expressed and exercised both by the prophets and Jesus and provides a welcome antidote to overly rationalistic approaches to ethical thought.

There are clear similarities as well between Levinas' understanding of human life and that expressed in historical Christian thought. Levinas' assertion of the "irreducible structure" of hospitality, his belief that authentic human life is discovered in the "welcoming of the Other," his emphasis on the basic sociality of human existence, is one that resonates deeply with the Christian understanding that humanity, made in the image of the Triune God, is, by its very nature, hospitable, created for relationships with the Other/others. So too, his understanding of the nature of personhood, the fact that the Other can never be completely understood or comprehended, but remains a mystery, beyond totalization, is one to be commended.

However, while there are convergences, there are also major distinctions between a Levinasian and an overtly Christian theory of ethics.

65. Despite the different conclusions drawn regarding the question or nature of Jesus' divinity, there is a growing consensus amongst scholars that Jesus' ethical program is inextricably connected to his socio-political agenda. Jesus' socio-politico program, seeking to respond to the challenges facing first-century Judaism posed by Roman political power and the encroachment of Hellenistic culture, expresses and enacts ethical behavior which differs from that espoused by his contemporaries—Pharisees, Zealots, Essenes—and ultimately leads to confrontation with these groups. See Borg, *Conflict, Holiness and Politics*; Crossan, *Historical Jesus*; and Wright, *Jesus and the Victory of God*.

66. Mark 1:41; 6:24; 8:2; 9:22; Matt 9:36; 14:14; 15:32; 17:15; 20:34; Luke 7:13.

Note Levinas' use of the words "entrails" in *Humanism of the Other*, used to describe the physical nature of responsibility and mercy that erupt within human subjectivity. See notes 27 and 29 above.

67. Matt 18:27; Luke 10:33; 15:20.

Firstly, while the Torah serves as the key source for his ethical philosophy and for his understanding of the priority of the "transcendence of the Other," Levinas' reading of the Torah is itself shaped by certain philosophical presuppositions, in particular the belief that the "intelligibility of transcendence is not ontological" and that the "transcendence of God can neither be said nor thought in terms of being."[68] While Levinas is correct in seeing the "priority of the other" as one of the key themes of the Bible, his philosophical presuppositions require him to disregard the theological foundations upon which this priority of the Other is grounded: that is, the holiness of Yahweh and his salvific action in history. Eschewing metaphysical or ontological claims, Levinas states that "ethical language seems to me closer to the adequate language" and argues that "ethics is not at all a layer that covers over ontology, but rather that which is in some fashion more ontological than ontology; an emphasis of ontology."[69] Subsequently, in contrast to a Christian reading of the Torah in which the priority of the Other is predicated on the Otherness—that is, the holiness of Yahweh—Levinas claims that ethical behavior stems from the human (subjective) experience of the preexisting responsibility that is owed to the Other. Thus, human ethics are not actions that find their source and basis in the prior actions of the Transcendent, Divine Other, but rather, according to Levinas, it is our ethical encounter with the Other which opens us to the Transcendent.

But can the Bible really be reduced merely to a communication of the universal basis of ethics? Can the narratives of the Torah be stripped of their metaphysical elements and thus be interpreted as primarily concerned with offering a meta-ethical theory, an expounding of the irreducible structure of hospitality that undergirds inter-human relations? It is the final ethical demand of Jesus' "excessive ethic" outlined in the Sermon on the Mount that reveals the major point of difference between Levinas' meta-ethical philosophy and that of an explicit Christian approach to ethical thought. The excessive ethical demands of the Sermon on the Mount are both summarized and find their basis in Jesus' final demand: "Be perfect, therefore, as your heavenly Father is perfect."[70] Ultimately, the extreme demands that constitute Jesus' ethical manifesto expressed in the Sermon on the Mount are grounded upon a theological foundation. That is, *Christian ethics is a*

---

68. Levinas, *Of God Who Comes to Mind*, 77.

69. Ibid., 89–90.

70. Matt 5:48 NRSV. Or, as expressed in Luke 6:36: "Be merciful, just as your Father is merciful."

call to respond to the "mercy" of the Father, to imitate the mercy that has been bestowed upon us. The biblical imperatives laying out the priority of the other, the primacy of the alien, stranger, and orphan, are predicated upon the holiness of Yahweh, grounded in his divine mercy and compassion which He has demonstrated in his salvific acts.[71]

Furthermore, the very philosophical presuppositions which shape Levinas' reading of the Torah are themselves highly questionable. Levinas' philosophy of ethical metaphysics, as noted earlier, is motivated by two concerns: Firstly, that in attempting to speak of the Transcendent, God ceases to be transcendent, in that human language inevitably leads to a form of conceptual idolatry. And, secondly, that such a "metaphysical relation with God," leads to an "ignorance of men and things." *But is the exercise of theology, of speaking about God inherently violent and totalizing? Does a concern with ontological questions presuppose a disregarding of ethical matters?*

While sympathetic to Levinas' critique, ultimately our contention is that in authentic Christianity, the "metaphysical relation with God" does not lead to "the ignorance of men and things." Holding to the theological understanding that all God-talk and human ethical action takes place in an *a posteriori* fashion, and is simply a response to God's prior speech and action, we will argue that orthodox biblical faith avoids such idolatrous and unethical tendencies. Levinas' critique of theology, we will maintain, is aimed not at biblical Christianity, but rather against the god that emerges from a certain form of philosophical metaphysics. Ultimately, Levinas' critique is intended for, and finds its target in, the thought of his former mentor and later unspoken nemesis, Heidegger.

Our concerns regarding Levinas' interpretation of the Torah and the philosophical presuppositions that shape his thought point ultimately to a deeper disquiet regarding Levinas' thought. Despite claims to the contrary, Levinas' philosophy of "ethical metaphysics," is of course, implicitly at least, shaped by certain ontological assumptions. We will elaborate further on this point in chapter 3, but for now will note briefly how Levinas'

---

71. The constant refrain throughout the Torah, to care for the *alien and stranger*, is predicated on *the prior* salvific and compassionate actions of Yahweh. Israel, repeatedly reminded of their own plight, as "aliens in the land of Egypt" are told time and again that their ethical treatment of the *alien and stranger* in their midst is the appropriate *imitative response* to Yahweh's initial liberating actions. It is the fact that "I am the LORD your God, who brought you out of the land of Egypt, out of the house of slavery" (Exod 20:2) that establishes the basis for Yahweh's instructions that Israel now do likewise to the alien and stranger in their midst. See: Exod 20:2; 20:10; 22:21–27; 23:9; Lev 19:9–10, 33–34; Deut 10:17–19.

philosophical method seems to call into question the concept of identity itself and therefore puts at risk the very notion of an ethical relationship between the Self and the Other.

Questions of Identity and Discernment

While Christian ethics are grounded in the character and actions of the Triune God, Levinas argues that moral obligation stems not from metaphysical foundations nor from a universality and intelligibility grounded in reason, but rather, exists in unmediated obligation stemming from a particularity. A problem arises, however, in that as Fabio Ciaramelli points out, "the prescriptive power of the appeal [of the Other] and its pretention to concern each and every one of us, always and everywhere" means that the Transcendent Other becomes itself a universal.[72] While Levinas argues that moral obligation stems from the uniqueness of each moral situation, the irony is that his idea of the "Other" itself becomes elevated to the form of a Universal.[73] The criticism then arises that this generalized Other, which has lost its particular identity, is an "undifferentiable alterity" and therefore "entails an empty universal."[74]

This criticism of the vacuous nature of Levinas' Other is especially significant when one seeks to apply Levinas' thinking to the actual practice of hospitality. All ethical relationships involve questions of discernment and in the practice of hospitality in our contemporary world this process of discernment is especially important. In an age of "terror" where the stranger may be the refugee seeking sanctuary or the suicide-bomber who comes as the harbinger of death, how does one discern between the Other who comes in peace and the Other who comes to bring destruction? In the context of civil or ethnic conflict in which many different Others are in conflict with one another, how does the subject in a bond of "infinite

72. Ciaramelli, "Levinas's Ethical Discourse," 85.

73. The irony being of course that Levinas, in his critique of the totalizing "philosophy of power" which is ontology, states: "Universality presents itself as impersonal; and that is another inhumanity." Levinas, *Totality and Infinity*, 46.

74. Wyschogrod, "Language and Alterity in the Thought of Levinas," 192. See also John Milbank's concern at the vacuous nature of such a "generalized otherness" in Milbank, *Word Made Strange*, 223. Feminist philosopher, Luce Irigaray, is also critical of Levinas' "nondefinition of the other," asking, "Who is the other, if the other of sexual difference is not recognized or known?" For Irigaray, Levinas' use of words such as Other (*autre*) "without always defining or redefining them . . . gives a very insistent hermeneutical, metaphysical, or theological tone to his writings." Irigaray, "Questions to Emmanuel Levinas," 112–13.

responsibility" to the Other(s) determine which of the Other's needs/demands/rights are most pressing? Are the demands of the Kurds more significant than those of the Shia or the Sunni? Is the desire for a home-land amongst the Palestinians any less valid than that same desire amongst Israelis? That is, how does the universal demand of the Other of Levinas' account get worked out in the particularities of a world of competing claims amongst different Others? Increasing technological advances in the areas of media and communication mean that in the course of each day one is exposed to multiple tragic events with impacts on many "Others." If, as Levinas believes, we have "infinite responsibility" for the countless Others in each of these situations, how, with the finite resources we have at our disposal, do we discern *to whom*, and *how* we respond?

In each of these scenarios, an ethical response to the Other requires a process of discernment in assessing and deciphering the claims of each of the Others in the particular situation. Yet, Levinas' thought in offering no criteria to guide the process of critical reflection inherent to all ethical relations, leaves us still requiring another theory of justice.[75]

Such questions could well be perceived as unfair. After all, as we have outlined, Levinas does not seek to offer an account of ethical reasoning, but rather simply seeks to give an account of the basic ethicity that constitutes humanness. However, not only does the universalizing and generalizing nature of Levinas' "Other" raise the question of the process of discernment, but the priority given in Levinasian thought to affection and sensibility likewise appears problematic in our contemporary world. What happens once the bombardment of images and stories of the Others reaches saturation point—when rather than being "moved" by the plight of the Other, the subject reaches what some term "compassion fatigue" leading to a form of ethical paralysis? How do we, as ethical subjects, ensure that we remain open and vulnerable to the face and call of the Other? What are the obstacles that prevent us responding to the plight of the Other? Once again, Levinas' thought, by and large, stays silent on such important ethical questions and one is left to wonder how Levinas' powerful demand to "infinite responsibility" is actually outworked in a world of conflicting and infinite needs.

75. Merold Westphal highlights this same point. See Westphal, review of *Of God Who Comes to Mind*, 524.

Identity and the Nature of Relationships

As well as concerns over the identity of the Other and related questions of discernment, likewise the very nature of the relationship between ethical subjects envisaged by Levinas also leads to a certain unease. Levinas posits an asymmetrical and non-reciprocal relationship in which the Other approaches the subject not as an equal, but rather as "Lord" and "Master." To overcome the potential risk of the Other being incorporated into a totality, to prevent the abuse of the Other by the conscious subject, Levinas inverses the ethical relationship. The transcendent Other approaches the subject from height and "commands" and the subject is "infinitely responsible" for the Other. But what is the effect of this reversal of power?

We have noted the irony that in focusing on the "transcendence of the Other," the Other potentially becomes a faceless, generalized universal, devoid of a particular identity, thereby complicating questions of discernment that are critical within the practice of hospitality. Likewise, Levinas' thinking also appears problematic with regard to the identity of the subject itself. In Levinas' thought, the base structure of heteronomy means that the Other is the very basis of *sense*.[76] Without the Other there is no basis/foundation for the subject to express themselves. As a consequence, Levinas believes that the identity of the subject is "host"/"hostage" and the subject is formed by its ethical actions. The poststructuralist assumption which shapes Levinas' thinking does not merely mean that the world is constructed by our language-discourse, but further, Levinas' understanding that heteronomy is the basis of identity means the subject itself only exists as a constitution of its ethical actions toward the Other. Levinas' statement that the subject is "stitched of responsibilities" conveys the imagery of a quilt in which each ethical action becomes a new piece of material added to the whole.[77] The biblical ethical imperative: "Love your neighbor as yourself"[78] is, Levinas argues, shaped by his hermeneutic of the priority of the Other and the multi-interpretability of the Hebrew syntax, translatable as: "Love your neighbour; all that is yourself; this work *is* yourself; this love *is* yourself."[79]

76. Levinas, *Humanism of the Other*, 30.

77. Ibid., 67.

78. Lev 19:18.

79. Levinas, *Of God Who Comes to Mind*, 90–91. Emphasis added. While in this passage Levinas sees the identity of the subject as constituted in ethical actions, it is not always clear whether Levinas is also open to a possible monist understanding of identity. Some Levinasian commentators do see a monist perspective within his work.

Once again there is a disturbing irony that arises in Levinas' work. Levinas' account of the subject's existence being established in ethical actions is designed to overcome ethical imperatives which are rooted in self-love and self-interest. The ethical maxim "Do unto Others as you would have them do unto you" would be anathema to Levinas, placing as it does the subject at the centre of the ethical action. But Levinas' response, in placing the Other at the centre of the ethical event and arguing that the subject's existence is constituted by ethical action leads to new difficulties. If Levinas' ethico-constructionist understanding of identity were to be adhered to, what would this mean for our understanding of those who act unethically—though this begs the question as to what basis and criteria is used for deciding what is and is not ethical/hospitable?—or those, such as infants or others, who are not self-aware of their ethical encounters? In a strange twist, Levinas' philosophy in raising the Other to a generalized universal and making the subject a "hostage" to this unknowable Other, seems to commit the very act of totalization and dehumanization he is seeking to overcome. Is Levinas' philosophy simply an inversion of the totalizing power structure that he sees at work in Western philosophy with the only difference being now that the subject is at the mercy of the Other? Indeed, even the notion of the ethical subject as "hostage" while admittedly hyperbolic, seems to insinuate that the asymmetrical ethical relationship also contains an element of antagonism. But how appropriate or helpful is it to conceive of the ethical subject as "hostage" in a world of hostage-taking where those offering humanitarian assistance can experience a "hospitality" hosted by masked gun-men which is then recorded for others to witness? Or, where daughters, held captive in their own homes, become "hosts" to the children fathered by their own father?[80]

Richard A. Cohen writes: "One is not called on to 'love thy neighbour *as* oneself,' according to the biblical precept, as if self-love preceded other-love and were the measure of other-love. Rather, the proper formulation of Levinas's thought is more extreme, an infinite demand never satisfied even in its fulfilment: to 'love thy neighbour *is* oneself.' The moral self is the self-emptying, the 'fission,' the 'denucleation,' of selfhood in and as responsibility for the other—up to the ultimate self-sacrifice, to die for the other's welfare. Care for the other trumps care for the self, *is* care for the self. Nothing is more significant." Cohen, introduction to *Humanism of the Other*, xxvii.

80. We refer here to the shocking cases of Irish aid-worker Margaret Hassan and many others like her, in Iraq and other conflict-zones, who have been kidnapped, held hostage and murdered during the last decade; and, to the case of Austrian woman, Elizabeth Fritzl, who, held in captivity for twenty-four years by her own father Joseph Fritzl, gave birth to seven children fathered by him, before gaining freedom in April 2008.

These questions regarding identity and relationality are complicated further if we take Levinas' philosophical methodology of *emphasis*, discussed earlier, and apply it to his concept of the Other. In expressing the idea that "the real world is the world that is posited, its manner of being is the thesis," Levinas appears to conceive of the world as a linguistic construction, in which the ideas we posit are more real than the world of *being*.[81] But what happens if in the interests of consistency, Levinas' methodology of *emphasis*, this linguistic-constructionist approach, is applied to his concept of the Other. If the world we encounter is the world that we have posited in language, is this not also true of the Other? Is the Other that we encounter simply a linguistic construction that we have posited into existence? The problem arises not only in that Levinas' methodology of *emphasis* is grounded upon the presupposition that our positing will always be positive[82] but if adhered to, the idea of the linguistic construction of the Other undermines the priority of the Other upon which Levinas' "infinite responsibility" is based. That is, if the Other, like the world, is a linguistic construction, arising from the positing of the subject, then the Other is no longer prior to, but rather is subservient to language.

Derrida, in commenting on Levinas' philosophy of hospitality, draws the distinction between Kant's philosophy which "retains the trace of natural hostility" and Levinas' philosophy of peace.[83] But to what extent does the asymmetrical, non-reciprocal nature of inter-human relationships that Levinas posits really provide a basis for hospitality and peace? Does a philosophical account of hospitality based on a structure of asymmetrical and non-reciprocal relationships offer hope to a world in which such asymmetries, inequalities and inequities already exist? "Isn't there a need" Merold Westphal writes, "especially in a thinker who evokes messianic peace as Levinas does, to talk about the kind of reciprocity that represents both a moral and a social ideal?"[84] As we will see later, the doctrine of the Trinity offers such a vision of reciprocity in which both personal identity and re-

---

81. Levinas, *Of God Who Comes to Mind*, 89.

82. This again suggests there is an element of idealism within Levinas' philosophy. The reality is that we live in a world of propaganda in which the Other can be posited either as a deserving widow, orphan, stranger, or, as a terrorist, depending on who is doing the positing. A novel by Richard Flanagan powerfully portrays the ways in which an unsuspecting innocent Other, living in a contemporary Western society consumed by fear—nurtured and propagated by the media—of the Other, is transformed into a "terrorist." Flanagan, *Unknown Terrorist*.

83. Derrida, *Adieu*, 88.

84. Westphal, review of *Of God Who Comes to Mind*, 524.

lationality are able to coexist, thus overcoming the problems of an account of hospitality rooted in autonomy (Kant) or heteronomy (Levinas).

Summary

In this chapter we have assessed Levinas' philosophy noting that there this is much in Levinas' thought which show the potential to enrich the theological account of hospitality we seek to offer. Clearly Levinas' dependence on the Torah and his emphasis on the key motif of the "priority of the other" derived from this text provide immediate points of correlation with an explicit theological basis for hospitality. Similarly, Levinas' understanding of ethics as an adjective based in human sensibility and affection is a necessary critique of Western ethical approaches in which ethics have often been grounded in practical reason and reduced to a set of procedural laws, and likewise, bears some resemblances to the ethics exercised by the prophets and Jesus.

However, problems emerge in that in attempting to articulate the Judaic ethics of hospitality in the language of Western philosophy, Levinas takes on board the presuppositions of Western philosophical thought. In eschewing the theological basis for the ethics of the Torah and in renouncing the totalising tendencies of ontological philosophy, Levinas seeks to argue that hospitality stems from a pre-ontological alterity discoverable in a phenomenological analysis of human subjectivity. The consequence of this is that Levinas' poststructuralist account of hospitality is ultimately subjective. Within such an account critical questions remain unanswered: If the "irreducible structure" is one of "welcoming the other" how does one account for the fact that ethical care for the Other is not always forthcoming? If one holds to Levinas' assertion of the "infinite responsibility" that the subject has before the face of the Other how does one discern which of the infinite Others we should, with finite resources, respond to? Further, Levinas' emphasis on the asymmetrical and non-reciprocal nature of inter-human relationships, in which one is held "hostage" to the Other, far from providing a "great messianic discourse on eschatological peace," arguably has the potential effect of perpetuating the inequalities and abuses which characterise the inhospitable actions in our world.[85]

---

85. Derrida, *Adieu*, 95.

2

Unconditional Hospitality, the Gift of Deconstruction?

The Philosophy of Jacques Derrida

LEVINAS' ETHICAL PHILOSOPHY HAS HAD A MAJOR IMPACT ON PHILO-sophical and religious thinking of the late 20th century. Notable amongst the number of writers who have been influenced by Levinas' thought is well-known and controversial French philosopher, Jacques Derrida. In this chapter, we will explore the ways in which Levinas' commendation of the priority of the ethical, manifested in concepts such as the "transcendence of the Other" and the "infinite responsibility" of the subject, are developed further by Derrida into the theme of "unconditional hospitality."

Defining and Delineating Derrida's Deconstruction?

Biographical Philosophy

While clearly pivotal to the development of his philosophy, his thinking "dominated by the presentiment and the memory of the Nazi horror," Levinas' life experiences are rarely explicitly mentioned in his writings.[1] In contrast, Derrida's unique form of writing blurs the boundaries of "academic' philosophy and autobiography/self-exposure. In *Monolingualism of the Other*, reflecting on the chaotic cultural configuration brought about by the displacement of French-speaking Jews in Algeria in the 19th and 20th century, Derrida speaks of the creation of what he calls a "disorder of

1. Levinas, *Difficult Freedom*, 291.

identity." Speaking of himself as a "Franco-Maghrebian," Derrida professes his love of "pure French," a language which paradoxically reinforces his cultural alienation as an Algerian Jew.[2] In *Circumfession*, his most auto-biographical work, Derrida reflects further on this sense of illegitimacy, of being the Other, an exile without a home.[3] This theme of Derrida's not *belonging*, of his *absence* even while being *present*, of his *marginality*, is observed too by Derridean commentators. Giovanna Borradori notes the way in which Derrida's life and writing exists "at the boundaries of multiple territories: Judaism and Christianity, Judaism and Islam, in Europe and Africa, mainland France and its colonies, the sea and the desert."[4]

Deconstruction and Différance

Lionized and loathed, Derrida's philosophical writings are often gathered under the term, "deconstruction."[5] The concept itself is still greatly debated and the impossibility of a clear definition of the term "deconstruction" is itself illustrative of its guiding principle and *modus operandi*. Like other poststructuralist theories, deconstruction declines the structuralist assumption that structuralist principles are essences. Eschewing any form of essentialism, "deconstruction" seeks to reveal the way in which philosophical language, rather than signifying essences or givens, is itself

---

2. Derrida, *Monolingualism of the Other*.

3. Derrida, "Circumfession: Fifty-Nine Periods and Periphrases."

4. Borradori, *Philosophy in a Time of Terror*, 11. See also Caputo, *Prayers and Tears*, 304.

5. The division between those who see Derrida's work as of important philosophical significance and those who, as Richard J. Bernstein suggests, see Derrida as a "clever intellectual fraud, a 'prophet' of nihilism, a whimsical destroyer of any 'canons' of rationality, a self-indulgent scribbler who delights in irresponsible word play, punning and parody," is perhaps most clearly evident in the obituaries written after Derrida's death in October 2004. (Bernstein, *New Constellation*, 172). *The Economist*, viewing Derrida's work as one of "weak puns, bombastic rhetoric and illogical ramblings" pandering to "a market for obscurantism" expressed sympathy for "his unfortunate disciples," in particular theologians, who have "started to show an interest in his work. God help them." (Obituary: Jacques Derrida, October 21st, 2004, *Economist*.) Similarly harsh in their assessment of Derrida's work were the *New York Times* and the *Wall Street Journal*. In contrast is the gracious obituary offered by one of these theologians, James K. A. Smith. See Smith, "In Memoriam: Jacques Derrida."

The strength of feeling that Derrida's work provokes is also illustrated by the controversy that arose in 1992 over the decision of Cambridge University to award him an honorary degree. For an outline of "The Derrida Affair" as it became known and Derrida's response, see Derrida, *"Honoris Causa: This Is Also Extremely Funny."*

historical, contingent and temporary. The structures of philosophical discourse and language are disassembled by a rereading of the text, in which attention is paid to the way in which philosophical constructions depend on seemingly-fixed meanings and definitions, and clear-cut binary relationships which are often hierarchically-ordered, for example: male and female, spiritual and material, universal and particular. Deconstruction operates by inverting these hierarchical structures thereby revealing their ideological or strategic function; by engaging in an etymological quest to find the hidden or suppressed trace within a word; and by playfully pushing words to their semiological limits to reveal the multiplicity and paradox inherent within language.

As with Levinas, Derrida is critical of Western philosophy for its focus on ontological questions. Such philosophy seeking a grounding of being in *essence* reveals itself as a history of totalizing violence in which the "Other" is reduced to the Same. In contrast to such philosophy, Derrida's deconstruction, according to John D. Caputo: "is rather the thought, if it is a thought, of an absolute heterogeneity that unsettles all the assurances of the same within which we comfortably ensconce ourselves."[6] At the heart of Derridean deconstruction is the idea of *différance*, a word coined by Derrida, which is itself a pun of the French word *"différer."*[7] In French, the word *différer* has two meanings: *to differ* and *to defer*, and thus, Derrida's invented word is illustrative of his understanding of language: that words have multiple meanings encapsulated within themselves, and that in each context one of these meanings has to be deferred. Implied within Derrida's concept of *différance* is a belief that openness and temporality, not *essence*, are at the heart of both language and existence itself.

However, in line with other post-structuralist thinking, Derrida does not grant a foundational quality to his concept of *différance*. In an interview with Richard Kearney, Derrida states:

> The notion of "differance," for example, is a non-concept in that it cannot be defined in terms of oppositional predicates; it is neither *this* nor *that*; but rather this *and* that (e.g. the act of differing and of deferring) without being reducible to a dialectical logic either. And yet the term "difference" emerges and develops as a determination of language from which it is

6. Caputo, *Prayers and Tears*, 5.

7. The term *différance* first appears in an article by Derrida, "La Parole soufflé," in 1965 and then later in a longer paper, "Différance," presented in January 1968 to the Société de Philosophie. These papers are available in English translations in Derrida, *Writing and Difference*, 169–95, and Derrida, *Margins of Philosophy*, 1–27.

inseparable. Hence the difficulty of translating the term. There is no conceptual realm beyond language which would allow the term to have a univocal semantic content over and above its inscription in language. Because it remains a trace of language it remains non-conceptual. And because it has no oppositional or predicative generality, which would identify it as *this* rather than *that*, the term "difference" cannot be defined within a system of logic—Aristotelian or dialectical—that is, within the logocentric system of philosophy.[8]

Caputo, who has attempted to offer a Christianized theological-ethical rendering of Derridean thought, suggests: "it would be a serious misunderstanding to think that *différance* is a master name, the secret, hidden name of Being beyond Being."[9] Far from being a mystical or transcendental bed-rock on which to ground Being, Caputo asserts that Derrida's *différance* operates as a quasi-transcendental.[10]

Using Caputo's interpretation of *différance* as a quasi-transcendental, one can see a strong correlation between Derrida's idea of *différance* and Levinas' conception of a pre-ontological structure of alterity, beyond essence and being. Both philosophers seek to overcome what they perceive as the fundamental fault of Western philosophy—its tendency to reduce the Other to the "Same"—by replacing ontological questions of Being with an analysis of the ethical encounter, thus giving philosophical priority not to *essence* but to heterogeneity.

While many critics see Derrida's deconstruction as a form of nihilistic-relativism, intent on destruction, Derrida himself states: "I cannot conceive of a radical critique, which would not be ultimately motivated by some sort of affirmation, acknowledged or not. . . . deconstruction is, in itself, a positive response to an alterity which necessarily calls, summons or motivates it. Deconstruction is therefore vocation—a response to a call."[11] In another interview, defending deconstruction from its detractors, Derrida asserts: "Deconstruction ... is not negative, even though it

---

8. Derrida, "Deconstruction and the Other," 110–11. Or, as Derrida writes in his essay "Différance": "'Older' than Being itself, such a *difference* has no name in our language . . . there is no *name* for it at all, not even the name of essence or of Being, not even that of '*difference*,' which is not a name, which is not a pure nominal unity, and unceasingly dislocates itself in a chain of differing and deferring substitutions." Derrida, "Différance," 26.

9. Caputo, *Prayers and Tears*, 9.

10. Ibid., 12.

11. Derrida, "Deconstruction and the Other," 118.

has often been interpreted as such despite all sorts of warnings. For me, it always accompanies an affirmative exigency. I would even say that it never proceeds without love."[12]

So, too, Caputo, one of Derrida's most sympathetic commentators, argues that deconstruction is not bent on destruction, but rather, is an attempt to open philosophical discourse up to the Other, serving as a voice of "prophetic expectation and prophetic passion."[13]

This impulse of deconstruction to open up the philosophical discourse, to prevent philosophy—and literature, ethics, institutions—from becoming totalizing and hegemonic, finds expression in three specific concepts which punctuate Derrida's writings: the idiom *tout autre est tout autre*; his understanding of the messianic structure; and, the idea of the *impossible*.

Tout autre est tout autre

Derrida's phrase *tout autre est tout autre* operates in a similar manner to the Levinasian concepts of *infinity* and the *transcendence of the Other*, in asserting that *the Other is always wholly other*, is beyond our comprehension. Whether "the Other" is God or another human,[14] Derrida's "*tout autre est tout autre*" serves as a constant reminder that the "Other" cannot be completely understood or comprehended. A "cookie-cutter" approach to relationships in which the particular Other is always understood in relation to other Others, is overturned by Derrida's prioritizing of the singular. In Derrida's thought the universal always gives way to the priority of the particular. Caputo concisely summarizes this idea:

> The *tout autre*, the wholly other: God, for example, or any singularity whatever, no matter what. Like the singularity of an event whose uniqueness makes of each occurrence both an

12. Derrida, "Almost Nothing of the Unpresentable," 83.

13. Caputo, *Prayers and Tears*, 114.

14. Whether Derrida—or, for that matter Levinas—sees the concept of the "Other" as encompassing non-human life, is an interesting aside. At times Derrida does hint that responsibility to the Other involves more than responsibility to humanity. See Derrida and Roudinesco, "Unforeseeable Freedom," 52; and Derrida, "Hostipitality," 363. For an interview in which Derrida deals specifically with questions regarding the ethical treatment of animals, see Derrida and Roudinesco, "Violence against Animals." For a reflection on whether Levinas understands one's infinite responsibility to the Other as extending to non-human life see Llewelyn, "Am I Obsessed by Bobby?" Levinas' own remarks on this question can be found in Wright et al., "Paradox of Morality."

unprecedented first time and an unrepeatable last time. . . . The wholly other is any singularity whatever, whoever, whose this-ness we cannot lift up, cannot generalize, cannot universalize, cannot formalize, any singularity which fixes us in this place so that we cannot look away, cannot look up to the *eidos* of which it would be "but an example" which would allow us to get on top of it, dominate it, enable us to envisage it instead of finding ourselves fixed by its gaze. Derrida here takes up a uniquely biblical sense of singularity, as opposed to a Greek sense of subsuming the less real particular under the truer universal. *Tout autre*—it does not matter what or who—*est tout autre.*[15]

Thus, Derrida's mantra *tout autre est tout autre* serves as both a plea and a structural device to keep philosophy open—prioritizing the uniqueness and singularity of the Other, over generalizations and philosophical universals.

The Messianic Structure

As well as this prioritizing of the singular, the particular over the universal, recurrent throughout Derrida's thought is the idea of the Messiah—of the Other as a Messianic figure. Derrida's thought here is strongly influenced by the writings of his friend Maurice Blanchot, who, in *The Writing of Disaster*, retells a story that recurs in Jewish lore:

If the Messiah is at the gates of Rome among the beggars and lepers, one might think that his incognito protects or prevents him from coming, but, precisely, he is recognized; someone, haunted with questioning and unable to leave off, asks him: "When will you come?" His being there is, then, not the coming. With the Messiah, who is there, the call must always resound: "Come, Come." His presence is no guarantee. Both future and past (it is said, at least once, that the Messiah has already come), his coming does not correspond to any presence at all. . . . And should it happen that, to the question, "When will your coming take place" the Messiah responds: "It is today," the answer is certainly impressive: so, it is today! It is now and always now. There is no waiting, although this is an obligation to wait. And when is now? When is the now which does not belong to ordinary time . . . does not maintain but destabilizes it? . . .[16]

15. Caputo, *Prayers and Tears*, 51–52.

16. Derrida, *Politics of Friendship*, 46n14. Refer also to Blanchot, *Writing of Disaster*, 141–42.

Derrida is fascinated by the idea of the messianic structure, implied within Blanchot's writing—the idea of the Messiah as the singular Other whom we await, but whose arrival never occurs. For Derrida, this messianic structure creates a new understanding of time leading to an ethical posture of openness. One awaits the arrival of the Messiah with longing and expectation, but the fact that the Messiah never actually arrives prevents time from being sealed off, the future from being foreclosed.

The Impossible

This concept of a messianic time forms the basis for Derrida's understanding of the future as the *impossible*. In contrast to the essentialism or idealism that Derrida sees as characteristic of Western philosophy, deconstruction articulates the *impossible* nature of the future. Refusing to be closed off, shut down, foreclosed, or reduced to the horizon of the Same, deconstruction is a philosophy of radical openness, an openness to the particular, to the Other as wholly Other, to a messianic hope of the *impossible*; a philosophy not of absolutes and certainty, but rather, a philosophy of faith.

Indeed, Caputo interprets deconstruction as a form of philosophy that stands within the tradition of "de-hellenization," a philosophy that has more in common with the Jewish-biblical-prophetic tradition than Greek onto-theology, more concerned with questions of ethics and justice than the theme of being and *ousia*. Far from being a nihilistic philosophy that delights in destruction, Caputo asserts that deconstruction in its openness to the *impossible* is the source of a true faith, stating: "Deconstruction takes the form of a general or non-determinable faith in the impossible. . . . Deconstruction comes down to an affirmation or hope or invocation which is a certain *faith* in *the* impossible, and something that pushes us beyond the sphere of the same, of the believable, into the unbelievable, that which exceeds the horizon of our pedestrian beliefs and probabilities, driving us with a passion of *the* impossible, *the* unbelievable. . . ."[17]

As with his close friend Levinas, whose writings he interprets as an "immense treatise of hospitality,"[18] Derrida's philosophy of deconstruction, has likewise, been interpreted as a philosophy of hospitality.[19] As

---

17. Caputo, *Prayers and Tears*, 54.

18. Derrida, *Adieu*, 21.

19. Caputo writes: "If you were intent on making deconstruction look respectable, it would not be a distortion to say that deconstruction is to be understood as a form

with Levinas, ethics and hospitality are not peripheral, but constitute the very heart of Derrida's philosophical enterprise. The interchangeability of the terms is captured by the passage below, where Derrida, commenting on the notion of an ethic of hospitality, writes:

> "To cultivate an ethic of hospitality"—is such an expression not tautologous? Despite all the tensions or contradictions which distinguish it, and despite all the perversions that can befall it, one cannot speak of cultivating an ethic of hospitality. Hospitality is culture itself and not simply one ethic amongst others. Insofar as it has to do with the *ethos*, that is, the residence, one's home, the familiar place of dwelling, inasmuch as it is a manner of being there, the manner in which we relate to ourselves and to others, to others as our own or as foreigners, *ethics is hospitality*; ethics is so thoroughly coextensive with the experience of hospitality.[20]

For Derrida, *ethics is hospitality* and *hospitality is ethics*.[21] So too, according to Caputo's reading, a philosophy of deconstruction—a Derridean philosophy—is in itself, structurally, a philosophy of *ethical hospitality*, a philosophy that refuses to be sealed or closed off, but rather that seeks to open itself to the Other and to remain open, waiting in expectation for the *tout autre*, the *Messianic* stranger, the *impossible*. Derrida himself makes this claim, writing:

> If every concept shelters or lets itself be haunted by another concept, by an other than itself that is no longer even its other, then no concept remains in place any longer. This is about the concept of concept . . . hospitality, the experience, the apprehension, the exercise of impossible hospitality, of hospitality as the possibility of impossibility (to receive another guest whom I am incapable of welcoming, to become capable of that which I am incapable of)—this is the exemplary experience of deconstruction itself, when it is or does what it has to do or to be, that is,

---

of hospitality, that deconstruction *is* hospitality, which means the welcoming of the other. Deconstruction would thus mean—again in a nutshell—'let the other come!' 'Welcome to the other.' If deconstruction had an international headquarters, say in Paris, it would have a large banner hanging over its front door saying '*Bienvenue!*'" Caputo, *Deconstruction in a Nutshell*, 109–10.

20. Derrida, *On Cosmopolitanism and Forgiveness*, 16–17.

21. As noted earlier, Derrida, referring to Levinas' thought, asserts: "hospitality is not simply some region of ethics . . . it is ethicity itself, the whole and the principle of ethics." Derrida, *Adieu*, 50.

the experience of the impossible. Hospitality—this is a name or an example of deconstruction.[22]

But what sort of hospitality does Derrida's deconstructive philosophy describe? While Levinas' philosophy is perhaps best seen as "structurally" a work of "hospitality,"[23] Derrida's writing, particularly his later work, deals explicitly with the concept and practice of hospitality.[24] It is to a closer reading of Derrida's account of the ethic of hospitality, and in particular his idea of "unconditional" hospitality, to which we now turn.

"Hospitality" Deconstructed

Through playing the usual binaries of hospitality discourse against each other and engaging in an etymological analysis, Derrida exposes the multiple meanings, tensions and aporia that exist within the vocabulary of hospitality. Following the etymology of French structuralist linguist Emile Benveniste,[25] Derrida notes the inherent tensions and paradoxes within the word "hospitality," which, derived from the Latin word *hospes*, combines the words of *hostis*—which originally meant stranger, but came to take on the meaning of "enemy" or "hostile" stranger—with *potis*, to have mastery or power. The multiple meanings of the Latin word *hostis* is paralleled by the polysemous nature of the French word *hôte* which means both the one who gives (*donne*) and the one who receives (*recoit*). Through a simple etymological analysis, therefore, Derrida raises a number of in-

22. Derrida, "Hostipitality," 364.

23. Derrida himself notes that the theme of "hospitality" in Levinas' work "is borne out less by the occurrences of the word 'hospitality,' which are, in fact, rather rare, than by the links and discursive logic that lead to this vocabulary of hospitality." Derrida, *Adieu*, 21.

24. From the late 1980s onwards Derrida's writing becomes increasingly and explicitly political, ethical and religious in character. While in *Given Time, Gift of Death* and *The Politics of Friendship* Derrida touches on "hospitality" as it relates to the topics of the gift and friendship, in the late 1990s in *Of Hospitality* and *Cosmopolitanism and Forgiveness* he is concerned overtly with the theme. However, it would be a mistake to see "hospitality" only as a later theme and to divide Derrida's work into an earlier hermeneutical period and later ethical-religious writing. Rather, from his earliest works concerned primarily with language and grammar, Derrida seeks to point out the way in which Western philosophy, with its emphasis on ontology, operates within the Same, and therefore excludes the Other. Being attentive to the "middle-voice" Derrida seeks to deconstruct this totalizing logocentrism, revealing the way in which the presence of such texts is dependent on "absence," thereby allowing silenced voices in texts to be heard.

25. Benveniste, "Hospitality," 71–83.

triguing, and potentially unsettling, questions: In the act of hospitality, who is the "host" and who is the "guest"? Who is assisting who?—That is, who gives and who receives? And, is it the "host" or the "guest" who poses a potential threat?

Derrida's etymological analysis provides him with evidence for two important conclusions he makes regarding hospitality. Firstly, the interchangeability of ideas such as "host" and "guest" are, for him, evidence of the law of heteronomy—the fact that "the other is my law."[26] Drawing from Levinasian thought, Derrida argues that the offering of hospitality is not an act of autonomous, sovereign freedom, but rather is a response to the Other, who is already within us. Heteronomy and alterity, not autonomous freedom, are the basis of human existence.[27] Secondly, Derrida uses another neologism "hostipitality" to express his understanding that inherent within hospitality is the potential for violence. Derrida's indication of the close relationship between "hostility" and "hospitality" is summarized well by Caputo, who writes:

> The *hospes* is someone who has the power to host someone, so that neither the alterity (*hostis*) of the stranger nor the power (*potentia*) of the host is annulled by the hospitality. There is an essential "self-limitation" built right into the idea of hospitality, which preserves the distance between one's own and the stranger, between owning one's own property and inviting the other into one's home. So, there is always a little hostility in all hosting and hospitality, constituting a certain "hostil/pitality."[28]

Derrida's deconstructive analysis, his listening to the "middle voice," in drawing attention to the in-built tension of the concepts of which the discourse of hospitality is constructed—ideas of "host" and "guest," "hostage" and "enemy," "stranger" and "benefactor"—leads to the posing of probing questions regarding the nature of hospitality. Does hospitality exist through the act of *invitation* of the host, or the *visitation* of the guest? Does hospitality depend on reciprocal giving between "host" and "guest"—if such distinctions exist—or does it revolve around an act of unreserved generosity? Is it necessary or desirable to establish boundaries

26. Derrida and Roudinesco, "Unforeseeable Freedom," 52.

27. Derrida writes: "What arises unforeseeably, what both calls upon and overwhelms my responsibility (my responsibility *before* my freedom—which it nonetheless seems to presuppose, my responsibility in heteronomy, my freedom with autonomy)." Ibid.

28. Caputo, *Deconstruction in a Nutshell*, 110.

and limits to acts of hospitality, or does hospitality require the acceptance of all-comers?

The Gift

These questions regarding the nature of hospitality first begin to emerge in Derrida's treatment of the idea of the "gift," the dominant theme in his works *Given Time: I. Counterfeit Money*, and *The Gift of Death*.[29] In *Given Time*, Derrida engages with the influential work of French anthropologist/sociologist Marcel Mauss: *The Gift: The Form and Reason for Exchange in Archaic Societies*.[30] Mauss' work, using empirical evidence from a number of societies, argues that gift-giving, grounded in obligations and reciprocity, establishes a moral bond enabling the functioning of societies. Derrida responds to Mauss' influential theory of social relations developed around the idea of *the gift*, arguing that Mauss' idea of the gift as an economy of exchange of gifts, based as it is in closed circles of obligation and reciprocity, "begins more and more to look like an essay not on the gift but on the word 'gift.'"[31] For Derrida, the "gift" cannot be a concept trapped within the circles of economy and reciprocity, but rather is a moment/event of excess and madness, which opens up closed circles to the *impossible*. Derrida states:

> Now the gift, *if there is any*, would no doubt be related to economy. One cannot treat the gift, this goes without saying, without treating this relation to economy, even to the money economy. But is not the gift, if there is any, also that which interrupts economy? That which, in suspending economic calculation, no longer gives rise to exchange? That which opens the circle so as to defy reciprocity or symmetry, the common measure, and so as to turn aside the return in view of the no-return? If there is gift, the *given* of the gift (*that which* one gives, *that which* is given, the gift as given thing or as act of donation) must not come back to the giving (let us not already say to the subject, to the donor). It must not circulate, it must not be exchanged, it must not in any case be exhausted, as a gift, by the process of exchange, by the movement of circulation of the circle in the form of return to the point of departure. If the figure of the circle is essential to economics, the gift must remain *aneconomic*. Not that it remains

29. Derrida, *Given Time*; Derrida, *Gift of Death*.

30. Mauss, *Gift*.

31. Derrida, *Given Time*, 55.

foreign to the circle, but it must *keep* a relation of foreignness to the circle, a relation without relation of familiar foreignness. It is perhaps in this sense that the gift is the impossible.

Not impossible but *the* impossible. The very figure of the impossible. It announces itself, it gives itself to be thought as the impossible.[32]

In response to Mauss' idea of the "gift" which operates within the closed circles of exchange and reciprocity, Derrida posits that:

The gift, if there is any, will always be *without* border. What does "without" mean here? The gift that does not run over its borders, a gift that would let itself be contained in a determination and limited by the indivisibility of an identifiable *trait* would not be a gift. As soon as it delimits itself, a gift is prey to calculation and measure. The gift, if there is any, should overrun the border, to be sure, toward the measureless and the excessive; but it should also suspend its relation to the border and even its transgressive relation to the separable line or trait of a border.[33]

Derrida sees the aporetic nature of the concept of a "gift" as a glimpse of the *impossible*, of the messianic future yet to come, a philosophical concept that prevents our circles of economy and reciprocity from becoming closed circles, but rather opens these circles up and exposes us to moments of *excess* and *madness*. This idea of the "gift" as a moment of excess, of madness, of a transgressing of borders, plays an important role as Derrida develops the concept of *unconditional* hospitality in his later works.

Invitation and Visitation; Conditional and Unconditional

The idea of limitations and borders inherent within Derrida's discussion of the "gift" is again prominent in Derrida's analysis of other concepts central to the discourse and practice of hospitality: *invitation* and *visitation*. Drawing attention to the practice of extending an invitation to another, Derrida notes that intrinsic to such an *invitation* is the ability of the host to set limitations on who is welcome, and when they are welcome, thereby retaining mastery and control. Such behavior, Derrida suggests, is hardly hospitable, noting: "If I welcome only what I welcome, what I am ready to welcome, and that I recognize in advance because I expect the coming of

32. Ibid., 7.
33. Ibid., 91.

the hôte as invited, there is no hospitality."[34] Instead, Derrida suggests that genuine hospitality would require a giving up of this mastery and control. He states that "to be hospitable is to let oneself be overtaken [*surprende*], *to be ready to not be ready*, if such is possible, to let oneself be overtaken, to not even *let* oneself to be overtaken, to be surprised in a fashion almost violent, violated and raped, stolen . . . precisely where one is not ready to receive—and not only *not yet ready* but *not ready*, *unprepared* in a mode that is not even that of the "not yet."[35]

In contrast to a hospitality of invitation, where the guest is expected, recognized and welcomed, Derrida asserts "that radical hospitality consists, *would have* to consist, in *receiving without invitation*, beyond or before the invitation,"[36] and posits an unconditional hospitality of *visitation*, where the guest, appearing as a messianic ghost-like figure, comes to disrupt and disturb our prearranged and formalized practices.[37]

But is such a hospitality, a hospitality of the *gift* and *visitation*, a hospitality without limits and borders, really possible? Or, is Derrida, reminiscent of Levinas, simply employing hyperbole, to emphasize the radical nature of genuine hospitality? To answer these questions and to gain a deeper appreciation of Derrida's thought regarding hospitality, it is essential to understand the relationship that Derrida poses between these two forms of hospitality: hospitality as *invitation* or *visitation*. For Derrida these two notions of hospitality are not moments or phases of the same phenomenon, but rather belong to two different dimensions. Derrida writes:

> It is as if there were a competition or contradiction between two neighboring but incompatible values: *visitation* and *invitation*, and, more gravely, it is as if there were a hidden contradiction between hospitality and invitation. Or, more precisely, between hospitality as it exposes itself to the visit, to the visitation, and the hospitality that adorns and prepares itself in invitation. These two hôtes that the visitor and the invited are, these two faces of hospitality, visitation and invitation, are not moments of hospitality, dialectical phases of the same process, the same

34. Derrida, "Hostipitality," 362.

35. Ibid., 361. It is worth noting Derrida's choice of vocabulary, and the notion—reminiscent of Levinas—that the visitation of the Other comes upon the subject *violently*.

36. Ibid., 360.

37. The theme of the ghost-guest is an evocative one particularly in light of the Christian tradition and the Emmaus road story (Luke 24:13–35).

phenomenon. Visitor and invited, visitation and invitation, are simultaneously in competition and incompatible; they figure the non-dialectizable tension, even the always imminent implosion, in fact, the continuously occurring implosion in its imminence, unceasing, at once active and deferred, of the concept of hospitality, even of the *concept* in *hospitality*. To wait without waiting, awaiting absolute surprise, the unexpected visitor, awaited without a horizon of expectation: this is indeed about the Messiah as hôte, about the messianic as hospitality, the messianic that introduces deconstructed disruption or madness in the concept of hospitality, the madness *of* hospitality, even the madness *of the concept* of hospitality.[38]

Underpinning Derrida's account of hospitality therefore is a philosophical structure in which Derrida distinguishes between two different dimensions. One dimension is the "finite, relative and historically grounded"[39] reality of politics and law of our everyday real world—a dimension of juridical, political and ethical limits—while the other dimension is that of the *messianic*, of the future to come (*l'avenir*), of the *impossible*.

For Derrida, Kant's *Cosmopolitanism*, with its account of hospitality based on universal rights, but subject to conditions, serves as the archetypal law of conditional hospitality.[40] Kant outlines his juridical law of universal hospitality writing:

> As in the preceding articles, our consent here is not with philanthropy but with *right*, and in this context *hospitality* (hospitableness) means the right of an alien not to be treated as an enemy upon his arrival in another's country. If it can be done without destroying him, he can be turned away; but, as long as he behaves peaceably he cannot be treated as an enemy. He may request the *right* to be a *permanent visitor* (which would require a special, charitable agreement to make him a fellow inhabitant for a certain period), but the *right to visit*, to associate, belongs to all men by virtue of the common ownership of the earth's surface; for since the earth is the globe, they cannot scatter themselves infinitely, but must, finally, tolerate living in

38. Derrida, "Hostipitality," 362.

39. Borradori, *Philosophy in a Time of Terror*, 164.

40. Kant's juridical account of hospitality is outlined in the section entitled "Third Definitive Article for a Perpetual Peace: Cosmopolitan Right Shall Be Limited to Conditions of the Universal Hospitality," in *To Perpetual Peace*. Derrida engages explicitly with Kant's account in Derrida and Dufourmantelle, *Of Hospitality*, 65–71. See also Derrida, *Cosmopolitanism and Forgiveness*, 20–23.

close proximity, because originally no one had a greater right to any region of the earth than anyone else. . . . In this way distant parts of the world can establish with one another peaceable relations that will eventually become matters of public law, and the human race can gradually be brought closer and closer to a cosmopolitan constitution.[41]

Derrida points out the limits inherent within Kant's juridical account of hospitality, grounded as it is in natural law (droit). While Kant stresses the "common ownership of the earth's surface," the reality is that habitats, cultures, institutions and States are constructed upon this soil. As a consequence, hospitality is firstly limited to a right of visitation (Besuchsrecht) rather than a right to residence (Gastrecht), and secondly, hospitality becomes dependent on the State.[42]

For Derrida, however, the very existence of conditional hospitality, that is, hospitality in the world of concrete realities, as in the form of Kant's cosmopolitan law of universal hospitality, is dependent on the existence of a realm of pure unconditional hospitality and forgiveness. This belief is summarized succinctly in an interview where Derrida states:

> An unconditional hospitality is, to be sure, practically impossible to live; one cannot in any case, and by definition, organize it. Whatever happens, happens, whoever comes, comes (ce qui arrive arrive), and that, in the end, is the only event worthy of this name. And I well recognize that this concept of pure hospitality can have no legal or political status. No state can write it into its laws. But without at least the thought of this pure and unconditional hospitality, of hospitality itself, we would have no concept of hospitality in general and would not even be able to determine any rules for conditional hospitality (with its rituals, its legal status, its norms, its national or international conventions). Without this sort of pure hospitality (a thought that is also, in its own way, an experience), we would not even have the idea of the other, of the alterity of the other, that is, of someone who enters into our lives without having been invited. We would not even have the idea of love or of "living together (vivre ensemble)" with the other in a way that is not a part of some totality or "ensemble." Unconditional hospitality, which is neither juridical nor political, is nonetheless the condition of the political and the juridical.[43]

41. Kant, Perpetual Peace, 15–16.
42. Derrida, Cosmopolitanism and Forgiveness, 22.
43. Borradori, Philosophy in a Time of Terror, 129.

Derrida's thought here has strong similarities to Levinas' notion of the Saying and the Said. Like Levinas' *Saying*, for Derrida, *unconditional hospitality*, is beyond being, unable to be expressed in language or laws. And yet, to be brought into the world of being, both in language and ethical action, this unconditional hospitality must be thus rendered into rules and laws and thus become conditional, reduced, as with Levinas' *Saying*, to the *Said*. For Derrida, the relationship between these two hospitalities, a *conditional* hospitality manifested in the legal, juridical and political realities, and the transcendent *unconditional* hospitality which is *impossible* upon which it depends, is one of "paradox, aporia… at once heterogeneous and indissociable."[44] Unlike Hegel's dialecticism, in which tensions are synthesized and thus subsumed within an overarching philosophy, in Derrida's account it is the very paradox, the aporetic nature of hospitality which provides the impetus for philosophy, the motivation and stimulus for ethical action.

This idea—that it is this tension and aporia that provides the dynamic for philosophizing and ethical action—is captured by two recurring images within Derrida's thinking: poles and circles. Conceiving of the two dimensions of conditional and unconditional hospitality as poles, Derrida writes:

> These two poles, *the unconditional and the conditional*, are absolutely heterogeneous, and must remain irreducible to one another. They are nonetheless indissociable: if one wants, and it is necessary, forgiveness [*hospitality*] to become effective, concrete, historic, if one wants it to *arrive*, to happen by changing things, it is necessary that this purity engage itself in a series of conditions of all kinds (psycho-sociological, political etc.). It is between these two poles, *irreconcilable but indissociable*, that decisions and responsibilities are to be taken.[45]

While pure unconditional, messianic hospitality is *impossible*, the desire for such a reality to *arrive* necessitates and motivates acts of hospitality, even though such acts are limited by conditions. At the same time the dynamic tension between these poles means that the pole of unconditionality strains against the pole of conditionality, seeking to break free

44. Ibid.

45. Derrida, *Cosmopolitanism and Forgiveness*, 44–45. Our modification of the quotation, replacing the original word "forgiveness" with the word *hospitality*, demonstrates the basic structure of Derrida's philosophical thought, which draws distinction between the dimensions of legal-juridical-political realities and the *impossible* dimension of the *messianic future*.

from the constraints and limits that are inherent within legal-juridical-political notions of hospitality. Derrida explains the paradoxical relationship between these two laws—*conditional* and *unconditional*—thus:

> The law hospitality, the express law that governs the general concept of hospitality, appears as a paradoxical law, pervertible or perverting. It seems to dictate that absolute hospitality should break with the law of hospitality as right or duty, with the "pact" of hospitality. To put it in different terms, absolute hospitality requires only that I open my home and that I give not only to the foreigner (provided with a family name, with the social status of being a foreigner, etc.), but to the absolute, unknown, anonymous other, and that I *give place* to them, that I let them come, and I let them arrive, and take place in the place I offer them, without asking of them either reciprocity (entering into a pact) or even their names. The law of absolute hospitality commands a break with hospitality by right, with law or justice as rights. Just hospitality breaks with hospitality by right; not that it condemns or is opposed to it, and it can on the contrary set and maintain it in a perpetual progressive movement; but it is as strangely heterogeneous to it as justice is heterogeneous to the law to which it is yet so close, from which in truth it is indissociable.[46]

As with magnetic poles which, in constantly attracting or repelling each other, composes a dynamic magnetic field of energy, for Derrida, the two poles of conditional and unconditional creates the field of possibilities in which ethical action is performed.[47]

In a similar vein, the notion of the circle, particularly in relation to the "gift," frequents Derrida's work. In *Given Time*, Derrida writes: "For finally the overrunning of the circle by the gift, if there is any, does not lead to a simple, ineffable exteriority that would be transcendent and without relation. It is this exteriority that sets the circle going, it is this exteriority that puts the economy in motion. It is this exteriority that *engages* in the circle and makes it turn."[48]

---

46. Derrida and Dufourmantelle, *Of Hospitality*, 25, 27.

47. Precursory to themes we will raise and address later in this work, John Milbank, in his critique of Derrida's *différance*, asserts that Derrida's concept of dialectal poles and différance, far from breaking free from ontology, still stays within the "same" and thus constitutes an "ontology of violence." Milbank, *Theology and Social Theory*, 310.

48. Derrida, *Given Time*, 30.

In Derridean thought, the economy, the circle of exchange that is gift-giving, is put into motion by the *impossible* nature of the "gift"—the "gift" of excess and aneconomy. Caputo expresses this well:

> The dream and the desire for the gift, the passion that the gift impassions, are the passion and the desire to exceed the circle *even while not remaining entirely outside the circle.* . . . But it is no less true that the aneconomic gift keeps the circle turning, so that *the circle depends upon the very thing it excludes, the gift.* The circle needs the gift no less than the gift cannot avoid the circle. For Derrida's point is not to find a spot of simple exteriority to the circle, but to loosen the circle and to create an opening for the *tout autre.* . . . The circle cannot turn without the gift, and the gift has nothing to exceed without the circle. The gift will be inevitably drawn back into the circle, but the circle will not spin without gifts. Pure gifts without circles are empty; pure circles without gifts are blind. It is not a question of one or the other, of the gift pure and simple, if there were one, or of pure economy, if there were one, but of inhabiting the distance between the two with as much grace and ambiance and hospitality as possible.[49]

One way of envisaging what Derrida is trying to express here is to think of the structure of a bicycle wheel. *Conditional hospitality*—that is, the norms, laws and procedures which shape the operation and practice of hospitality in the real world—are the spokes which provide the structural strength to the wheel, while the rim of the wheel is the realm of *unconditional hospitality.* Without the rim, there is no recognizable wheel, but similarly without the spokes—hospitality operating within and under conditions—it would be impossible for the wheel to actually function as a wheel, to hit the ground and revolve.

Indeed, it is this notion of the *possible* being sustained by its *impossibility* which is one of the central tenets of Derrida's idea of *différance.* In *Of Grammatology,* Derrida writes: "Différance produces what it forbids, making possible the very thing that makes it impossible."[50] For Derrida, the impossibility of an *unconditional* hospitality does not therefore, lead to paralysis. Rather, it is the very aporetic nature of hospitality, its *impossibility,* which makes it possible. Caputo again expresses this concisely:

> Like everything else in deconstruction, the possibility of hospitality is sustained by the impossibility; hospitality really starts to

49. Caputo, *Prayers and Tears,* 171–73.
50. Derrida, *Grammatology,* 143.

get underway only when we "experience" (which means to travel or go through) this paralysis (the inability to move). Hospitality *is* impossible, what Derrida calls *the* impossible (the im-possibility of hostil-pitality), which is not the same as a simple logical contradiction. Hospitality really starts to happen when I push against this limit, the threshold, this paralysis, inviting hospitality to cross its own threshold and limit, its own self-limitation, to become a *gift beyond hospitality*. Thus, for hospitality to occur, it is necessary for hospitality to go beyond hospitality. That requires that the host must, in a moment of madness, tear up the understanding between him and the guest, act with "excess," make an absolute gift of his property, which is of course impossible. But that is the only way the guest can go away feeling as if he was really made at home.[51]

In his deconstructive attentiveness to the binaries of which the practice of hospitality is composed: host-guest, exchange-excessive gift, invitation-visitation, conditional-unconditional, Derrida illustrates the inherent paradox within the concept of hospitality and points to its antinomic nature. This aporetic relationship between the two dimensions—the real finite world of conditions and limits and the messianic future of the impossible—is not a problem to be resolved by complicated philosophical maneuvers, but rather, for Derrida, is the very structure that ensures that philosophical discourse remains open. Likewise, the fact that the messiah will never show up, the *impossibility* of a pure gift, or an unconditional hospitality of visitation, rather than leading to paralysis or inaction, is the very dynamic which empowers ethical action, the practicing of hospitality.

An Evaluation

Having given a general sketch of Derrida's "deconstruction" and his account of hospitality, we now turn our attention to assess the strengths and weaknesses of his account. In what follows, our evaluation of Derrida's thought will be guided by three questions:

1. What is the nature of ethical action as conceived within Derrida's thought?

2. What understanding of human identity and human-relationality is conveyed within Derrida's philosophy?

3. What is Derrida's understanding of *faith*?

51. Caputo, *Deconstruction in a Nutshell*, 110–11.

In each of these three areas we will observe that while there are potential compatibilities and coherences between Derrida's thought and a Christian-theological account of hospitality, there are also clear dissimilarities.

Hospitality as Excessive and Risky Performance

Like Levinas, Derrida is uneasy with universal moral projects which ground ethics in metaphysics, espousing universal laws which the moral subject is bound by *duty* or *obligation* to obey. For Derrida, *duty and obligation* grounded in a general law to all men—as in Kant's juridical account of a Cosmopolitan law—are inappropriate motivations for the ethical practice of hospitality. Similarly, contractual understandings of hospitality as in Rawl's "theory of justice"—in which ultimately the motivation for hospitality stems from debt to a social contract or self-interest, are, for Derrida, likewise a violation of the very nature of hospitality.[52] Derrida writes:

> For to be what it "must" be, hospitality must not pay a debt, or be governed by duty: it is gracious, and "must" not open itself to the guest [invited or visitor], either "conforming to duty" or even, to use the Kantian distinction again, "out of duty." This unconditional law of hospitality, if such a thing is thinkable, would then be a law without imperative, without order and without duty. A law without law, in short. For if I practice hospitality *"out* of duty" [and not only *"in conforming with* duty"], this hospitality of paying up is no longer an absolute hospitality, it is no longer graciously offered beyond debt and economy, offered to the other, a hospitality invented for the singularity of the new arrival of the unexpected visitor.[53]

For Derrida, the attempt to frame hospitality in legal, political or contractual clauses, rules and maxims, that is, the attempt to formalize ethics in a programmatic and procedural form, while necessary, must be constantly deconstructed. Ethical behavior, Derrida argues, is hardly ethical if we simply seek to apply preestablished conduct or laws in each ethical encounter. To genuinely encounter the singular particularity of the *tout autre*, means to give up one's preconceived conceptions of ethics based on knowledge and to allow one's ethical behavior to be guided by the request of the other. For Derrida, true moral behavior entails a move beyond the

52. Rawls, *Theory of Justice.*
53. Derrida and Dufourmantelle, *Of Hospitality,* 83.

realm of knowledge and a Kierkegaardian leap of faith into the abyss of madness, into the experience of "undecidability."

Therefore, according to Derrida, one's ultimate *duty* is not the following of laws and ethical duties, but the absolute responsibility one holds to the other who is wholly Other. "Ethics," Derrida asserts: "must be sacrificed in the name of duty. It is a duty not to respect, out of duty, ethical duty. One must behave not only in an ethical or responsible manner, but in a non ethical, nonresponsible manner, and one must do that *in the name of* duty, of an infinite duty, *in the name of* absolute duty."[54]

For Derrida, Abraham is the exemplary figure of such ethics, one who sacrifices his *duty* to ethics, and demonstrates his absolute duty not to a *universal* law, but to the singular particularity of *tout autre*. Derrida suggests that one's ethical action should imitate that of Abraham, whose actions, in being prepared to sacrifice his son Isaac are based, Derrida believes, not on knowledge but on faith. Thus, Derrida writes: "The knight of faith must not hesitate. He accepts his responsibility by heading off towards the absolute request of the other, beyond knowledge. He decides, but his absolute decision is neither guided nor controlled by knowledge. Such, in fact, is the paradoxical condition of every decision: it cannot be deduced from a form of knowledge of which it would simply be the effect, conclusion, or explicitation."[55]

In contrast to law-based approaches to ethics which presuppose a universal knowledge, Derrida emphasizes the contingency of knowledge and points to the fundamental personal nature of ethics. Ethics, rather than being a fulfillment of duties or obligations, is fundamentally about a personal encounter with a particular/singular individual. Derrida turns the traditional understanding of ethics upside-down by asserting that it is the very alterity, that is, the singularity of the Other, which is the true law of ethics. Hence, he states: "Linking alterity to singularity or to what one would call the universal exception or the law of the exception—*tout autre est tout autre* signifies that every other is singular, that everyone has a

---

54. Derrida, *Gift of Death*, 67.

55. Ibid., 77. Elsewhere Derrida states: "The only possible decision possible is the impossible decision. It is when it is not possible to *know* what must be done, when knowledge is not and cannot be determining that a decision is possible as such. Otherwise the decision is an application: one knows what has to be done, it's clear, there is no more decision possible; what one has here is an effect, an application, a programming." Derrida, "Dialanguages," 147–48.

singularity, which also means that everyone is each one, a proposition that seals the contract between universality and the exception of singularity."[56]

This understanding of ethics expressed not in laws, maxims and procedures, but rather embedded in and shaped by actual physical encounters with the Other, of ethics not as a bound and sealed tome of knowledge, but an action which inhabits the space of temporality and contingency—Derridean ethics so to speak—has strong similarities with Levinasian thought. It also has certain resonances with the kingdom ethics espoused and practiced by Jesus. One of the striking features of Jesus' ministry is the *particular* nature of the miraculous episodes which punctuate his public ministry. Far from being run programmatically and having a procedural inevitability, Jesus' ministry, in Lukan terms, of "preaching good news, proclaiming freedom for the prisoners, recovering sight for the blind, releasing the oppressed, and proclaiming the year of Jubilee," is as diverse and varied as the particular people and communities that Jesus encounters.[57] It is the very singularity and particularity of Jesus' ministry and the way in which his ethical behavior bends the established laws and customs, which leads to his ongoing conflict with the religious leaders of his day. Two obvious examples are the healing of the man with a shriveled hand on the Sabbath and Jesus' response to the woman caught in adultery.[58] In each case, Jesus' understanding of the appropriate ethical response, reinterprets or bypasses the legal framework, and adheres to a higher ethical standard. Jesus "deconstructs" the law by revealing the way in which duty to the law, with its disregard for the singularity of the Other, runs the risk of "destroying, rather than saving life."[59] Derrida's understanding that what is important is not one's adherence to law or a fulfillment of legal duties, but rather how one's ethical behavior accords with the transcendent nature of pure "justice," "hospitality" and "forgiveness," echoes Jesus' scathing rebuke of the Pharisees for the way in which their stringent adherence to the law blinded them to "the more important matters of the law—justice, mercy and faithfulness."[60]

Derridean ethics then, cannot be reduced to a program or a set of predetermined actions applicable to different contexts, but rather is best understood *performatively*—a response not to legal, juridical or political

---

56. Derrida, *Gift of Death*, 87.

57. Luke 4:18–19.

58. See Matt 12:1–14; Mark 3:1–6; Luke 6:1–10; and John 8:1–11.

59. Luke 6:9.

60. Matthew 23:23.

duties, but to the absolute *obligation* one has to the *tout autre*. One's obligation to the *tout autre*, like Levinas' *infinite responsibility*, means that one's ethical duties are never fulfilled no matter how well one upholds or administers laws or procedures. The active nature of this *performative experience* of ethics is particularly important. In Derrida's thought, the problem which arises with many ethical schemas is that so much time is spent discussing and debating what is the appropriate ethical response that nothing is done. In contrast, Derrida's account of ethical hospitality calls not for endless pontificating, but rather is a summons to ethical action. Caputo expresses it this way:

> Derrida likes to say that we do not know what hospitality is, not because the idea is built around the difficult conceptual riddle, but because, in the end, hospitality is not a matter of *objective knowledge*, but belongs to another order altogether, beyond knowledge, an enigmatic "experience" in which I set out for the stranger, for the other, for the unknown, where I cannot go. I do not know what is coming, what is to come, what calls for hospitality or what hospitality is called. The aporia is not conceptually resolved by a bit of intellectual adroitness but strained against *performatively*, by an *act* of generosity, by a giving which gives beyond itself, which is a little blind and does not see where it is going. . . . it does not come down to *knowing anything*, but to *doing something*.[61]

As with Levinas' emphasis on *affection*, Derrida's emphasis on ethics as *performance* stems from his contention that ethics stems not from the exercising of reason but from human subjectivity itself. Like Levinas, Derrida stresses that such performing of *unconditional* hospitality, a leap into the unknown, is, by corollary, a risky undertaking. Derrida's awareness of and his advocating of ethical action which is inevitably excessive and risky, is made clear when he writes: "Pure, unconditional or infinite hospitality cannot and must not be anything else but an acceptance of risk. If I am sure that the newcomer that I welcome is perfectly harmless, innocent, that (s)he will be beneficial to me . . . it is not hospitality. When I open my door I must be ready to take the greatest of risks."[62]

Such an emphasis on the risky and excessive nature of ethical performance is again, one to be commended. In a world where the media

---

61. Caputo, *Deconstruction in a Nutshell*, 112. Emphasis added.

62. Derrida, "Debat: Une Hospitalité sans condition," quoted in Rosello, *Postcolonial Hospitality*, 11–12.

is constantly highlighting the potential danger that waits outside one's hermetically-sealed homes, and where risk-aversion seems to have become the key determining factor for how many order their lives, Derrida's reminder of the risky nature of hospitality, while discomforting, is also an important reality-check. As we will consider in more depth later, crucial to hospitality is an acknowledgement and acceptance of the risk involved in such a practice.

However, while Derrida's description of ethics as a risky and excessive performance, a movement of faith beyond the knowledge-based confines of law and duty, does have some similarities with a Christian-theological account of ethics, there are also elements of Derrida's account which are problematic. Firstly, while Derrida makes much of Abraham as the exemplar of faith, there are aspects of Derrida's interpretation of this narrative—as offered in *The Gift of Death*—which are clearly questionable. In Derrida's thinking, *knowledge* is an activity which in totalizing, systematizing and reducing the Other to the Same often leads to inaction. Genuine ethical behavior he therefore asserts requires the relinquishment of *knowledge* and an embracing of *faith*.[63] But is *knowledge* always totalizing and does faith consist of a complete abandonment of knowledge? While Derridean thought seems to create an exaggerated dichotomy between *faith* and *knowledge*, the Christian tradition has always emphasized the ways in which these two elements work together. While *knowledge* can be oppressive and totalizing, the Christian tradition has stressed that knowledge and understanding have an appropriate role if built upon the foundation of faith.[64] Likewise, central to Christian thought is the belief that the essence of such faith—the knowledge of God—is not inactivity,

63. Derrida does recognize that there is a relationship between *faith* and *knowledge*, but stresses the heterogeneous nature of this relationship. He writes: "Decision, an ethical or a political responsibility, is absolutely heterogeneous to knowledge. Nevertheless, we have to know as much as possible in order to ground our decision. But even if it is grounded in knowledge, the moment I take a decision it is a leap, I enter a heterogeneous space and that is the condition of responsibility." Derrida, "Hospitality, Justice and Responsibility," 73. While Derrida's phrase "Je ne sais pas. Il faut croire" ("I do not know. One has to believe") has been picked up by sympathetic commentators, as evidence of Derrida's affirmation of *faith*, like his emphasis on the distinction between a pure realm of unconditional hospitality and conditional hospitality, for Derrida, these two realms of faith and knowledge are bifurcated from one another. Derrida offers no hope that the realm of faith in some way overcomes and transforms the hostility contained within human knowledge. Also, as we note later, it is not exactly clear *what*, or *who*, Derrida, has faith in. Derrida, *Memoirs of the Blind*, 129.

64. One only needs to recall Anselm's famous dictum: *fides quaerens intellectum*—faith seeking understanding.

but rather active obedience. As Karl Barth states: "Knowledge of God is obedience to God. Observe that we do not say that knowledge may also be obedience, or that of necessity it has obedience attached to it, or that it is followed by obedience. No; knowledge of God as knowledge of faith is in itself and of essential necessity obedience."[65]

Secondly, as well as these differing conceptions of knowledge, there is also a contrast between Derridean and Christian thought with regard to their respective understandings of faith. While Derrida is to be applauded for highlighting the degree of madness inherent in faith what he fails to recognize is the extent to which such leaps of faith are episodes in ongoing faith journeys. While correct in stressing the element of madness in Abraham's faithful actions, Derrida fails to take into account the extent to which this action—in this case of preparing to sacrifice his son—takes place after a series of other acts of "madness"/faith, such as leaving his homeland and negotiating with God over the future of Sodom and Gomorrah. For Derrida, *faith* entails a leap into an abyss of not-knowing, with each ethical action being seen as a singular decision cut off from the rest of time and experience. In contrast, the Christian tradition sees faith as on ongoing relationship with the Triune God. Faith so construed, still involves an element of risk, of stepping out into the unknown, but with an assurance that the personal and faithful God who calls and guides, will continue to remain true to his promises. Based on one's previous experiences of God's faithfulness one can be confident that one does not take the leap of faith alone. As the writer of Hebrews reminds us, Abraham's actions are those of a faithful man, one whose leap of faith is based on the confidence that Yahweh is faithful—that is, that Yahweh will stay true to his promises.[66]

It is this understanding that Abraham's moments of madness/leaps of faith stem from an ongoing relationship with Yahweh which is missing from Derrida's interpretation. While Derrida speaks of Abraham's *duty* to the "nameless name of God,"[67] the biblical story sets Abraham's leap of madness in the context of his ongoing relationship with Yahweh—with the God who has called, promised, and "supped" with Abraham. In disconnecting the story of Abraham and Isaac from the wider narrative, Derrida fails to recognize the *relational* component of *faith*—that faith is founded on faithfulness—and therefore fails to uncover the motivation that under-

65. Barth, *Church Dogmatics* II/1, 26.

66. See Heb 11:8–9, 11, 17.

67. Derrida, *Gift of Death*, 67.

lies Abraham's faith, expressed in ethical action. Could we venture that the underlying basis for Abraham's ethical actions, shaped in the crucible of an ongoing relationship with Yahweh, is one of *love*?

This failure of Derrida to understand that *faith* is not primarily to be construed as a leap beyond knowledge, but rather as a summons to enter into relations of faithfulness and trust with others, leads on to a consideration of the second of our questions—that is: How does Derrida conceive of human identity and human-relationality? While Derrida's belief in hospitality as an excessive and risky ethical practice, beyond *duty*, shows potential for integration within an explicit Christian understanding of hospitality, his understanding of identity and the nature of relationships, are, we suggest, less amenable to a theological account of hospitality.

Identity and the Nature of Relationships

At the heart of Derrida's account of hospitality and his understanding of relationships and identity is the concept/non-concept of *différance*. According to Derrida's account, hospitality is only possible due to *différance*. That is, "as master and host, the self, in welcoming the other, must interrupt or divide himself or herself. *This division is the condition of hospitality*."[68] In Derridean thinking, the identity of the subject is not one of unity, but rather, identity is composed of "self-interruption" and "division."[69] The significance of this notion of "division" for both an understanding of self-identity and therefore relationality becomes clear in the extract below, where Derrida outlines the two meanings "division" has for him:

> The meaning of division itself divides. On the one hand, it is fate, seen in its painful aspect: the inability to bring together in the one. It is necessity, inevitable. In this sense it is what exposes to dissociation, to dehiscence; and at the same time, on the other hand, in another meaning, division can also be a line of strategy, a profound movement of keeping itself. From the moment one divides oneself, one keeps something always in reserve, one doesn't expose oneself all at once to the threat. There is always another place, there is not just one side, just one place; there are always several places, and this differentiation is a protection, a strategy of the living. This is not a little calculation, it's a strategy of desire which divides itself in order to keep something in reserve: I remain free, I am not just there, you will

68. Derrida, "Hospitality, Justice and Responsibility," 81. Emphasis added.
69. Ibid.

see that I am also elsewhere, and thus that I have resources, I still have a reserve, some life, and that you will not kill me off so quickly. From this point of view, division, inasmuch as it is a structural phenomenon of the living, which can live only by dividing itself *up to a certain point* (death is also a division, a dissociation), a certain type of division of the living is at once exposure to suffering, but also a measure taken to save and to keep, a kind of reserve or holding back.[70]

While in Christian anthropology there is a recognition that the subject evolves and changes, identity is grounded in a fixed given—that is, the subject's unitive identity is grounded as a relational being, created in the image of God. In contrast, in Derridean thought, with its emphasis on "division," identity is a constantly changing reality, without a fixed centre or foundation. The subject is, in Derridean thought, both inevitably and of necessity, a *divided self*.

This conceptualization of the subject as a *divided self* has important consequences for one's understanding of relationality. While the term "division" expresses Derrida's understanding of identity, the term "dissociation" describes his conception of the underlying structure of relationality. Like Levinas, Derrida's philosophy articulates an account of relationality which stresses the transcendence and unknowability of the Other. This radical distinction and difference of the Other is again communicated simply and succinctly by Derrida in an interview format:

Once you grant some privilege to gathering and not to dissociating, then you leave no room for the other, for the radical otherness of the other, for the radical singularity of the other. I think, from that point of view, *separation, dissociation is not an obstacle to society, to community, but the condition. . . . Dissociation, separation, is the condition of my relation to the other.* I can address the other only to the extent that there is a *separation, a dissociation,* so that I cannot replace the other and vice versa. . . . The structure of my relation to the other is of a "relation without relation." It is a relation in which the other remains absolutely transcendent. I cannot reach the other. They cannot know the other from the inside and so on. That is not an obstacle but the condition of love, of friendship, and of war, too, a condition of the relationship to the other. So, *dissociation is the condition of community,* the condition of any unity as such.[71]

---

70. Derrida, "Dialanguages," 146–47.

71. Caputo, *Deconstruction in a Nutshell,* 14. Emphasis added.

As with Levinas, Derrida is suspicious of any ethical behavior which finds its basis in the consciousness and reasoning of the ethical subject, seeing such ethical action as inevitably self-serving. In *Given Time*, Derrida draws particular attention to what he calls the *auto-affective* nature of ethical behavior, that is, ethical behavior where the subject performs a certain ethical action—such as offering hospitality—on the understanding and hope that they will get something back in return, i.e., a reciprocal invitation/a reward from God. Derrida suggests the need for an ongoing vigilance and awareness that the action of offering hospitality can itself be a form of violence, the practicing of hospitality being motivated by a desire for *appropriation*. Thus, Derrida writes: "To dare to say welcome is perhaps to insinuate that one is at home here, that one knows what it means to be at home, and that at home one receives, invites, or offers hospitality, thus appropriating for oneself a place to *welcome* [*accueillir*] the other, or, worse, *welcoming* the other in order to appropriate for oneself a place and then speak the language of hospitality. . . ."[72] For Derrida, it is separation and dissociation, the radical difference between the subject and the Other in the face of such inherent violent self-interest, which ensures that the Other is not captured or categorized by the subject.

While Derrida's description is motivated by a desire to ensure that the Other is protected from totalizing violence, such a structural account raises a number of significant questions: Does an understanding of identity in terms of "division" and relationality in terms of "dissociation" and "separation," provide an appropriate and fitting structure for the development of an ethic of hospitality? How do Derrida's idea of "division" and the themes of keeping in "reserve" and "holding back" relate to the ideas of excessiveness and risk-taking, which we have observed? And, perhaps most importantly, to what extent is such a structure based on a "divided" self and radical "separation" compatible with the theological understanding of a Triune God—a God of unity and relationality, who in the event of the Incarnation does not "hold Himself back"?

As we saw in the previous chapter, Derrida commends Levinas' thinking as a philosophy of peace in contrast to Kant whose "institution of an eternal peace, of cosmopolitical law, and of universal hospitality, retains the trace of natural hostility."[73] But is Derrida's description of identity and relationality inherently peaceful? Despite his condemnation of transcendental and metaphysical philosophy, Derrida's philosophy can be

---

72. Derrida, *Adieu*, 15–16. See also Rosello, *Postcolonial Hospitality*, 17–18.
73. Derrida, *Adieu*, 88.

seen itself as a form of metaphysical philosophy which, it has been argued, takes the shape of ontological violence.[74] While Derrida's description of the "hostility" which inheres within the concept of hospitality and his understanding that the self must divide itself as a condition for hospitality clearly relates to the finite *conditional* dimension of hospitality, it is not clear whether Derrida also conceives of these same "hostilities" and "divisions" existing within the dimension of *pure unconditional* hospitality. *Do hostility and division constitute the ontological essence of hospitality or are they simply evident in the operation of hospitality in the finite-conditional world? And, crucially, is there any hope that this inherent hostility can be overcome?*

Ultimately, like Levinas, Derrida's emphasis on "separation" and "dissociation" stems from a desire to ensure that the Other is not consumed, assimilated and violated by the subject. Yet, one wonders whether such a description of the relational structure based on these core principles can really provide a peaceful, harmonious, and stable basis on which to develop the ethical practice of hospitality.

"Religion without Religion" and Ethics without Foundation

Thus far, in evaluating Derrida's understanding of the nature of ethics and his conception of identity and relationality we have noted both areas where his thought offers potentially useful insights, while also observing areas of dissonance. But what of Derrida's own religious thought? To what extent can Derrida's religious philosophy, and in particular his notion of *faith*, be incorporated into a theological account of hospitality?

We have noted how Derrida's philosophical schema and his description of the ethical action of hospitality distinguishes between two dimensions: the "finite, relative and historically grounded" dimension of juridical, political and ethical limits, and the dimension of the *messianic*, of the future to come (*l'avenir*), of the *impossible*.[75] For Derrida, the existence and practice of hospitality in the world—though limited by the conditions of the legal-political world—is dependent on the existence of the *idea* of a pure, unconditional hospitality. But what is the site/source/origin of this *pure hospitality* that Derrida envisages? Perhaps surprisingly,

---

74. See Milbank, *Theology and Social Theory*, 306–11. Milbank's contention that Derrida's philosophy is a form of dialectic Hegelianism and thus, itself, a form of metaphysical philosophy, is one we will examine in more detail in the next chapter.

75. Borradori, *Philosophy in a Time of Terror*, 164.

Derrida does not avoid such questions. In reflecting on the nature of the *gift*, Derrida asks what it is that, "while not simply belonging to the circle, engages in it and sets off its motion. What is the gift as the first mover of the circle? And how does it contract itself into a circular contract? And from what place? Since when? From whom?"[76]

In seeking to respond to such questions, in developing the concept that the *possible* is conditional on the *impossible*, in affirming a belief in a realm of *absolute hospitality, pure forgiveness,* the *pure gift*, Derrida is led constantly, much to the horror of many other philosophers, back to the religious and the transcendent.[77] Caputo's assertion that "Jacques Derrida is a man of tears, of faith and tears, for faith is driven by passion and tears are the passion of faith" is perhaps a more accurate portrayal than that of Derrida as the harbinger of nihilistic anarchy as some others would maintain.[78] Nevertheless, while heavily influenced by Jewish-biblical religious thinking, and while significant Christian theologians act as interlocutors in his philosophical work, there are major differences between Derrida's post-structuralist faith, interpreted by Caputo as a "religion without religion," and the historical Christian faith.[79] Perhaps the starkest example of the divergence between Derridean post-structuralist faith and orthodox Christian faith can be seen in Derrida's concepts of the *messianic structure* and *the future as the impossible.*

Messiahs, Messianic Structures, and the Telos-less Future

Derrida's understanding of the visitation of the stranger as a messianic-figure concurs with a rich tradition within the Christian history, in which the receiving of the stranger was commended on the understanding that

76. Derrida, *Given Time*, 31.

77. In this sense Derrida is simply representative of the broader "theological turn" within French phenomenological thought, evident in the work of our interlocutors, and also Paul Ricoeur, Jean-Luc Marion, Jean-Louis Chrétien and Michel Henry. Dominique Janicaud argues against this "turn," asserting that the "new phenomenology" practiced by such writers is no longer phenomenological. See Janicaud, *Phenomenology and the "Theological Turn."*

78. Caputo, *Prayers and Tears*, 308.

79. Two Christian theologians in particular figure prominently in Derrida's philosophy: Søren Kierkegaard and St. Augustine. While the influences of these theologians are evident throughout Derrida's work, they explicitly appear in his close reading of Kierkegaard's *Fear and Trembling* in *The Gift of Death* and through his commentary on St. Augustine's *Confessions* in *Circumfession.*

such a visitor may be a messianic figure or theophany.[80] But beyond these surface similarities there are fundamental differences between Derrida's understanding of the Messiah and conception of messianic time and that of orthodox Christian thought.

Central to Derrida's account of hospitality is his understanding of the messianic structure. It is the openness of time created by an expectation and waiting for the Messiah, which, according to Derrida, prevents foreclosure and therefore keeps us open to a future of the *impossible*. Derrida's position seems to characterize—and arguably caricature—historical messianisms as movements in which adherents are closed to new possibilities, whose "waiting" for the potential arrival of their promised Messiah leads to either ethical paralysis, or worse, a totalizing violence towards those of other messianic faiths/traditions.[81] In contrast, Derrida proposes a messianic structure—without the historical messianisms which contribute to the wars and woes which beset the world—a structure that keeps us perpetually open to the future that is yet to come. But does the arrival of a/the Messiah really close down time and close the "faithful" from the openness of the future? And, can you have a generalized "ontological" messianic structure without a particular "historical" messiah?[82]

To answer these questions it is necessary to understand Derrida's conception of time, which is integral to his idea of the messianic structure. In *Of Grammatology*, Derrida argues that the Western conception of time is "linearist," centered around a temporal conception of "presence."[83] In the revolt of deconstruction against the tradition of Western metaphysics which grounds meaning in presence, Derrida notes how the "linearist" conception of time gives way to a "delinearized temporality."[84] Derrida

---

80. Biblical examples of this include Abraham's hosting of the three angels (Gen 18), Elijah being hosted by the widow of Zarephath (1 Kgs 17:7–24), and most significantly, the hosting by two disciples of the resurrected Jesus (Luke 24:13–35). Most notable amongst the historical tradition whose practices of hospitality were shaped by the themes of these narratives is "The Rule of St. Benedict." Benedict, echoing Matthew 25:35, writes: "All guests who present themselves are to be welcomed as Christ, for he himself will say: 'I was a stranger and you welcomed me.'" See Benedict, *Rule of St. Benedict*, 51.

81. For this explicit criticism that the "three . . . religions of the Book" are engaged in a "war of messianic eschatologies," and that the "war for the 'appropriation of Jerusalem' is today the world war," see Derrida, *Specters of Marx*, 58.

82. For a discussion on this conundrum within Derrida's thought, see: Caputo, *Deconstruction in a Nutshell*, 169.

83. Derrida, *Grammatology*, 72.

84. Ibid., 87.

concludes that modern philosophy must abandon the classical vocabulary and conception of time, positing that: "The concepts of *present, past,* and *future,* everything in the concepts of time and history which implies evidence of them—the metaphysical concept of time in general—cannot adequately describe the structure of the trace."[85]

While no theory of time is explicitly outlined by Derrida in either *Of Grammatology* or later works, hints of his conception of time are noticeable throughout his writings, in particular, in *Given Time.* Here, in contrast to the "linearist" view in which time is orientated towards its end, Derrida posits a circular understanding of time, stating: "One of the most powerful and ineluctable representations, at least in the history of metaphysics, is the representation of time as a circle."[86]

As mentioned earlier, it is this notion of the circle which is illustrative of Derrida's belief that the *possible* is nourished and sustained by its *impossibility.* For Derrida it is the very *impossibility* of the gift breaking into the economic circle or the Messiah turning up and entering time which sustains and makes possible both hospitality as gift-giving and *time itself.* Derrida states this explicitly:

> That wherever there is time, wherever time predominates or conditions experience in general, where *time as circle* is predominant, the gift is impossible. A gift could be possible, there could be gift only at the instance an effraction in the circle will have taken place, at the instant all circulation would have been interrupted and *on condition* of this instant. What is more, this instant of effraction (of the temporal circle) must no longer be part of time. . . . There would be a gift only at the instant when the *paradoxical* instant (in the sense in which Kierkegaard says of the paradoxical instant of decision that it is madness) tears time apart. In this sense one would never have the time of a gift.[87]

It is this sense of the *impossible,* the circular nature of time, in which the future is unknown and therefore always open, which for Derrida prevents the totalization and universalization inherent in Western "linear" metaphysical thinking.

But does such an understanding of time—of a messianic time in which the messiah never shows up—really provide the basis for ethical

---

85. Ibid., 67.

86. Derrida, *Given Time,* 8.

87. Ibid., 9.

action as Derrida envisages? Can one really speak of ethical action, or ethics itself, without an account of the Good, and the *telos* to which ethical action is directed? While Derrida and other post-structuralist thinkers see the disappearance of *telos* as a major philosophical advance, other moral philosophers see the loss of teleology as the single most contributory problem to the fragmented and exclusionary world we inhabit.[88] While we will return to this question later in this work, for now, it is worth simply asking: To what extent do Derrida's conceptions of the messianic and his notion of time accord with a Christian-theological understanding?

Derrida's conception of a messiah without presence and of the impossibility of an "irruptive" event / gift which "interrupts the continuum of the narrative,"[89] is in stark contrast to the claim of Christianity that Jesus of Nazareth is the Messiah who has entered historical time. Coming to earth, suffering under Pontius Pilate, being crucified, dead, and buried, the creeds of Christian faith assert that this crucified Messiah has been resurrected, has ascended into heaven, and, *will come again*. Christian teleology, far from being totalizing, with a fixed-determined future which closes down possibilities and results in ethical paralysis is thoroughly eschatological. In the Christian theological tradition the messianic future is neither a Derridean *impossibility* nor a fixed *telos* functioning like a regulative Kantian *ideal*, but rather is a *present-reality* that has burst into history with the resurrection of Jesus. While Derrida's messianic structure is founded upon a form of "dogmatic agnosticism," which asserts that the possible is sustained and nourished by the impossible, it is the claim of Christian faith that with God *all things are possible*.[90] It is in the visitation of the Messiah, in doing what *we* perceive as the *im*possible and taking on human flesh that the Triune God has opened time to new possibilities. God has revealed himself in *presence*, and the *telos* of the future has broken into the present. It is this irrupting of divine hospitality into the world of presence and time which provides the foundation for Christian hope and therefore establishes the basis for human actions of excessive and risky hospitality.

In contrast to a Christian theology of hospitality grounded in the historical events of the life, death and resurrection of a singular-particular Messiah—the entrance of the "gift," of *pure* hospitality into the world of *being*—Derrida's two-dimensional understanding of hospitality has strongly

88. In particular, see MacIntyre, *After Virtue*.

89. Derrida, *Given Time*, 123.

90. Luke 1:37, 18:27.

Platonistic tendencies, with an aversion to any kind of incarnation.[91] In his preference for a generalized concept—that of some sort of ontological "messianic structure"—over the *particular, temporality* of the phenomenon of historical messiahs, Derrida seems to jettison his own philosophical *modus operandi*—of stressing the *particular* over the *universal!* As well as being ironic, such action is symptomatic of his post-structuralist approach, which seeks a version of faith, religion and morality, without committing oneself to any dogma.

Bruce Ellis Benson captures well the extent to which this "undecidability," heralded by Derrida as authentic faith, can alternatively, be seen as a failure to take "the idea of undecidability seriously enough." Benson writes:

> True, dogma can be a way of avoiding responsibility if one says, "I believe whatever the creeds say. I really haven't thought about it myself. I just believe the stuff." But dogma can also be a way of taking responsibility, of saying "Here I stand." In saying "Here I stand," one does not necessarily say "All that I believe is 100 percent right: I am unwilling to think about this any further." One does say, "I am making a commitment to a body of belief and, more important, to God." After all his talk of responsibility as something that one cannot ultimately justify, it seems odd that Derrida would be so afraid of dogma. For dogma just is that which cannot be ultimately justified. And commitment to it is a way of taking responsibility.[92]

Derrida's deconstructive post-structuralist faith, with its belief in the circular nature of time and thus an understanding that every ethical decision is a new singular moment, is ultimately not merely a "religion without religion," but also a faith without content, or foundation. In contrast, as we will expand upon in this work, Christian dogma recounts the narrative of the hospitable Triune God, a God who, remaining faithful to his promises, incarnates himself into *time* and *presence* as the Messiah and, in doing so overcomes our hostility. Taking responsibility and committing oneself to the identity-shaping nature of this dogma, one's life becomes grounded upon a firm foundation. It is from such a launching pad that one can thus,

---

91. This aversion to a God of Being, of the possibility of an incarnate God, perhaps explains Derrida's fascination with a spectral-like Messiah. See esp. Derrida, *Adieu*, 111–12. For the same critique of the ultimately Platonizing impulse of Derrida's thought see Benson, *Graven Ideologies*, 167.

92. Ibid., 165–66.

with confidence, take the leap of faith to engage in the risky and vulnerable practice of unconditional hospitality.

Summary

Our dialogue with Derrida's deconstruction and his account of *unconditional* hospitality has provided us with some important insights. According to Derrida, ethical behavior requires more than the observance of juridical laws, the following of universal maxims or adherence to contractual agreements. Influenced by Levinas' concepts of the "transcendence of the Other" and "infinite responsibility," Derrida asserts that genuine ethical behavior is an absolute *duty* to the particularity of the *tout autre*, an Other that has to be encountered in all their otherness. Such an approach to ethics—by its very nature hospitable—cannot be measured, formalized in programs or contained in tidy procedures. Rather, authentic hospitality is a *performance* constituted of risk-taking and vulnerability; a radical *gift* of *excess*, a moment of *divine* madness, an ethical performance which is always pushing the boundaries, seeking to break through the encirclements and conditions placed upon it.

While elements of this description resonate with theological themes and could potentially contribute to an explicitly Christian account of the ethic of hospitality, there are also aspects of Derrida's thought that are clearly less compatible. Derrida's understanding of identity and relationality, expressed in concepts such as "separation," "division," and "dissociation," appears based upon an ontology of hostility and difference. Such an ontology seems a less than appropriate basis for an ethic of hospitality. Similarly, the assumptions of his post-structuralist faith—the eschewal of knowledge and the denial of a *telos*—are problematic for any theological understanding of the world.

3

Levinasian and Derridean Hospitality

Ethics beyond Ontology?

IN SEEKING TO OFFER A THEOLOGICAL ACCOUNT OF THE ETHICAL PRAC-
tice of hospitality we have begun our journey by reflecting on the work of
Emmanuel Levinas and his friend and compatriot, Jacques Derrida. The
choice of Levinas and Derrida as interlocutors is not arbitrary. As well
as the far-reaching influence of Levinasian and Derridean thought, not
unimportant is the extent to which their respective philosophies have
been shaped by their own life experiences of inhospitality, exclusion and
violence. Such experiences have led them to the conclusion that not only is
Western thought ill-equipped to respond to the inhospitable and unethical
events of the late twentieth—and we could now posit, early twenty-first—
century, but further, they assert that it is Western philosophical thought
itself that is to blame for the quandary we find ourselves in.

According to Levinas and Derrida, the problem, is twofold. Firstly,
they contend that Western thought with its obsession with ontological
concerns is a philosophy of totalization and sameness. Secondly, within
such a structure, ethics is seen as a subset or derivative of philosophy. Their
response is to call for something of a Copernican revolution in Western
thought. Rather than ethics being of a secondary, subsidiary nature, they
seek to replace a metaphysic of transcendental ontology with a metaphysic
of ethical response. In response to what they regard as philosophies of
inhospitality and sameness, Levinas and Derrida offer philosophies of
hospitality, in which heterogeneity is emphasized and the "Other," rather
than being excluded, is "welcomed." Such philosophies, stemming from
the ontic reality of inter-subjectivity, overcome, they claim, the "totalizing" and idolatrous nature of ontological philosophy and lead to ethical
obedience.

To what extent can the philosophical insights of Levinas and Derrida be incorporated into a more explicitly theological account of hospitality? In what follows we will briefly reiterate Levinas' and Derrida's key emphases, noting particular areas of resonance and then turn our attention to areas where there appears to be clear disjuncture between Levinasian-Derridean and Christian theological thought. We will reflect further upon areas we have already expressed concern—in particular their notions of identity, inter-subjective relations and eschatology. As will become clear, our concerns stem from a deeper disquiet regarding the implicit ontology which underlies their respective works.

Revisiting Our "Jewish-French" Hosts

The Otherness of the Other and Ethics as a Leap of Faith

In our contemporary world the very concept and practice of hospitality is one that faces significant challenges. How does hospitality proceed in an "age of terror," where the stranger on one's threshold may be either the refugee seeking sanctuary or the suicide-bomber bringing unwanted gifts of death? Is it possible to practice a radical "unconditional" hospitality in a world where the ability to discern between the malevolent and benevolent Other is so difficult? What happens to the concept of hospitality in a "marketized" world of consumption where inter-human relations are reduced to monetary transactions between "consumers" and "clients"—where hospitality consists of the fulfillment of contractual obligations?

Both Levinas and Derrida in their respective works are sensitive to these concerns. For both writers, in the process of seeking to discern and recognize, the Other is brought within the totalizing gaze of the self. The otherness of the Other is no longer affirmed but rather captured and subsumed within the consciousness of the self and its desire to "know," "comprehend" and "categorize." It is this very violation of the transcendence of the Other, the placing of rationality and ontology before subjectivity and ethics, that our interlocutors seek to overcome. Thus, for Derrida, in genuine ethical hospitality:

> It is necessary to welcome the other and his alterity, without waiting, and thus not to pause to recognize his real predicates. It is thus necessary, beyond all perception, to receive the other while running the risk, a risk that is always troubling, strangely troubling, like the stranger (*unheimlich*), of a hospitality offered

to the *guest* as *ghost* or *Geist* or *Gast*. There would be no hospitality without the chance of spectrality.[1]

The belief in the absolute otherness of the Other—that the Other is beyond comprehension—is applied not merely to the human Other, but to God. Derrida continues:

> But spectrality is not nothing, it exceeds, and thus deconstructs, all ontological oppositions, being and nothingness, life and death—and it also gives. It can give [*donner*], give order(s) [*ordonner*] and give pardon [*pardonner*], and it can also not do so, like God beyond essence. God without being, God uncontaminated by being—is this not the most rigorous definition of the Face of the Wholly other? But is this not then an apprehension that is as spectral as it is spiritual?[2]

It is Levinas' and Derrida's shared belief that human rationality, in attempting to comprehend, represent and categorize the Other, dehumanizes the human Other and turns God into an idol, which leads them to stress the radical exteriority of the Other. Accordingly, Levinas and Derrida posit human relationships as being of an asymmetrical and unilateral nature, and secondly, they advocate a form of "metaphysical atheism," a "religion without religion."[3]

While Levinas' work stresses the radical exteriority and separation of the Other, Derrida's thought moves between this Levinasian notion of alterity—which stresses distance and separation—and a more traditional phenomenological conception of alterity, in which alterity is, at least to some extent, dependent on and relative to the self.[4] For Derrida, "there is an irreducible otherness that divides the self-identity of the living present."[5] Thus Derrida writes: "The other is in me before me: the ego . . . implies alterity as its own condition. There is no 'I' that ethically makes room for the other, but rather an 'I' that is structured by the alterity within it, an 'I' that is itself in a state of self-deconstruction, of dislocation. . . . the other is there before me, that it comes before me [*previent*], precedes and

---

1. Derrida, *Adieu*, 111–12.

2. Ibid.

3. Levinas, *Totality and Infinity*, 77.

4. For a discussion of these changing conceptions of alterity within the work of Derrida see Reynolds, "Other of Derridean Deconstruction."

5. Derrida, "Time of a Thesis," 40.

anticipates me. . . . Which means that I am not proprietor of my 'I,' I am not a proprietor of the place open to hospitality."[6]

Levinas and Derrida are to be commended for their affirmation that the Other—regardless of their identity or history—is one to be welcomed. While not basing their assertions upon theological grounds, their emphasis on the *unconditional* welcoming of the Other, is one that accords with the Christian understanding of the universality of God's grace. The Triune God does not distinguish between "deserving" and "undeserving" Others, but rather we are all "strangers" who through the "gift" of Christ are forgiven and summoned to participate in God's ultimate action of hospitality. Similarly, the Levinasian and Derridean understanding that ethical action is not dependent on the development of a comprehensive theory of ethics, but rather precedes such theory as a *response* to the "call of the Other," is likewise, to be endorsed. Resonating with the Christian tradition, both Levinas and Derrida see this response to the prior call of the Other, as therefore being by its very nature, excessive and risky. To practice radical *unconditional* hospitality requires a leap of faith, perhaps even a touch of madness.

However, whether stressing the radical exteriority of the Other, or positing a conception of alterity in which "the other is somehow always already within the self . . . always, already encroaching upon the self"[7] there is a disturbing aspect to the asymmetrical and unilateral relational structure offered by Derrida and Levinas. Our unease revolves around two different but inter-related matters that we have already traced briefly. Firstly, the extent to which Levinasian-Derridean conceptions of alterity potentially lead to a dissolution/dissolving of both an understanding of self-identity and of otherness; and secondly, the fact that in Levinasian and Derridean thought, inter-subjective relationality tends to be understood in adversarial terms.

Responsibility to Any or All?

In *The Gift of Death* Derrida contends that an act of responsibility to the one means a sacrificing and betraying of our responsibility to all the Others, and that such a choice, of one over another, can never be justified. Reflecting on this, David Wood wonders whether such thinking contains

6. Derrida and Ferraris, *Taste for the Secret*, 84–85.
7. Reynolds, "Other of Derridean Deconstruction," 1.

an element of "hubris."[8] What worries Wood is that Derrida's thinking "seems to deny my situatedness, it seems to return us to occupying a universal space in which we could be anywhere."[9] Wood argues that Derrida's "infinite obligation" is actually "deactualizing obligation" in that it fails to give "privilege to those obligations, precisely that we have not willed, but that we find ourselves in, to those we have voluntarily acquired, to those expectations we have allowed others to have of us."[10] Derrida's move in absolutizing "absolute duty" and calling the Abrahamic sacrifice "the most common and everyday experience of responsibility," of arguing that every duty is an absolute duty and every choice is a sacrifice, rather than affirming the singularity and particularity of the Other, reduces all Others to the same level. Mary-Jane Rubenstein, commenting on the same passage, writes:

> It is astounding that a thinker so concerned with difference could efface it so completely. If every other is just as other as every other, then God is different from Fred in the same way that Fred is different from his cat in the same way that the cat's ball of yarn is different from God. And if all otherness is identical to all other otherness, then every otherness is the same, the singular is no longer singular, the finite no longer finite, and all difference is identity. Without different kinds of difference, there *is* no difference.[11]

A further concern raised by Wood is the extent to which Derrida's "infinite obligation" seems to slide from a responsibility for *any* to a responsibility to *all*. *But, who is capable of having "infinite responsibility for all"? Who is able, as host, to offer unconditional hospitality to all?* To understand "infinite responsibility" as a responsibility for *all* is, as Wood suggests, "surely a huge exaggeration of one's own importance."[12] Indeed, such an understanding, arguably, requires one to have something of a "messianic complex."[13] And, how would one actually stay sane if one were

8. Wood, "Much Obliged," 136. For Derrida's discussion on the sacrifice involved in our infinite obligation and the inability to justify our ethical choices, see Derrida, *Gift of Death*, 53–81.

9. Wood, "Much Obliged," 136.

10. Ibid.

11. Rubenstein, "Relationality," 78.

12. Wood, "Much Obliged," 137.

13. This, overemphasis, arguably, on one's own importance is evident too in Levinas' thought when he writes, "From a responsibility even more ancient than that *conatus* of substance, more ancient than the beginning and the principle, from the anarchic, the

to hold to a Derridean understanding that in each ethical choice one was sacrificing and betraying all other obligations?[14] Wood wonders whether he is alone in hearing in these words the "voice of guilt"?[15] Indeed, does the Derridean "infinite responsibility" run the risk of becoming a "bondage to an insatiable monster,"[16] which, rather than leading to ethical openness and care of the Other results in a sense of being overwhelmed, and thus to ethical paralysis?

A similar critique is offered by James Olthuis, who expresses concern that Levinas' emphasis on the priority of the other may "give birth—albeit contrary to intention—to a guilting moralism."[17] While the Levinasian emphasis on an asymmetrical relationship with its ethic of self-sacrifice has some resonance with specific Biblical themes, Olthuis wonders whether Levinas' position has the affect of bringing "into ethical disrepute all concern for self-interest."[18] If this is the case, then does not Levinas, in his concern to challenge "narcissistic self-interest" threaten the very concept of an identity and therefore the very basis for his inter-subjective ethics?[19] The problematic nature of Levinas' unilateral relationship, in which the self's only interest is that of the Other, is noted too by Paul Ricoeur. Ricoeur asks: "Is not a moment of self-dispossession essential to authentic selfhood? And must one not, in order to make oneself open, available, belong to oneself in a certain sense?" He concludes: "If my identity were

---

ego returned to self, responsible for Others, hostage of everyone, that is, substituted for everyone by its very non-interchangeability, hostage of all the others who, precisely *others*, do not belong to the same genus as the ego because I am responsible for them without concerning myself about their responsibility for me because I am, in the last analysis and from the start, even responsible for that, the ego, I; I am man holding up the universe 'full of all things.' Responsibility or saying prior to Being and beings, not saying itself in ontological categories." Levinas, *Humanism of the Other*, 57.

14. Derrida, *Gift of Death*, 69.

15. Wood, "Much Obliged," 137.

16. Ibid.

17. Olthuis, "Face-to-Face," 143. David F. Ford seeks to overcome the potential burdensome sense of "obligation" in Levinas' "infinite responsibility" by synthesizing it with Eberhard Jüngel's notion of "joy." Ford, *Self and Salvation*.

18. Olthuis, "Face-to-Face," 136. Levinas writes: "It is my inescapable and incontrovertible answerability to the other that makes me an individual 'I.' So that I become a responsible or ethical 'I' to the extent that I agree to depose or dethrone myself—to abdicate my position of centrality—in favor of the vulnerable other. As the Bible says; 'He who loses his soul gains it.' The ethical I is a being who asks if he has a right to be, who excuses himself to the other for his own existence." Levinas, "Ethics of the Infinite," 62–63.

19. Olthuis, "Face-to-Face," 136.

to lose all importance in every respect, would not the question of others also cease to matter?"[20]

Adversarial Relationality and the Charge of Ontological Violence

Not only does such an advocating of a unilateral, asymmetrical relationality, an emphasis on an ethic of self-sacrifice, seem to rob the self of any essential, inherent moral right, but similarly disturbing is the extent to which Levinasian and Derridean conceptions of alterity tend to view interpersonal relationships in adversarial terms. James K. A. Smith observes that "because hospitality *is* ethics for Derrida, what is at stake in considering hospitality *as such* is not just international law or immigration but also the nature of intersubjective relationships. It is in the consideration of hospitality, we might suggest, that we get something like Derrida's philosophical anthropology."[21] And what is the nature of this anthropology and the understanding of inter-subjective relationships offered to us by Levinas and Derrida? Derrida's understanding of the essential adversarial nature of inter-subjective relationships is encapsulated well in an interview with Richard Kearney where Derrida states: "the rapport of self-identity is itself always a rapport of violence with the other; so that the notions of property, appropriation and self-presence, so central to logocentric metaphysics, are essentially dependent on an *oppositional relation* with otherness. In this sense, identity *presupposes* alterity."[22] Derrida's attempt to overcome the potential violence of the Kantian autonomous individual seems itself therefore to be embedded in a violent relationality.[23]

Likewise, as noted earlier, Levinas' conception of inter-human relationality also appears to be construed in adversarial terms. Levinas' understanding that *being* itself is constitutively violent, a struggle for existence, is expressed concisely in an interview, where Levinas states: "This is my principal thesis. A being is something that is attached to being, to its own being. That is Darwin's idea. The being of animals is a struggle for life. A struggle for life without ethics. It is a question of might. . . . the living being struggles for life. The aim of being is being itself. . . . The law of evil is the

20. Ricoeur, *Oneself as Another*, 138–39. For a similar critique see also Ogletree, *Hospitality to the Stranger*, 53–54.

21. Smith, *Derrida: Live Theory*, 69.

22. Derrida, "Deconstruction and the Other," 117.

23. Smith, *Derrida: Live Theory*, 41.

law of being."[24] For Levinas, the Face of the Other does not appear in this world of *being*, characterized by struggle. "Being persisting in being, that is nature" but the face is a "rupture with nature," an in-breaking of "generosity," "charity," "grace," "love" into being. Levinas contends that "in the conatus essendi, which is the effort to exist, existence is the supreme law. However, with the appearance of the Face on the inter-personal level, the commandment 'Thou shalt not kill' emerges as a limitation of the *conatus essendi*."[25]

While at one level his ethical account of subjectivity clearly asserts for the pre-priority of the Good—contra the Hobbesian characterization of nature as war—Levinas' concept of the Face irrupting into the struggle of being seems to presuppose a primordial, original state of hostility. In *Totality and Infinity*, Levinas suggests that the temptation to kill the Other—"The Other is the sole being I can wish to kill"—is one which is resisted by the "epiphany of the face."[26] Levinas writes:

> This infinity, stronger than murder, already resists us in his face, in his face, is the primordial *expression*, is the first word; "you shall not commit murder." . . . The epiphany of the face brings forth the possibility of gauging the infinity of the temptation to murder, not only as a temptation to total destruction, but also as the purely ethical impossibility of this temptation and attempt.[27]

Thus, Levinas' contention that "war presupposes peace, the antecedent and non-allergic presence of the Other; it does not represent the first event of the encounter" appears to be belied.[28] His logic, in stating that the primordial *expression*, the first word is "you shall not commit murder," suggests rather, the primacy of violence. Judith Butler makes the same point when she observes that while "Levinas cannot accommodate the notion of a primary set of needs or drives he gestures towards an elementary

24. Wright et al., "Paradox of Morality," 172, 175. Levinas' assumption here—that "life" consists of an inherent conflictual struggle for survival—is itself one that is now being overtaken. There is increasing recognition that while predation and death (conflictual relationality) play a role in the functioning of healthy ecosystems, complimentary, cooperative, collaborative relations are just as significant to the existence and continuation of the bio-diversity of life.

25. Ibid., 175–76.

26. Levinas, *Totality and Infinity*, 197–98.

27. Ibid., 198. See also Levinas' essay "Ethics and Spirit," in Levinas, *Difficult Freedom*, 8.

28. Levinas, *Totality and Infinity*, 198.

notion of aggression or murderous impulse when he grants that killing the Other is the temptation against which ethics must work."[29]

Others, attentive to the way in which alterity within Levinasian-Derridean thought is conceived of in "oppositional" or non-relational terms, argue that such an understanding of inter-human relations is representative of an undergirding "ontology of violence."[30] The belief that human inter-subjective relationships contain violence, that inherent within hospitality is a little hostility—vividly expressed in Derrida's neologism, "Hostipitality"—is, such writers aver, symptomatic of a less than peaceful ontology. James K. A. Smith believes that despite all its richness, Levinas' assertion that "infinity is 'as primordial as totality,' (*TI*, 23) . . . seems to still entail that totality is primordial. *Hence, there is a way in which relationality is always already inscribed with war.*"[31]

So too, Olthuis suggests that Levinas' philosophy "seems to valorize the often adversarial quality of interpersonal relations as the inexorable human condition (which we then need to transcend to be ethical), rather than to envisage such opposition itself as the breakdown of relations of mutuality in which my self-interest and the self-interest of the other may interface with each other to the harmonious enjoyment and enrichment of both parties."[32]

But is the self totally incapable of being in relation with the Other without violating them? Is ontological self-interest and egoism the sum total of the human self? Does the relationship with the Other, to protect the Other from totalizing violence, have to be one of asymmetry, distance, separation? And, if the relationship between the self and the Other does contain an element of tension, then what of the future? Do Levinas or Derrida envisage an end to inter-subjective conflict? That is, to what extent do their respective philosophies offer a hope of redemption, a move beyond tension and oppositional conflict, to a bright messianic future? Such questions inevitably lead us to a brief but necessary foray into a consideration of Levinas' and Derrida's understandings of eschatology and teleology.

---

29. Butler, *Giving an Account of Oneself*, 98.

30. Smith argues that the fact Levinasian thought "operates on the basis of an oppositional notion of difference (or 'differential ontology') . . . means that an 'ontology of violence' continues to undergird his project, even if it is offered in the name of peace." Smith, "Call as Gift," 219. Others who accuse Levinas and Derrida of offering philosophies of "ontological violence" include Milbank, *Theology and Social Theory*, 278–325, and Pickstock, *After Writing*.

31. Smith, "Call as Gift," 223. Emphasis added.

32. Olthuis, "Face-to-Face," 136.

Eschatology and Teleology

Eschatological and teleological ideas are constantly at play, either implicitly or explicitly, within Levinas' and Derrida's thinking, leading commentators such as Richard Kearney to propose that their philosophies are a "sort of Messianic eschatology."[33] However, as one would expect, the Levinasian and Derridean understanding of such ideas is complex. Derrida states that while interrogating "the idea of an *eschaton* or *telos* in the absolute formulations of classical philosophy . . . that does not mean I dismiss all forms of Messianic or prophetic eschatology. I think that all genuine questioning is summoned by a certain type of eschatology, though it is impossible to define this eschatology in philosophical terms."[34] Similarly, Levinas states,

> I must express my reservations about the term eschatology. The term *eschaton* implies that there might exist a finality, an end (*fin*) to the historical relation of difference between man and the absolutely Other, a reduction of the gap which safeguards the alterity of the transcendent, to a totality of sameness. To realize the *eschaton* would therefore mean that we could seize or appropriate God as a *telos* and degrade the infinite relation with the other to a finite fusion. This is what Hegelian dialectics amounts to, a radical denial of the rupture between the ontological and the ethical.[35]

For Levinas, "the danger of eschatology is the temptation to consider the man-God relation as a state, as a fixed and permanent state of affairs." In contrast to his theme of ethical responsibility, described "as *insomnia* or *wakefulness* precisely because it is a perpetual duty of vigilance and effort which can never slumber," Levinas argues that "ontology as a state of affairs can afford sleep."[36]

Once again, both Levinas and Derrida express the concern that eschatology and teleology, as traditionally understood, stem from an ontology of totality, one which closes down and fixes the future, thereby offering the foundation for ethical irresponsibility and inaction.[37] *But do*

33. Levinas, "Ethics of the Infinite," 66.

34. Derrida, "Deconstruction and the Other," 119.

35. Levinas, "Ethics of the Infinite," 66.

36. Ibid.

37. In his essay "Ends of Man," Derrida asserts that "the Greek thinking of *telos* . . . such a discourse, in Hegel as in the entirety of metaphysics, indissociably coordinates teleology, with an eschatology, a theology, and an ontology. *The thinking of the end of man, therefore, is always already inscribed in metaphysics, in the thinking of the truth of man.*" Derrida, "Ends of Man," 121.

eschatology and teleology have to be construed in such ways? Are eschatology and teleology of necessity totalizing and therefore exclusive of the Other, the Infinite? To what extent does a theological account of eschatology and teleology overcome this Levinasian-Derridean critique? We will return to these questions later, but for now, having noted the Levinasian-Derridean concerns, we return to our major consideration—that of Levinas' and Derrida's understanding of inter-subjective relationships and the ontology that underpins such thinking. Our anxiety over particular features of their philosophy—the seeming loss of self-identity, the non-reciprocal and adversarial understanding of inter-subjective relationships, and the lack of hope for redemption from such hostility—ultimately appear symptomatic of what some term, an "ontology of violence." To understand this nuanced critique it is necessary to pause momentarily and clearly define what is understood by the terms "metaphysics" and "ontology" in their respective philosophies.

Ontology and Metaphysics

For Levinas, ontology is the totalizing discourse that legitimates and reifies the sphere of the Same. Whether it be Heidegger's discourse of Being, or Hegel's philosophy of Spirit, Levinas rails against an ontology in which the Being of our subjective *cogito* or the Being of the immanent and finite cosmos is given an all-encompassing universality. Robyn Horner observes: "Instead of following the ontological path, Levinas suggests that we pursue a genuine metaphysics, one that has an eye, or perhaps an ear for transcendence and the ethical. . . . Levinas characterizes metaphysics as a radical aiming at exteriority (transascendence), an exteriority that is beyond our theoretical comprehension, beyond the realm of being and of knowledge, beyond what can be reduced to the Same."[38]

Adhering to his contention that ontological thought totalizes and causes violence, Levinas offers a metaphysic that gives preeminence to the lived experience, to the ethical encounter with the Other. While initially Levinas embraced the thinking of his earlier teacher Heidegger in seeking a philosophy that gave priority to questions of embodied lived experience and existence, he soon turned away from and became critical of Heideggerian thought due to the way in which Heidegger's thought became an "all encompassing strategy for grasping life in understanding."[39] As John

---

38. Horner, *Rethinking God as Gift*, 60.
39. Ibid., 55.

Llewelyn notes: "Levinas's ontology calls into question the fundamentality of the 'ontological difference,' the distinction between being and beings, between the ontological and the ontic upon which [Heidegger's] *Being and Time* takes its stand. . . . Levinas's ontology stands for the ontological significance of concrete empirical, hence ontic experience."[40] While for Heidegger the horizon by which all things are judged is *being*, for Levinas the horizon is the *Other*.

Important to note here is that Levinas uses the term "metaphysics" in a positive sense. For Levinas, "metaphysics" is the relationship with the Infinite Other that overcomes the totalizing violence of ontology. In place of an ontology of *sameness*—a totality—Levinas offers a metaphysic of *otherness* and *difference*—an alternative ontology of infinity. This Levinasian project of developing a philosophy of ethical metaphysics is fundamentally different from Derrida's project of deconstructing the "metaphysics of presence." While in Levinas' writing the term "metaphysic" is used positively—in opposition to ontology—in Derrida's writing, the term "metaphysics" has negative connotations, with Derrida's "metaphysics of presence" being akin to Levinas' ontology of *sameness*.

Derrida's and Levinas' critique of the totalizing nature of Western ontological philosophy leads them to attempt to overcome the capacity for violence that both philosophers see in transcendental, universal accounts reliant on ontological claims. "Metaphysics begins," Derrida argues, "when theory criticizes itself as ontology, as the dogmatism and spontaneity of the same, and when metaphysics, in departing from itself, lets itself be put into question by the other in the movement of ethics. Although in fact it is secondary, metaphysics as the critique of ontology is rightfully and philosophically primary."[41] In this sense, therefore, both Levinas' and Derrida's philosophy can be seen as continuing in the stream of the larger philosophical attempts to overcome metaphysics.

But is such a philosophy—a post-metaphysical philosophy—really possible, or for that matter ultimately necessary? And, what are the implications of such a quest for theology?

David Wood points to the fact that Derrida's philosophy, while seeking "not to retread too many of the paths of metaphysics . . ." is ultimately itself inescapably metaphysical by nature, contending that "Derrida's deconstructive strategy . . . [is] wedded to transcendental modes of thought. . . ."[42]

40. Llewelyn, *Emmanuel Levinas*, 108.

41. Derrida, "Violence and Metaphysics," 96.

42. Wood, *Deconstruction of Time*, 297, 311. While observant of the distinction

Indeed, even while seeking to overcome metaphysics of presence, Derrida himself acknowledges the impossibility of escaping from metaphysics. In his essay, "Structure, Sign and Play in the Discourse of the Human Sciences," reflecting on Nietzsche's, Freud's and Heidegger's critique of metaphysical concepts such as truth, consciousness and being as presence, Derrida concludes that all such "destructive discourses are trapped in a kind of circle." He continues:

> This circle is unique. It describes the form of the relation between the history of metaphysics and the destruction of the history of metaphysics. There is no sense in doing without the concepts of metaphysics in order to shake metaphysics. We have no language—no syntax and no lexicon—which is foreign to this history; we can pronounce not a single destructive proposition which has not already had to slip into the form, the logic, and the implicit postulations of precisely what it seeks to contest.[43]

Derrida concedes that "we cannot do without the concept of the sign, for we cannot give up this metaphysical complicity without also giving up the critique we are directing against this complicity."[44] Elsewhere, he admits that "*différance* remains a metaphysical name, and all the names that it receives in our language are still, as names, metaphysical."[45] In an interview, he candidly states: "the idea that we might be able to get outside of metaphysics has always struck me as naïve."[46]

This impossibility of escaping from the discourse of metaphysics, the impossibility of escaping ontological concepts, is likewise one acknowledged by Levinas. For Levinas, the emergence of the Third person necessitates a shift from a "pure" ethical relationship into the realm of the "political" and therefore of ontology. Levinas states:

> The temporality of the interhuman opens up the meaning of otherness and the otherness of meaning. But because there are more than two people in the world, we invariably pass from the ethical perspective of alterity to the ontological perspective of

---

between Derrided and Kantian understandings of the transcendental, Horner also notes the way in which Derrida's thought slips into a transcendental mode in his reflections on the gift. Horner asks why in referring to the gift as the "first mover of the circle" (*Given Time*, 30) Derrida uses language "that has resonated so forcefully in the context of 'onto-theology?'" Horner, *Rethinking God*, 189.

43. Derrida, "Structure, Sign and Play," 280–81.

44. Ibid., 281.

45. Derrida, "Différance," 26.

46. Derrida, "Deconstruction and the Other," 111.

totality. There are always at least three persons. This means that we are obliged to ask who is the other, to try to objectively define the undefinable, to compare the incomparable in an effort to juridically hold different positions together. So that the first type of simultaneity is a simultaneity of equality, the attempt to reconcile and balance the conflicting claims of each person. If there were only two people in the world there would be no need for law courts because I would always be responsible for, and before, the other. As soon as there are three, the ethical relationship with the other becomes political and enters into the totalising discourse of ontology. *We can never completely escape from the language of ontology and politics. Even when we deconstruct ontology we are obliged to use its language.*[47]

Important to note therefore, is that while highly critical of the totalizing nature of ontological philosophies, and seeking to continue the Heideggerian task of overcoming metaphysics, both Levinas' and Derrida's philosophies of hospitality, like all philosophical discourses, are themselves, trapped in the "circle" of metaphysics. Even their attempts to articulate ethical-hospitable philosophies, in which primacy is given to the ontic ethical encounter with the Other and inter-human subjectivity, while subordinating ontology are still dependent on an ontology. Wood concludes:

Derrida has transformed the way we think about, and read (or perhaps write), philosophy, he has transformed our understanding of the relationship between the inside and the outside of philosophy, but his strategic dependence on such metaphysical values as "authorial intention" and on formally transcendental arguments essentially limit his achievement. . . . his lesson, or the lesson to be drawn from him, is *not merely* that as he says, there is no sense in doing without metaphysical concepts in trying to overcome metaphysics, but there is no prospect whatever of *eliminating* metaphysical concepts and strategies. Rather the project of overcoming metaphysics (Merlau-Ponty said of the phenomenological reduction) must be repeated indefinitely.[48]

47. Levinas, "Ethics of the Infinite," 57. Emphasis added. This understanding that it is the emergence of the Third that leads us into the necessity of the "political" is likewise, expressed in Derrida, *Gift of Death*, 68.

48. Wood, *Deconstruction of Time*, 317. In this sense, the philosophical work of Levinas and Derrida can be interpreted in two ways. While some read Levinas' and Derrida's attempt to escape metaphysics as an enterprise inevitably doomed to failure—i.e., Milbank—others take a more sympathetic view and argue that the work of Levinas, Derrida and Marion functions at the limits of phenomenology. See particularly Horner, *Rethinking God*, 153–83.

Our analysis and evaluation of the work of Levinas and Derrida ultimately lead to a number of important questions and observations: *To what extent is Levinas' and Derrida's critique of the totalizing, logocentric, nature of Western philosophy also true of the theological enterprise? That is, is theology—the attempt to give an account of the character and actions of God— likewise a discourse of totality and sameness, one that therefore excludes the Other? To what extent is all theology of necessity a form of onto-theology? Do sameness and otherness have to be seen as mutually exclusive or in a constant state of oppositional conflict? Is it possible to conceive of an ontology in which sameness/unity and otherness/difference coexist peacefully?*

As Olthuis asks: "Is an ethical asymmetry (with priority of the other person) the only alternative to either manipulative relationships (with the other as object) or the balanced exchange of economic transactions?"[49] Or, can we envisage an ethical relationality of genuine mutuality and reciprocity? Might it be that part of the Levinasian-Derridean critique of ontology stems from an assumption that knowledge of what is Other, entails "power-over"[50] this Other; that *knowledge of* the Other is inevitably violent and violating; that is, that in Levinasian and Derridean thought it is supposed that epistemology subverts relationality? *But is human knowledge and theorizing of necessity violent? Is the very act of conscious representation, of recognizing and discerning the Other inherently an act of totalization and violation?* What if knowledge was not understood as "power-over," but rather "power-with," if epistemology, rather than being primary, was seen as inextricably dependent on a prior ontological relationality? What if one began with an ontology that privileged relationality over epistemology, and mutuality and exchange over distance and asymmetry? Rubenstein suggests that: "Only if ontology is understood as always-already relational can the self give without subsuming the other or destroying it. Only within a non-oppositional scheme of selfhood and otherness (and a non-identical scheme of otherness and Otherness) does the self find itself in the interplay of giving, given selves, constituted and maintained through their participation in divine intersubjectivity, a constant play of unity and difference."[51]

Such an ontology, as Ricoeur suggests, is "one that does justice in turn to the primacy of self-esteem and also to the primacy of the convocation

49. Olthuis, "Face-to-Face," 153.

50. Ibid., 146.

51. Rubenstein, "Relationality," 78.

to justice coming from the other."[52] In such an ontology the Same and the Other, rather than being in a state of oppositional conflict interpenetrate one another, and "communication," "reciprocity" and "exchange" are construed as the essential and constitutive elements of the relationship between the self and the Other.[53] Such an ontology, one of *"benevolent spontaneity"* in which "receiving is on an equal footing with the summons to responsibility,"[54] is apparent in the Christian accounts of the doctrines of Creation and the Trinity. It is the distinct ontology that stems from these doctrines which will be the theme of our next chapter.

Summary

We commenced this work contending that in a world where the Other is increasingly seen as a threat, and where professionalization and commercialization are rife, there is the urgent need for a reinvigoration of an ethic of hospitality. The work of Emmanuel Levinas and Jacques Derrida seeks to respond to such a world by offering an alternative account of human ethical behavior.

However, while providing an initial stepping stone, a closer analysis of the philosophies of Levinas and Derrida, has raised a number of concerns. Put succinctly, in seeking to overcome the imperialism of the self, Levinas and Derrida offer an account of human relations in which the elevation of the Other appears accompanied by "a necessary disinterest in self-concern."[55] That is, the Levinasian-Derridean account of hospitality stresses ethical asymmetry, and relationships of uni-directionality. Underlying such an account, appears to be the belief that not only are inter-subjective relationships inevitably of an adversarial and conflictual nature, but also that such conflict is embedded in the very fabric of the created world?

In contrast to such thinking, in section two of this work we will offer a theological account in which the human capacity for the practice of hospitality stems from an ontology of peace and communion. From the doctrines of the Creation and the Trinity emerges an ontology of *communion* in which human existence is understood not as primordial struggle, but rather as gift; where relationality is understood not in adversarial or

52. Ricoeur, *Oneself as Another*, 331.

53. Ibid., 339.

54. Ibid., 190.

55. Olthuis, "Face-to-Face," 146.

oppositional terms but as characterized by mutuality and reciprocal gift-exchange. The supreme performative action of divine hospitality—the incarnation of Jesus Christ and his life and death—is to be understood not as an act of self-sacrificing violence, but rather as a gift offered back to the Father, which therefore overcomes human hostility. Those who, taking the leap of faith have their lives re-narrated according to this meta-narrative, participate in God's eschatological hospitality and thus offer nourishing hope to the world. It is to an exposition of this narrative that that we now turn our attention.

4

Gifted, Called, and Named

Trinitarian Personhood and
an Ontology of Communion

Man, made in the image of the Trinity, can only realize the divine like-
ness if he lives a common life such as the Blessed Trinity lives: as the three
persons of the Godhead "dwell" in one another, so a man must "dwell" in
his fellow men, living not for himself alone, but in and for others.

    —Timothy Ware[1]

THE WORK OF EMMANUEL LEVINAS AND JACQUES DERRIDA HAS BEEN OF
major significance in its critique of the modern Western understanding of
selfhood and identity. For both Levinas and Derrida, Western conceptions
of human identity and personhood post-Descartes are deeply disturbing.
In placing the *cogito* at the centre of his philosophy, Descartes and his successors give primacy to consciousness and conceive of the human person
as a self-constituted entity. Philosophy which gives primacy to consciousness has, argue Levinas and Derrida, always given priority to the "I" and
turned the Other into an object. They conclude that such philosophy leads
ultimately to the dehumanization of humanity and the death camps of the
holocaust.

    In response to such thinking, Levinas and Derrida present phi-
losophies which offer a radically different conception of personhood and
identity. In Levinasian and Derridean thought the autonomous *cogito* of
the self at the centre of philosophical thought is replaced by the Other.
Philosophy and ethics, argue Levinas and Derrida, do not begin with the

1. Ware, *Orthodox Church*, 241.

self-reflexive consciousness of the "I" but rather begin with the call, the address, of the Other. The relationship between the self and the Other is not one of symmetry, of understanding and comprehension, but rather is a relationship characterized by excess. The excess of the Other entails a relationality of asymmetry, in which sameness gives way to separation and the radical exteriority of the Other.

However, while endorsing this critique of the Cartesian-self, the alternative conception of the self that Levinas and Derrida offer, we have contended, is somewhat troubling. The "deconstructed self," put forward by post-structuralist thought, ultimately appears to be a non-self. Such an understanding of selfhood is lauded by Mark C. Taylor, who, in *Erring: A Postmodern A/theology*, speaks of such a deconstructed self as a "careless wanderer." For Taylor, the self is a "serpentine character . . . rootless and nomadic (originless), as well as ex-centric and exorbitant (centreless), the erring trace is purposeless and aimless (endless)." "The wanderer," Taylor declares enthusiastically, "has no certain destination, goal, aim, purpose, or end."[2]

But does self-hood and identity so conceived, really provide the basis for an understanding and practice of genuine hospitality? While agreeing with the post-modern rejection of the Cartesian self, Olthuis believes "Taylor's erring wanderer is a scary, sad, desolate figure, nameless, impersonal, and incurably wounded" and asks whether it is possible for "such a postmodern person, without home and without purpose," to be "called to responsibility?" Is not "such an anonymous person," Olthuis wonders, "a difference that makes no difference—a difference that is the same, because there is no longer any uniqueness?"[3] Indeed, far from assisting the development of an ethos and culture of hospitality, it has been argued that the non-self of post-modern thought is the inevitable product of late modern capitalism, that the deconstructed post-modern self is the inescapable consequence of the skepticism of the Cartesian self turned upon itself.[4] Or, as Colin Gunton puts it: "postmodernism is modernity come home to roost."[5] Does a post-modern conception of self—one with no fixed identity, no sense of "home"—rather than responding to our contemporary malaise in which people are rebranded and labeled, and hospitality reduced to a marketable commodity, actually potentially perpetuate

2. Taylor, *Erring*, 157.
3. Olthuis, "Crossing the Threshold," 28.
4. Boyle, *Who Are We Now?*
5. Gunton, *One, Three and Many*, 124.

such tendencies? Elizabeth Newman, noting this connection between the empty non-self of post-modern thought and contemporary consumerism, writes: "The very idea of hospitality requires not only a "hospice," a home, but also a particular kind of giving and receiving. An empty self is unable to conceive of the fact that he or she has something to give, something to offer. Such a self is also, oddly enough, unable truly to *receive*. . . . the empty self consumes in order to feed or fix the emptiness. But consuming is different from receiving. Consuming has about it an air of desperation as the consumer seeks to create a persona or satisfy a fabricated need.[6]"

This association between the fragmented empty self of post-modern thought and the culture of consumerism of the contemporary world is also made by Oliver Davies. Davies writes: "In the modern world our encounter with otherness, with the alien or strange, begins not at the borders of the self, but rather *within the self*, at the very core of our identity, and in a way that challenges the self-possession of the subject. Lacking an uncontested centre, the self comes to its own self-awareness through its acquisitive demands: we exist unequivocally as consumers. Our appetite for goods defines our existence, and is reflected in the enticements of the commercial cosmos of advertising and sales.[7]"

Arguably, the fragmented self is both the *product*, and simultaneously, the philosophical *impetus/basis* for the culture of commoditized consumerism which prevails particularly in Western societies in the global village. If personhood is not something we intrinsically *are*, but rather is an added quality—a new product that we acquire, a new "lifestyle" we adopt—is it any wonder that hospitality becomes reduced—and debased—to a series of consumptive exercises which aesthetic individuals participate in, and that the highest personal virtue emphasized is one of *tolerance*?[8] Could it be that the homeless, deconstructed non-self offered to us by post-structuralist thought, with its accompanying ethos of *tolerance* and rituals of acquisitive consumption, far from offering hope to the problems of the

---

6. Newman, *Untamed Hospitality*, 37–38.

7. Davies, *Theology of Compassion*, xvi.

8. For an outline of the theological justification for the practice of tolerance, see Fergusson, *Church, State and Civil Society*, 72–93. Luke Bretherton argues that the problem with tolerance understood as substantive good, is that such accounts of tolerance are based upon a liberal conception of the good and the liberal conceptions of rationality upon which this itself is based. Bretherton sees the theologically specified notion of hospitality as preferable to tolerance in fostering respect for the "Other." See Bretherton, "Tolerance, Education and Hospitality," and Bretherton, *Hospitality as Holiness*.

contemporary world, actually exacerbates the misunderstanding and divisions which seem to beset us and lead to conflict?

While strongly sympathetic with aspects of the post-structuralist project, the conception of selfhood offered by Levinas and Derrida, and the ontology upon which this self is based, are less than satisfactory. Can we speak of a non-self, a self, which ironically, appears to be obliterated of its particularity and uniqueness? Can a self with no fixed identity, devoid of uniqueness, nameless and wounded—really be a hospitable self? Does one not require a metaphysical "home" if one is to provide hospitality to the Other?

Orthodox theologian John Zizioulas maintains that the problem with many conceptions of the self is that they start with the presupposition that personhood is "a quality to be added, as it were, to being." In contrast, Zizioulas argues that if we assume that *personhood* is something that someone *is*—then "the assertion of personal identity," the question "Who am I?," "has the claim of absolute being, that is a metaphysical claim, built into it."[9] For Zizioulas, "the expression 'I *am*', cannot be understood apart from some kind of transcendence, from what might be called 'metaphysics.'"[10] Like Zizioulas, we believe that far from being an intellectual dead end, or the major contributor to the moral morass of our day, metaphysics is central to any attempt to develop an understanding of a hospitable self.[11] In what follows, we will argue that rather than being implicated in the Levinasian and Derridean critique of ontology, Christian theology—particularly in the doctrines of the Trinity and Creation—provides an alternative ontology which protects the uniqueness and particularity of both the Other and the self, while simultaneously positing peaceful human relationality and communion/unity as possibilities.

The Doctrine of Creation: Freedom and Otherness

Seeking to continue our conversation with our "Jewish" interlocutors, our starting point for developing a theological account of hospitality and

9. Zizioulas, *Communion and Otherness*, 100.

10. Ibid., 100–101.

11. In a similar vein Oliver Davies states: "The historical Christian commitment to an implicit metaphysic is such therefore that the wholesale renunciation of an explicit metaphysic would be the significant loss of a higher language by which the Christian and perhaps other religious communities can offer a controlling resource for the shaping of the implicit self who lives and acts in a world of God's making." Davies, *Theology of Compassion*, 9.

the elaboration of an alternative ontology of personhood, begins appropriately with a shared narrative, that of the Judeo-Christian doctrine of Creation.[12] Creation accounts reveal one's ontological views, and from its earliest origins, the Judeo-Christian account of creation was illustrative of an ontology radically divergent from other religions and philosophies. While sharing stylistic similarities with other Ancient Near East creation narratives the Judeo-Christian description of creation in Genesis operated as a polemic against these alternative accounts. Despite their differences, Ancient Near East cosmologies, shared similar conceptions of both divinity and humanity and were grounded in a similar ontology. That is, the world was created from existing material, out of the *conflict and struggle* of the gods, and human beings were either seen as an afterthought, or were created to serve as slaves to the lazy and unpredictable gods. In contrast to these polytheistic cosmologies with a low view of humanity, in which conflict and violence are seen as primordial, the Judeo-Christian account of creation speaks of a world that came into existence not through violence or death but rather through the creative word of *Elohim*. Humanity, in the Biblical account, far from being inconsequential, or consigned to slavery of the gods, is the climax of the creative activity of God.

The Genesis creation accounts served a polemic function in providing a distinct and contrasting understanding of personhood from those of the surrounding Ancient Near-Eastern cultures. So too, the doctrine of creation, and the underlying ontological assumptions upon which such an account was founded, were of significant import to the Christian theologians of the first centuries as they sought to reconcile their biblical faith with the assumptions of ancient Greek philosophy. While not univocal, all ancient Greek philosophy, from Parmenides, the grandfather of Greek philosophy, through to Plato and Aristotle, essentially held to an ontological monism, in which the *real is One* and is *eternally existent*. Parmenides states in *Way of Truth:*

---

12. As we have already noted, both Levinas' and Derrida's personal life experience—as "Jewish" exiles, who receive the "welcome" of France—and their subsequent writings raise intriguing questions regarding the notion of identity. The extent to which both Levinas and Derrida "live in the difference between the Jew and the Greek" is explicitly raised by Derrida in his "Violence and Metaphysics." For a biography on Derrida, which explores Derrida's in-between identity in Joycean terms, see Hélène Cixous, *Portrait of Jacques Derrida as a Young Jewish Saint.*

How could what *is* perish? How could *is* have come to be? For if it came into being, it is not; nor is it if ever it is going to be. Thus coming into being is extinguished, and destruction unknown.[13]

While Plato questioned this extreme view of the *Parmenidean One*, his recognition of the existence of others within his philosophy was still dependent on the One. Similarly, while Plato in his work *Timaeus* professes faith in a creator, the act of creation by the demiurge is not an ontologically free act of creation, but rather, the creative process involves preexisting material and is determined by adherence to ideas such as Beauty and Goodness and the circumstances and conditions of preexisting space.[14] Plato's most famous student, Aristotle, states: "Nothing could have come to be out of what is not, for there must be something present as substrate."[15]

It is these ontological assumptions upon which ancient Greek philosophy rested—*ex nihilo nihil fit* (nothing out of nothing), and the prioritizing of unity and Oneness over against otherness and the Many—which seem to underlie the thought of Derrida, in particular his concepts of *khôra* derived from Plato's *Timaeus* and his understanding of *différance*.

Caputo, drinking deeply from the well of *différance*, offers a Derridean-like interpretation of the Genesis creation narrative, positing that "creation is not a pure act without a patient, like a pure dance without a partner, not a pure perfect exnihilatory performance, an absolute act carried out entirely in a sphere all its own."[16] Rather, Caputo argues, "when *Elohim* began to create the world, things had evidently already begun."[17] For Caputo, "the act of creation is inscribed in something that received the creative operation. . . . the creative act is inscribed, or spoken, in a context or a container, in a receptive medium, received by a receiver."[18] While the Genesis passage may speak of *Elohim* as the *arche*, Caputo asserts, "there is something there with Elohim" and positing that this something, is Derrida's *khôra*, "which is a surname for *différance*."[19] For

---

13. Parmenides, *Way of Truth*, 6.10, in Melchert, *Great Conversation*, 27.

14. Zizioulas, *Communion and Otherness*, 14–19.

15. Aristotle, Phys. 191A, 23.

16. Caputo, "Before Creation," 93.

17. Ibid.

18. Ibid., 93–94.

19. Ibid., 93, 97. Elsewhere Caputo writes, Derrida's *différance* "is something like a *khôra*, a more maternal simulacrum, a non-originary origin." Caputo, *Prayers and Tears*, 168.

Caputo, this *khôra-différance*, "an inoriginate medium, or milieu, without truth or falsity, without good or evil, a kind of non-originary origin, a groundless ground,"[20]—*Elohim's* partner in the act of creation—is a "quasi-transcendental condition," is "our inescapable condition," "marked by a certain 'necessity.'"[21]

What emerges from Caputo's theology of creation is a Derridean world of deconstruction, a world with "no well demarcated beginning or end, no absolute *arche*, no tidy *telos*";[22] a world of binary oppositions held uneasily together in constant tension. In such a world: "*khora* provides an allegory of or a figure for the necessity that every unity of meaning—from the highest to the lowest—is under to be inscribed within *différance*, by which it is conditioned and precontained as are all the oppositions that are inscribed within it."[23]

Caputo's *theologized* reading of Derrida here, entailing a Platonic understanding of creation in which a demiurge works on preexisting material and where creation occurs through the medium, activity and presence of *khôra-différance*, while sophisticated, is both perplexing and problematic. Within such an account of creation, the self, like all *being*, has no clear beginning or end, nor a fixed sense of identity, but rather is constantly in the process of being formed, reformed and deformed; endlessly open to deconstruction and reconstruction.

In contrast to this Derridean-inspired account of Genesis offered by Caputo, and the endlessly "deconstructive" ontology upon which it is founded, the historical doctrine of *creatio ex nihilo* offers a distinct ontology which provides a more stable and secure grounding for an understanding of personhood and identity.

Creatio ex nihilo

According to John Zizioulas, it is the historical doctrine of *creatio ex nihilo* that offers us the first of two significant planks in the construction and articulation of a distinct Christian ontology. For Zizioulas, the assumptions

20. Caputo, "Before Creation," 98.

21. Ibid. In contrast to the doctrine of *creatio ex nihilo*, which he contends "is a creation of metaphysics, a fantasy of power and clean pure acts, a creature that was not formed in Genesis, but much later," Caputo argues that "*Elohim* is the everlasting comrade of the elements [earth, darkness, wind], not their cause or explanation." Caputo, "Before Creation," 93, 95. A more thorough analysis of Derrida's own thinking regarding *khôra* is contained in his essay "Khôra."

22. Caputo, "Before Creation," 97.

23. Ibid., 98.

upon which ancient Greek philosophy rested—*ex nihilo nihil fit* (out of nothing, nothing comes), and the prioritizing of unity and Oneness over against otherness and the Many—were a significant challenge for the earliest Christian theologians as they sought to communicate biblical faith to the world of Greek philosophy. The problem these theologians encountered was the implication of Greek philosophical thinking: that God and the world were not seen as distinct—*other*—and therefore, logically following, this would mean God's action in creating was not an act of *freedom*, but rather one of *necessity*. Such thought, in which *Being* was seen as *necessary* and *eternally existent*, Zizioulas maintains, was the antithesis to the Judeo-Christian belief that creation "did not always exist but came into being out of a free act of the free and transcendent God."[24]

The ontological implications of these two contrasting accounts of *creation* are spelt out by Zizioulas, who writes:

> *The absence, therefore, of freedom in the act of creation would amount automatically to the loss of ontological otherness, for both the Creator and his creation.* Otherness as an ontological category for both the Creator and his creation emerges as a logical imperative when creation is conceived as an act of freedom, that is, as an act that cannot be explained by being itself; it cannot be attributed axiomatically to being itself, but to a factor other than being itself which causes being to be. Creation *ex nihilo* implies that being does not come from being, which would make it necessary being. This, therefore, is the reason why otherness and freedom are interwoven in ontology with regard, in the case under consideration, to the being of creation. Otherness in this case has to be ontological in character or else freedom in the ontological sense disappears: the Creator would be bound up ontologically with his creation.[25]

Put simply: According to the assumptions of Greek ontological thought—in which Being is seen as natural and eternal—creation is construed as an act of *necessity* and otherness as a diminution from the One. Yet, in the Christian doctrine of *creatio ex nihilo*—in which God is understood as separate and distinct from the world and creates out of *nothing*—creation is conceived as an act of *freedom*. As Zizioulas asserts, an ontology of "freedom and otherness, are interdependent."[26] Zizioulas summarizes: "Otherness is necessary for freedom to exist: if there is no

24. Zizioulas, *Communion and Otherness*, 15.

25. Ibid., 16.

26. Ibid., 16.

absolute, ontological otherness between God and the world, there is no ontological freedom allowing each of these two 'beings' to be *themselves* and thus to be at all."[27]

Furthermore, in ancient Greek philosophical thought—as evidenced in Caputo's Derridean creation theology—*Being*, understood as eternally existent, has no clearly defined beginning or end and thus lacks a specific *telos*. In contrast, the Christian doctrine of *creatio ex nihilo* as well as providing an ontology grounded upon *otherness* and *freedom*, also offers—with its conception that creation has both a distinct beginning and therefore a distinct ending—a clear *teleology*. Such an emphasis upon *telos*, in stark contrast to the *telos-less* nature of Levinasian and Derridean thought, is an important theme to which we will return later.

Creation as Violence?

The ontological assumptions one holds in approaching the doctrine of creation are also significant with regard to one's understanding of power and relationality. The doctrine of creation *ex nihilo* has in recent times become unfashionable as theologians—particularly process and feminist theologians—express concern at what they see as the problematic "power" dynamics inherent within the doctrine of *creatio ex nihilo*. Common to many of these theologies is the belief that the doctrine of *creatio ex nihilo* provides the basis for the domination of both the non-human world of nature and women. In response, such theologians seek to reinterpret the biblical account, replacing what they perceive as the power-discourse of creation from nothingness, with a *creatio ex profundis*.[28] In their belief that Genesis offers a "masculine" account of the world in which "the Divine exists beyond it, symbolized as a combination of male seminal and cultural power (word-act) that shapes it from *above*"[29] such approaches often jettison the biblical account altogether, grounding their theology in alternative creation narratives.[30]

---

27. Ibid., 19.

28. See Keller, *Face of the Deep*.

29. Ruether, *Sexism and God-Talk*, 77. Emphasis added.

30. Both Ruether and Keller have a strong affinity for Babylonian and Canaanite cosmologies, suggesting that the mythologies of the Ancient Near-East, in which "the Divine is within, not transcendent to, the matrix of chaos-cosmos" provides the material for a more ecological and feminine affirming ethic. See ibid., 76, and Keller, *Face of the Deep*, 103–23.

But a number of ontological assumptions lie beneath these critiques. Firstly, *creatio ex nihilo* can only be construed as an act of violence, if one construes non-being, the "feminine" *chaos*, as having some form of ontological status—i.e., akin to Caputo's Platonic-Derridean reading of creation. Yet, as Rowan Williams puts it: "Power is exercised by x over y; but creation is not power, because it is not exercised on anything." Williams posits that far from imposing "a definition" on us, God's act of creation, actually "creates an identity."[31]

Secondly, in their belief that any exercise of power implies forced control and domination and the accompanying belief that any "hierarchical chain of being and chain of command" leads automatically to a violation and domination of those lower down the hierarchy,[32] these critiques of the doctrine of *creatio ex nihilo* hold to the questionable ontological assumption that power and hierarchy are, of necessity, violent. But do power and hierarchy have to be seen, in and of themselves, as violent?

While the doctrine of *creatio ex nihilo* challenges the assumptions of Greek philosophy regarding the eternal existence of being, it is in the distinctively Christian doctrine of the Trinity, that we are offered an ontology which responds particularly to this critique of power and hierarchy.

The Doctrine of the Trinity: Communion and Personhood

In *Totality and Infinity*, Levinas mounts a strident critique of the totalizing nature of Western thought. Implicated in Levinas' critique is Western theology in which, he argues, substance and sameness are central concepts. But what role does the Doctrine of the Trinity play in assisting in the formation of an ontology in which unity and difference, communion and otherness are seen not as mutually exclusive, but as interdependent?

It is no accident that the post-structuralist critique of Western philosophy, and in particular the negative appraisal of the self-positing *cogito*, has coincided with a reemergence of theological interest in the Doctrine of the Trinity, and in the implications this doctrine has for an understanding of personal identity. According to Zizioulas, it was in the emergence of

31. Williams, *On Christian Theology*, 68.

32. Ruether argues that "the whole Western theological tradition" is based upon a "model of hierarchy that starts with non-material spirit (God) as the source of the chain of being and continues down to nonspiritual 'matter' as the bottom of the chain of being and the most inferior, valueless, and dominated point in the chain of command." Ruether, *Sexism and God-Talk*, 85.

the Trinitarian tradition within the patristic period, as the patristic theologians engaged with the cosmologies of the Greek philosophers, that one sees the formation of a distinctive Christian ontology. While according to the patristic understanding of *creatio ex nihilo*, *freedom presupposes otherness and otherness presupposes freedom*, such thinking was impossible to conceive of in Greek philosophical thought, where *being* was understood as substance or *ousia*. However, it was the Cappadocian Fathers, Zizioulas contends, who, through their replacement of a *substantialist* ontology with a *personalist* ontology, fundamentally changed the nature of Greek philosophy and therefore offered an ontology in which freedom and otherness is possible.

Zizioulas argues that while early philosophical Patristic theologians such as Justin Martyr, Clement, and Origen, struggled to "avoid the pitfalls of a monistic ontology," pastoral theologians such as Ignatius of Antioch, Irenaeus, and Athanasius, approaching the question of the being of God, not primarily through the employment of academic philosophy, but rather "through the experience of the ecclesial community of *ecclesial being*," began to develop a new ontological framework.[33] According to Zizioulas, it was out of the Eucharistic experience of the life of the church that these pastoral theologians concluded that "the being of God could be known only through personal relationships and personal love. Being means life, and life means *communion*."[34]

It is, in particular, in the writings of the Cappadocian Fathers—Basil of Caesarea (ca. 330–379), Gregory of Nazianzus (ca. 325–389) and Gregory of Nyssa (ca. 330–ca. 395)—as they grappled with how to describe the Holy Trinity that we see the emergence of a radical rethinking of the concept of Being. The Cappadocians, as theologians of the Greek-speaking East, had concerns with the language that the Latin-speaking Western section of the Church was using to describe the Holy Trinity. Tertullian's *una substansia, tres personae*, while gaining wide acceptance in the West, caused alarm in the East due to the fact that the Latin term *personae*, used by Tertullian, was translated into Greek as "*prosōpon*," a term which lacked any ontological content. While safeguarding the unity of the Divine Godhead, to the Cappadocians, Tertullian's theology tended towards a form of Sabellianism.

The response of the Cappadocians was to take the concept of "hypostasis" with its ontological significance and to identify this with the

33. Zizioulas, *Being as Communion*, 16.
34. Ibid.

term *"prosōpon."*[35] In identifying these two terms, the Cappadocians transformed the significance of both words and gave them new fields of meaning.[36] While *prosōpon* in Greek thought had been seen as secondary to being, the Cappadocians, in amalgamating these terms, asserted (i) that a *prosōpon* is not secondary to being, but its *hypostasis*, and (ii) the ontological category of a *hypostasis*, is, by its very nature, an irreducible relational entity. That is, it is *prosōpon.*[37]

The effect of this Cappadocian thought, Zizioulas argues, was both to introduce "a revolution into Greek ontology,"[38] and also to shape the long-term direction of Eastern theologies of the Trinity. According to Zizioulas, the effect of the theology offered by the Cappadocians, was an understanding that *Being* is ultimately *personal* and "that person is now the *ultimate* ontological category we can apply to God."[39] Within Cappadocian theology therefore—as interpreted by Zizioulas—the Trinity is best understood as a *communion of persons.*[40] Zizioulas writes: "The being of God is a relational being: without the concept of communion it would not be possible to speak of the being of God. . . . The Holy Trinity is a *primordial* ontological concept and not a notion which is added to the divine substance or rather which follows it. . . . The substance of God, 'God', has no ontological content, no true being, apart from communion."[41]

---

35. Within Greek thought the term "hypostasis" was closely linked to and explicitly identified with "substance." Indeed, St. Athanasius in his Letter to the bishops of Egypt and Libya states: "*Hypostasis* is *ousia* and has no other meaning apart from being itself. . . . For *hypostasis* and *ousia* are existence: it is and it exists." Ibid., 36n23.

36. While Zizioulas attributes the linking of the terms "*prosōpon*" and "*hypostasis*" and the subsequent transformation of their meaning to the Cappadocians, John Wilks argues that this development actually came about through the Western tradition. See Wilks, "Trinitarian Ontology of John Zizioulas," 74.

37. Zizioulas, *Communion and Otherness*, 186. Zizioulas summarizes with more clarity, the significance of the Cappadocian thinking in his earlier book, *Being as Communion*, when he states: "The person is no longer an adjunct to a being, a category which we *add* to a concrete entity once we have verified its ontological hypostasis. *It is itself the hypostasis of the being.*" Zizioulas, *Being as Communion*, 39.

38. Zizioulas, *Communion and Otherness*, 186.

39. Ibid.

40. While achieving broad acclaim, Zizioulas has been criticized for his interpretation and use of the patristic texts. Zizioulas' constructive theology, which engages particularly with questions of personhood and inter-subjectivity, remains valid even if his claims for patristic warrant are called into question.

41. Zizioulas, *Being as Communion*, 17.

A key component to this understanding that the being of God is a *communion of persons* and therefore of Being itself "as communion," is the patristic concept of *perichoresis*.

Perichoresis: Particularity and Love

Originating in the writings of John of Damascus and grounded in the words of the Johannine Jesus, the patristic concept of *perichoresis*, while originally used to reflect on divine unity, offers a significant theological motif for the development of an ontology of personhood. According to the notion of *perichoresis*, the divine persons are not independent, nor even interdependent identities who influence one another, but rather, the divine persons of Father, Son and Spirit are *personally interior* to one another. Within this conception of the Trinity and the belief that "in eternity Father, Son and Spirit share a dynamic mutual reciprocity, interpenetration and interanimation,"[42] relations between the divine persons are not seen as secondary to the divine *ousia*, but rather are *constitutive* of the very being of God. Colin Gunton, responding to the problem of particularity posed by Platonic thought, states that "the persons [of the Trinity] do not simply enter into relations with one another, but are constituted by one another in the relations."[43] For Gunton, "God is not God apart from the way in which Father, Son and Spirit in eternity give to and receive from each other what they essentially are. The three do not merely coinhere, but dynamically constitute one another's being."[44]

The doctrine of *perichoresis*—the dynamic interrelatedness of the three persons of the Trinity—is an important theological concept offering the ability to express "the unity and plurality of the being of God," while preserving "both the one and the many in dynamic interrelations."[45] Gunton suggests that if we understand the concept of perichoresis as having

---

42. Gunton, *One, Three and Many*, 163.

43. Ibid., 214. Gunton, concurring with Levinas, believes it is the failure of Western thought to engage with the problem of particularity inherent in Platonic philosophy which lies behind the intellectual and moral problems of our modern age. Gunton writes: "Thus it is that that the modern failure of Plato to give due place to particularity in his vision of things is replicated both in modernism's suppression of the particular through the universal and in postmodernism's homogenizing tendency to attribute to all particulars essentially the same value." Ibid., 70.

44. Ibid., 164. Gunton here suggests that the Latin derivative, *coinherence*, is less satisfactory than the Greek *perichoresis*, in that it seems to suggest "a more static conception" in comparison to the dynamic mutuality of *perichoresis*.

45. Ibid., 163–64.

a transcendental status, then we are presented with an understanding of being—an ontology—which is able to hold together the one and the many, the universal and the particular.

According to Zizioulas, it is only this personal-relational understanding of the Trinity—particularly as offered by the Cappadocians and the Eastern theological tradition—that is able to provide us with an ontology which overcomes the monism of Greek philosophy. To speak of freedom and thus love is impossible within the monistic universe of Greek philosophical thinking—grounded as it is in its impersonal substantialist ontology of necessity. In contrast, a Trinitarian ontology—grounded in the free love offered between the Father, Son and Spirit—provides such an ontology. Zizioulas summarizes this point thus:

> The only exercise of freedom in an ontological manner is *love*. The expression "God is love" (1 John 4:16) signifies that God "subsists" as Trinity, that is, as person and not as substance. Love is not an emanation or "property" of the substance of God . . . but is *constitutive* of His substance, i.e. it is that which makes God what He is, the one God. Thus love ceases to be a qualifying—i.e. secondary—property of being and becomes *the supreme ontological predicate*. Love as God's mode of existence "hypostasizes" God, *constitutes* His being. Therefore, as a result of love, the ontology of God is not subject to the necessity of the substance. Love is identified with ontological freedom.[46]

The Question of "Causation"

Eastern-Cappadocian theologies have begun to have a significant impact on contemporary Western Trinitarian thought. A number of Western theologians offer visions of a perichoretic God who makes room and space for the Other—a Trinitarian God whose Being is constituted by the mutual giving and receiving that takes place between Father, Son and Spirit. Nevertheless, even theologians who have drunk deeply from the Cappadocian-Zizioulian well express concern at the role that the Cappadocian notion of "monarchy" plays in Zizioulas' theology. Alan Torrance suggests that Zizioulas' contention that the Father is the "cause" of the Son and Spirit in the immanent Trinity of personhood, "involves projecting a causal ordering into the Godhead."[47]

46. Zizioulas, *Being as Communion*, 46.

47. Torrance, *Persons in Communion*, 289. Torrance's critique of Zizioulian

On a close analysis, it becomes clear that underlying these concerns expressed regarding Zizioulas' use of the Cappadocian notion of "monarchy" is a belief that causality, hierarchy, or any form of subordination is antithetical to the concept of communion and therefore to be viewed pejoratively. But is causality, or are forms of hierarchy or subordination, by their very nature contrary to the notion of communion, that is, inhospitable? Zizioulas argues not, and bearing in mind that this critique of causation, hierarchy and subordination has already arisen in the process-feminist assault on the doctrine of *creatio ex nihilo* discussed earlier, and will appear again later in our discussion on the nature of relationality, it is appropriate and necessary at this point to outline the argument Zizioulas employs as a rejoinder to his critics.

For Zizioulas, causation, hierarchy and subordination are only to be construed as negative if approached from within substantialist ontology. Yet, according to Zizioulas, it is the Cappadocian insistence on the Father as "cause," origin, *arche* of the Trinity, which underpins their understanding of ontology, not in *substantialist*, but rather *personalistic* terms. By understanding the concept of "causation" within the Godhead not at the level of *ousia* but rather at the hypostatic or personal level, causality becomes a *relational* term. Subsequently, causation becomes an act of *relational freedom*, rather than one of *substantial necessity*. As Zizioulas puts it: "Causation is precisely part of God's dynamic being; it involves movement, not however a movement of substantial necessity, but a movement initiated freely by a person."[48]

For Zizioulas therefore, causation and hierarchy are not to be seen negatively, but rather are an inherent feature of a personalist ontology. Such a perspective has significant implications for our theological anthropology. Firstly, for Zizioulas, the belief that "the Father is the cause of personhood in God's being" means

> that there is not and should not be personal existence which is self-existent, self-sufficient or self-explicable. A person is always a *gift from someone*. It is demonic to attribute one's own personal identity to oneself or to an a-personal something. The notion of self-existence is a substantialist notion, not a personal one. Persons have a "cause", because they are the outcome of love and freedom, and owe their being who they are, their distinctive otherness / as person, to another person. Ontologically, persons

"monarchianism" can be found in 288–95. Similar critiques are evident in Volf, *After Our Likeness*, and T. F. Torrance's *Trinitarian Faith* and *Christian Doctrine of God.*

48. Zizioulas, *Communion and Otherness*, 131.

are givers and recipients of personal identity. Causality in Trinitarian existence reveals to us a personhood which is constituted in love.[49]

Secondly, and significant in echoing one of the insights of Levinas, Zizioulas argues that "divine causality teaches us that personal otherness is not symmetrical but *a-symmetrical*." Zizioulas writes: "There is always in this otherness a 'greater' one (John 14:28) not morally or functionally but ontologically. Otherness is, by definition, 'hierarchical' since . . . we are not 'other' by ourselves but by someone else, who in this way is 'higher', that is, ontologically 'prior' to us, the giver of our otherness."[50]

For Zizioulas therefore, hierarchical ordering is inherent in personhood as all personal relations are asymmetrical, since persons are not self-existent, but "caused" by another who is there ontologically "prior" as "giver."[51] Zizioulas notes that while hierarchy has taken on a pejorative term in our world, it is not hierarchy *per se* that is problematic. Rather, *asymmetrical* relations and *hierarchy* are only ontologically problematic, and thus evil, when the "cause" brings forth an "inferior"—that is, when the "cause" fails to allow the other to be *fully Other*. If however, "causation" is understood as the "cause," or the ontologically prior, bringing forth another ontologically "free" and equal Other, then asymmetry is not incompatible with equality.

In summary, Zizioulas offers an account of Trinitarian relations in which there is a formal ordering within the Divine Godhead, and yet simultaneously, an ontological equality. Order does not imply inequality or domination. The very fact that the term "Father" is a relational term means that when we speak of the "Father" we automatically think of the Son and the Spirit, and of the relationship that exists between the Father, the Son and the Spirit.[52] That is, the identity of the *hypostases* within the Trinity is not identical with their relations, but rather is *constituted* by their relations, one with another. The divine communion of the Trinity is composed of particular persons-hypostases, in free relationship with one another.

Our brief survey of the doctrines of creation and the Trinity provides us with a distinct ontological view. In Greek philosophical thought *Being* is conceived of as *eternally existent* and understood *substantially*, leads to

49. Zizioulas, *Communion and Otherness*, 141–42.

50. Ibid., 143.

51. One only need think here of the example of parenthood and of how parents are ontologically prior to and therefore the "cause" of their children.

52. Zizioulas, *Communion and Otherness*, 122n33.

an ontology of *necessity* and *sameness*. However, the Christian belief that *Being* is primordially the *communion of Divine persons* presents an ontology in which *unity* and *difference* are seen not as mutually exclusive, but rather as mutually constitutive. It offers an ontology not of *necessity* and *sameness* but rather of *freedom* and *otherness*.

Zizioulas claims that "There is no model for the proper relation between communion and otherness either for the Church or for the human being other than the Trinitarian God."[53] Our agreement with Zizioulas' assessment that the "relation between communion and otherness in God is the model both for ecclesiology and for anthropology," requires that our attention now be turned towards tracing out the implications of such an ontology for our conception of human personhood, identity and relationality.[54] How exactly does the Trinity—or more precisely, the dynamic relationality that is the communion of divine persons, in which particularity and communion are seen as mutually constitutive—act as the model for our understanding of human identity and personhood? What does an elaboration of *being as communion* mean for our attempt to offer a theological anthropology? In reinterpreting motifs that punctuate the work of our philosophical interlocutors—that of gift, call, and address—we will lay down some preliminary guiding lines in our sketching of the "hospitable" self.

Tracing the Hospitable Self

There are similarities between Levinas' philosophical reflections on *personhood* and the theological anthropologies of the Eastern Orthodox tradition. Both start, in the words of Corneliu Boingeanu, with the premise "that the person cannot be defined, it cannot be captured, by conceptual thought."[55] With obvious parallels to Levinasian thought, Eastern Orthodox anthropologies propose an understanding of personhood based not on rationality but rather "on a personal, existential encounter with the divine."[56] This shared starting point of an active renunciation of the attempt to understand the Other rationally and an emphasis on the constitutive role of the *call* or *election* leads Zizioulas to state that "with Levinas we come closer to the patristic understanding of otherness than with any

---

53. Ibid., 4.

54. Ibid., 5.

55. Boingeanu, "Personhood in Its Protological and Eschatological Patterns," 3.

56. Ibid.

of the philosophers."[57] Nevertheless, there are also subtle but significant distinctions.

Called, Elected, and Named by the Other

In *Otherwise Than Being or Beyond Essence*, Levinas writes: "The word I, means *here I am*" while elsewhere he writes: "I am, as if I had been chosen."[58] For Levinas, it is not self-consciousness that constitutes the self, but rather, as he states: "my inescapable and incontrovertible answerability to the other . . . makes me an individual 'I.'"[59] Such statements are illustrative of the extent to which the understanding of human identity and personhood offered by Levinas are steeped in the biblical motifs of *call* and *election*. Terry Veling summarizes Levinas' thought succinctly, writing:

> The priority is not with the *I* constituting itself, but with the call of the other who asks after me. It is this call that comes first, that is always prior, that is always before me, and constitutes my identity as a response-ability and answer-ability. Levinas is converting the "I think, therefore, I am" of modern, Western thought into the "here I am" of biblical, prophetic response. This is the election of the *I* as chosen and responsible before the face of God and neighbour.[60]

While Veling is correct in stressing the biblical and prophetic dimensions of Levinas' work, there are however nuanced differences between the Levinasian notion of *call* and *election* and how these concepts are understood from within the Christian theological tradition.

Central to Levinas' philosophy is the concept that the call/address of the Other is not expressed *within* relationship but rather is one that is issued from a place of transcendence and distance. While there are resonances with the dialogical philosophy of Martin Buber, Levinas is deeply suspicious of the potential violence within symmetrical relations. Accordingly, he develops a philosophy which prefers *separation* and *distance* over relationship, a philosophy in which the Other remains Transcendent.[61] In

---

57. Zizioulas, *Communion and Otherness*, 48.

58. Levinas, *Otherwise than Being*, 114. Levinas, *Outside the Subject*, 35.

59. Levinas and Kearney, "Dialogue with Emmanuel Levinas," 27.

60. Veling, *Practical Theology*, 85.

61. While for Levinas the Other is primordial, for Buber the "Other" and the "I" are given equal primordiality and it is the relationship between the *I* and *Thou* which is seen as having ontological basis. See Buber, "What Is Man?," 242, and *I and Thou*.

Levinas' work, *the call* is issued by the Other, transcendent and *distant*, a call which arises beyond relationship, calling the self to its fundamental *responsibility* and *answerability* to an unknown Other.

But are there only two options available for construing our engagement with the Other? Both the Buberian and Levinasian accounts seem incapable of giving an understanding of the self which, while constituted by the Other, possesses a distinctive and unique identity. The choice of Buber or Levinas only appears necessary however, if one holds to a *substantialist* ontology in which relationality is seen as potentially "violent," an ontology which struggles conceptually with *particularity*. In contrast, we have already contended that Christian theology offers a different ontology—one in which the Divine Other, as a communion of particular persons, remains both transcendent while simultaneously engaging in relationship with his created world and humanity, not as an act of "power over" but rather as an act of "love and freedom." Thus, in Genesis 2:7 the narrative paints a picture of YHWH, the Divine Other, tenderly and intimately sculpting a creature from the earth (*adamah*) and then exhaling the breath of life into the nostrils of *Adam—the earth Creature*. While the Genesis account may offer us a Face which "cannot be comprehended" or "encompassed,"[62] the emphasis is not on *distance* and *separation*, but rather on intimacy and closeness. It is in receiving the breath of life as *gift* that *Adam* becomes a living being. In contrast to the Levinasian call, the call of the Trinitarian God is issued by the God who, while beyond total comprehension or encompassing, joyously reveals Godself to that which is other. Such a call is not a generalized call, but rather a call issued to *particular* recipients; a call which *elects* the particular recipient of the call, and *establishes* them within a covenantal relationship of faithful love.[63] Thus, the call and election issued by the Trinitarian God institutes a relationship with the subsequent call to *responsibility* and *answerability* taking place within the context of this relationship.[64]

The Hebrew Scriptures, of which Levinas himself is so fond, are full of material illustrative of such a notion of *call* and *election*. At the foundation of all three of the Abrahamic faiths is the *call* and *election* of Abram. Called by YHWH to leave his own country, to become a pilgrim, the renaming of Abram to Abraham both signifies the covenantal relationship that has been instituted by the call/address of YHWH, while also

62. Levinas, *Totality and Infinity*, 194.
63. See Barth, *Church Dogmatics* III/1.
64. See McFadyen, *Call to Personhood*.

reiterating the promise inherent within this call/address. Abram, *high Father*—whose name, in light of his lack of progeny, would have sounded like a bad joke—becomes Abraham, *ancestor of a multitude*. The relationship established between Abraham and YHWH is of an asymmetrical nature, characterized by the *responsibility* and *answerability* of Abraham to the radical promise of YHWH. But again, this response-ability and answerability takes place not within a mode of distance and separation, but rather occurs within a relationship in which the Divine Other reveals Himself as the God of gracious gift, promise and proximity—a God who arrives uninvited to eat at Abraham's place and who then enters into negotiation regarding his future actions (Genesis 18). As noted earlier, the "leap of madness" of Abraham—not merely of leaving his homeland in response to the call and promise of a previously unknown God, but also the [un]ethical obedience in following through the command to sacrifice his Son Isaac—can only be understood through the eyes of faith. That is, Abraham's actions only make sense—though not sense according to human sensibilities or rationality—if framed within this broader context of gift and gratitude, promise and obedience, call and response, that is, within a relationship of faithfulness and love. The biblical conception of *call* and *election*, grounded upon a *personalist* ontology, takes place not *outside* of relationship, but rather founds the self *within* its relationship with the Other, establishing a covenantal relationship between two particularities.

Perhaps the clearest way to observe this subtle difference between the Levinasian notion and the understanding of *call* and *election* that we are advocating is through a closer reflection on the actual word, *address*. The word "address," whether used as a noun or a verb, refers to a *particular* and *specific* identity.[65] Thus, one goes to one's *address* book to find "the place where a person lives or an organization is situated" and especially the *"particulars of this"* if one intends sending a letter (noun). Or, understood in a different context: one delivers an *address*—that is a *specific* discourse (noun), by actively (verb) directing one's attention and speech to a *specific* audience or individual. In contrast to the biblical notion of *call/address* which takes place between two particular and unique identities, Levinas' notion of otherness seems to struggle with such specificity or particularity. The Levinasian notion of *address*, in its occurrence outside of relationship, at times appears analogous to one of the scourges of our contemporary technological world—that of e-mail spam. Levinas' call/address from the Other, proceeds from a *distant*, and unknown Other with whom we have

---

65. *Concise Oxford Dictionary*, 8th ed., s.v. "address."

no prior relationship nor any hope of the development of genuine relationality or intimacy.

Defining the Other: Naming as Violence?

Yet, some critics have asked whether the dynamic of election evident in the Biblical narrative implies favoritism and therefore entails an exclusion of the Other. Is not the forming of a covenantal relationship between YHWH and Abraham, Jacob and the other patriarchs, and with the people of Israel an act of either implicit—and at times—explicit violence? After all, does not the instituting of such relationships of *particularity* and *uniqueness* ultimately lead to the exclusion of others such as Abel, Hagar, Ishmael and Saul, who are not God's "chosen"?[66] And, in the case of the tribes already occupying the "promised land," does not this failure to be "elected" finally lead to explicit violence as God's "chosen" people commit their own form of ethnic cleansing?[67] Likewise, does not "naming," an activity integral to each of these episodes of "call" and "election," as Levi-Strauss has demonstrated, consist of the exercising of symbolic power by the addressee/ "the one who names" over the one who is named

Following in the legacy of Levi-Strauss and his theory of "the symbolizing power of language,"[68] much twentieth century biblical scholarship has indeed understood the practice of "naming" in terms of "power." Gerhard von Rad reflects the consensus of biblical scholarship when stating that: "name-giving in the ancient Orient was primarily an exercise of sovereignty, of command."[69]

But have theologians and biblical scholars been correct in taking on board the assumption that the ritual of "naming" in the Biblical narrative is primarily concerned with power and command over the Other? That is, is Levi-Strauss's understanding of the "symbolic power of language" always the appropriate hermeneutic for understanding the biblical activity

---

66. Indeed, it would not be difficult to imagine such questions being raised by our interlocutors, especially Derrida, for whom the biblical doctrine of "election" would appear as anathematic to his call for an "absolute hospitality."

67. Regina Schwartz sees the nexus between land, monotheism, and monogamy as leading to "a doctrine of possession, of a people by God, of a land by a people, of women by men." Thus, Schwartz argues that monotheism contains the seeds for the violence perpetrated by humanity upon humanity, by humanity upon creation and by men over women. Schwartz, *Curse of Cain*, 71.

68. Kearney and Rainwater, *Continental Philosophy Reader*, 305.

69. Von Rad, *Genesis*, 81.

of "naming"? Does not Levi-Strauss' structuralist approach—in which he seeks to classify all relations—itself act in a totalizing fashion, robbing identities and their relations of their uniqueness and particularity? Can the mystery and wonder of relationships between unique and particular identities be simplified into generalized and comprehensible laws? Indeed, the thought of our post-structuralist interlocutors, and their emphasis on an unclassifiable and transcendent Other, is itself, a response to these generalizing and therefore totalizing tendencies of structuralist thought. And secondly, even if "naming" does in some sense contain an aspect of the issuing of sovereignty and control by the "namer" over the "named," do such relationships—relationships of an asymmetrical or hierarchical nature, where one partner of the relationship has "power" or primacy over the other—have to be understood as inherently *violent* by nature?

Once again there are two recurring and questionable underlying assumptions which are at play in the debate regarding naming. Firstly, as noted in the previous chapter, there is a privileging of epistemology over ontology and thus the conception that language is distinct/separate from relationality. And secondly, flowing from this there is the recurring Foucauldian presupposition that power is to be understood pejoratively, as an act of "power-over" the Other. With such presuppositions, the action of naming within the biblical text, divorced from a relational-personalist ontology, is therefore understood as an exercise of power, and power is understood pejoratively, as an act of violence. That is, criticisms of both *election* and *naming* only have validity when such notions are detached from a personalist ontology of communion.

In contrast, the distinctive Christian ontology we have delineated does not give primacy to epistemology over ontology nor conceive of language outside of, or independent of, a prereexisting relationality. Language is neither independent of *being* nor creates reality, but rather is itself another gracious gift offered by the Trinitarian God to humanity to aid the development of relationships between the self and the Other. In such thinking, in which language is understood as gift which flows *ek-statically* from an ontology of relational peace, "naming" is construed not as an assertion of one's power or control over another, but rather, as a celebration of the underlying relationship that exists / has been instituted.

To illustrate this point, one only need think of the activity of naming that takes place in the context of families. Is the naming of children by their parents an act of violent control, an assertion of their sovereignty over their off-spring, or rather, is it best understood as a symbolic action that expresses the joy of the parents, their delight at the new life received as gift, and evidence of the bond of love that exists between parent and child? The very act of choosing a name involves both an intuitive sense of who the child already *is*, and a hope for who they will yet become. Likewise, consider the naming that takes place between friends and, in the even more intimate setting between lovers, where "nick-naming" becomes a sign of the affection and endearment shared by the two parties.

Similarly, the names of "Father," "Son" and "Spirit," which refer to the three *hypostases* of the Trinitarian God, do not connote dynamics of power and control, but signify the existing intimate relationship of communion that exists within the Godhead. The divine actions of communion/communication—begetting and being begotten, sending and proceeding—which take place within the Godhead, are not functions of a monistic substance but are relational events. The Trinitarian names refer, therefore, not to functionary roles, but to the particular personal identities in their *communion* with one another. The Father is Father to the Son; the Son is Son to the Father; the Spirit is the Spirit of Christ, the go-between God, the very breath of the Father.[70]

Such an ontology undergirds the biblical poem of Song of Songs, where the relationship of intimacy and mutual constitution between the two lovers is expressed in the repeated formula: "My beloved is mine and I am his" [2:16] / "I am my beloved's and my beloved is mine" [6:3]. Within such a relational ontology, as Phyllis Trible recognizes: "Naming is ecstasy, not exercise; it is love, not control. And that love marks a new creation."[71]

Ultimately, despite the corporeal nature of Levinas' writing and his notion of the self's existence being dependent upon the *address* of the Other, the intimacy and mutuality of the relational ontology that we have outlined here is foreign to his thought. In spite of the motif of "the caress" that punctuates his thought, it appears, as Irigaray suggests, that "Levinas does not ever seem to have experienced the transcendence of the other which becomes im-mediate ecstasy.... For Levinas, the *distance* is always maintained with the other in the experience of love." Levinas, Irigaray suggests, "knows nothing of communion in pleasure."[72]

---

70. In describing the Trinitarian relations in such a way—with allusions to both the Western emphasis on the Spirit as the Spirit of Christ and Augustine's "bond of love," and simultaneously with the emphasis of the Greek Fathers on the Spirit proceeding as breath (*ekporeusis*) from the Father—it is not our intention to offer a distinct position with regard to the *filioque* controversy. We seek simply to point to the underlying relational nature of the Trinitarian names.

71. Trible, "Depatriarchalizing in Biblical Interpretation," 44.

72. Irigaray, "Questions to Emmanuel Levinas," 110–11. Emphasis added.

Election and the Blessing of the Other

And what of God's election of specific characters in the biblical narrative? Is election, in its very specificity, therefore, an act of violent exclusion of others? To respond to such a criticism we will briefly return to the story of Abraham.

From its inception the covenantal relationship instituted by YHWH's call of Abram is not an exclusionary election. Rather, Abram is promised that YHWH will bless him, "so that you will be a blessing" (Gen 12:2). Indeed, shaped by this understanding that chosen by YHWH he is summoned to a responsibility for others, and in the security derived from the divine *call*, Abraham's life is characterized by the practice of radical hospitality. While Abraham's action of welcoming the unknown Others who appear at Mamre in Genesis 18—famously depicted in Rublev's icon—is usually perceived as the exemplary event, this event is surrounded by other significant hospitable events.

The first of these episodes appears in Genesis 14. It is confidence in his identity stemming from his *call* and *election* by the Divine Other which enables the monotheistic Abraham to accept humbly the blessing of the pagan king, Melchizedek. Having himself been a recipient of the hospitality of the people of the land, it is inappropriate for Abraham to accept the bounty due to him for his defeat of King Kedorlaomer and his allies, and he instead offers it back as a return-gift to those who have *hosted* him in the land to which he has migrated.[73]

A second significant moment of Abraham's life comes immediately after the well-known theophany in Genesis 18. While Abraham offers hospitality to the unknown strangers who appear outside his tent, arguably the genuine test of his hospitality is how he will respond to those whom he knows best. Having been assured of an heir, the question the narrative implicitly poses is whether Abraham will continue to stay loyal to his nephew Lot and the inhospitable hosts of his kin. And yet, despite the sheer depravity which characterizes the city of Sodom—Genesis 19 in graphic detail outlines how within Sodom the sacred cultural practice of hospitality has itself become laced with violence—Abraham has the confidence to enter into negotiation with YHWH over what he perceives

---

73. Norman Habel contends that the relations of mutuality that Abraham as the immigrant, the *other*, builds with his hosts in his new land constitute a radically different land ideology than that ventured within the book of Joshua. "The land ideology he [Abraham] represents," suggests Habel, "is depicted as accommodating rather than acquisitive." Habel, *Land Is Mine*, 126.

as YHWH's impending inhospitable actions towards the city. Having received God's gift of election and blessing, Abraham seeks now to offer the same graciousness to others and pleads for the survival of the city.

The gracious, hospitable character of Abraham, his understanding that his election is not for himself but is an election *for* the Other, is evident too even in the distressing account of Hagar's and Ishmael's exclusion (Gen 21:8–21). Sarah's inhospitality—manifest in her demand that Ishmael's legitimate inheritance rights should, after the birth of her own son Isaac, be revoked, and both Ishmael and Hagar sent away—is contrasted in the story with Abraham's anguish at casting away his own flesh and blood (v. 11–12). The passage suggests that Abraham has no intention of following Sarah's demands, and only acts in such an *unethical* and *inhospitable* manner, once God has conveyed to him that the protection and future inheritance of Ishmael will be of Divine concern. This offering up of his own son Ishmael to the hospitality of God, is preparatory for what is the more radical *call*—the sacrifice of Isaac—that awaits Abraham in the following chapter.

Such an understanding of election—not election *instead* of the Other, or, *apart* from the Other, but rather, *for* the Other—is central not just to the story of Abraham, but rather is a thread woven throughout the Biblical narrative. While having an obvious resonance with Levinas' understanding that the call of the Other is a call to *infinite responsibility*, nevertheless, the distinction we have highlighted is that such *responsibility for the Other* stems from the prior *reception* of the gift of self-identity, the gift of being *addressed*, *named* and *elected* by the Divine Other.

Human Personhood: Gifted, Unique, the Image of God

Three foundational theses of a theological anthropology stem from our reinterpretation of the motifs of call/address/election.

The first tenet that proceeds from the argument we have outlined is that *self-identity and personhood is a gift*. In contrast to the *impossible* Derridean gift—which comes from no-one and no-where and on reception is annulled—at the heart of the Christian doctrine of *creatio ex nihilo* is the belief that humanity does not come into existence due to *necessity*, but rather is a *free* act which overflows from the love shared between the communion of Divine persons. Creation, thus understood, is not an exercise in violent power "over" the Other, but rather is a movement of love and freedom, a moment of *ekstasis*, the free offering of a gift from the absolute

Other, an expression of divine hospitality. This understanding that our very biological existence is a gift of the Creator God, that our identity as a person is not self-constituted but rather is constituted by our relations, both with the Creator God and with others around us, is conveyed by Zizioulas, thus: "The person is an identity that emerges through relationship . . . ; it is an 'I' that can exist only as long as it relates to a 'thou' which affirms its existence and its otherness. If we isolate the 'I' from the 'thou' we lose not only its otherness but also its very being; it simply cannot be without the other."[74]

Accordingly, it is oxymoronic to speak of an *individual* person. Personhood is not something that happens in isolation. To be a person is to be involved in relationships of love and freedom. Genuine freedom is not freedom *from* the Other, but rather *for* the Other.

Secondly, in a personalist ontology *to be a person is to be unique and particular*. While in historical Western thought the human being has been understood primarily in substantial terms—according to nature (*ousia*)—the Eastern tradition, in its understanding of *Being* as personal, emphasizes the *particularity* of each hypostasis. In a theological anthropology influenced by the Orthodox tradition, each human is understood as sharing in the same nature of being human—that is, our very existence as humans is an existential fact of the prior relationship, of our being *gifted*. However, what it is that makes us persons is our *particularity* and *unique distinctiveness*. Orthodox theologian, Christos Yannaras, explains how such a personalist ontology works itself out anthropologically, in this manner:

> Man [humanity] is one in essence according to his nature, and in many hypostases according to his persons. Each man is a unique, distinct and unrepeatable person; he is an existential distinctiveness. All men have a common nature or essence, but this has no existence except as personal distinctiveness, as freedom and transcendence of their own natural predeterminations and natural necessity. The person is the hypostasis of the human essence of nature. He sums up in his existence the universality of human nature, but at the same time surpasses it, because his *mode of existence* is freedom and distinctiveness.[75]

Thus, when we speak theologically of "person" we are speaking not of generalities—as in Greek thought—but rather of particularities. To be a

---

74. Zizioulas, *Communion and Otherness*, 9.
75. Yannaras, *Freedom of Morality*, 19.

human person is to recognize both one's own uniqueness and particularity, but also the uniqueness and particularity of the Other.

Thirdly, *as humans made in the "image of God," we are designed to exist as God exists.* Central to our argument, and flowing from the tenet above, is the belief that humanity reflects the *imago Dei*, not through our nature—our substance/*ousia*—but rather through our mode of being. That is, it is not *what* we are but *how* we exist which is of the greatest significance. Humanity, as *created*, and therefore with a beginning and an end, can never be God by nature, but we are "called to exist in the way God exists."[76] *How* God exists as Father, Son and Spirit, who freely and in love "make room" and space for the Other establishes and discloses the ultimate and genuine form of human life.

Such an ontology of personhood as we have outlined has profound implications for our understanding of human identity. If our very existence is itself a result of the gift of life breathed into our nostrils, if our existence stems from the movement of *ekstasis* within the Godhead, then according to the Christian doctrine of *imago dei*, our very identity as created humans is one of being gift-receivers and thus gift-givers. If human gift-giving (hospitality) is predicated on the gift-giving (hospitality) of God, then, as Miroslav Volf suggests, "to live in sync with who we really are means to recognize that we are dependent on God for our very breath and are graced with many good things; it means to be grateful to the giver and attentive to the purpose for which the gifts are given."[77]

While the attempt to construct a theological anthropology and a conception of social relations by starting with an exploration and elaboration of the ontological Trinity has been critiqued[78] Zizioulas and other Trinitarian theologians offer, we believe, a compelling account of the way in which human relations are shaped by, and should reflect, Trinitarian relations. To be a person is to be a gift-giver and receiver, to acknowledge that we are constituted by the gift/call of the Divine Other, and to recognize that our lives are only fully human as we live, making space for others. Created in the "image of God" and therefore designed to participate in "how" God lives, human relationships should be characterized by freedom, mutual self-giving and love.

76. Zizioulas, *Communion and Otherness*, 165.

77. Volf, *Free of Charge*, 36.

78. Peters, *God as Trinity*, 186, and Kilby, "Perichoresis and Projection." For a response to these two common critiques of Trinitarian theology, see the preface to Gunton, *Promise of Trinitarian Theology*.

However, any approach to construct a theological anthropology based purely on the doctrines of creation and the Trinity would be problematic. While humanity, made in the image of God, bears the imprint of the relational-hospitable Trinitarian God, our createdness—the fact that we are not divine—and the fact that our lives "are inescapably marred by sin and saddled with transitoriness"[79] means that the ability for human relations to correspond with those of the Trinitarian relations has set limitations.

In what follows, we will propose that it is the failure of humanity to live as gift-receivers/givers, our inability to participate freely in divine hospitality, and thus our incapacity to enter into genuine "personhood," which provides the appropriate construal of the nature of sin. Adversarial relationality, characterized by *hostility*, *separation-distance* and *division*, is not, we will argue, to be understood as the creational intent, but rather stems from this failure of humanity to live *how* God does.

The Doctrine of Sin: Hostility and the Knowledge that Consumes

While the Christian scriptures begin with the declaration that humanity is made in the "image and likeness" of God (Gen 1:26), by chapter 3 of this Genesis account things have begun to go awry. Many historical interpretations of Genesis 3 tend to concentrate their reading of this passage around the series of dialogues that take place: Between the woman and the Serpent; the earth woman and the earth man; YHWH's questioning of the man and woman; and then, the subsequent monologue, delivered by YHWH to the man, woman and serpent. While there is much to be gleaned from such an analysis of the speech dynamics within the text, in what follows we will take a different approach. Central to an understanding of the narrative and therefore to our conception of "sin," we will suggest, is an appreciation of the emphasis that the narrative places on the *eyes*, the function of *sight* and their relationship to *knowledge*.

In Genesis 3:5, in his conversation with the earth woman, the serpent explicitly connects *knowledge* with the *eyes*, stating that should the earth creatures eat of the fruit of the forbidden tree their "*eyes* will be opened and you will be like God, *knowing* good and evil."[80] Subsequent to her conversation with the serpent the woman then "*saw* that the tree was good

79. Volf, "Trinity Is Our Social Programme," 107.

80. NRSV. Emphasis added.

for food and that it was a *delight to the eyes*" (Gen 3:6). The knowledge that the serpent offers is not however a genuine knowledge but rather, is distorted. As Nahum Sarna eloquently puts it: "There is an undertone of irony in the formulation that she 'saw that it was good,' for it echoes God's recurring judgment about his creation in chapter 1. Now, however, good has become debased in the woman's mind. Its definition is no longer God's verdict but is rooted in the appeal to the senses and in utilitarian value. Egotism, greed, and self-interest now govern human action."[81]

Rather than recognizing their *givenness*—that is, living in the *knowledge* of their existence constituted as gift from the Divine Other, and likewise, living in an appreciation of the gift of each other and the creation around them—appropriative *desire* is awoken within the earth creatures. Seduced by the cynical and manipulative conjecturing of the serpent, the "fall," is perhaps best understood as humanity's *desire* for an all-seeing, all-comprehending, all-encompassing, totalizing *knowledge*.

The consequences of such an appropriative desire—for a knowledge which is gained through one's *own eyes*, for an *epistemology/episteme* derived from the self and grounded in human experience/subjectivity, rather than embedded in and stemming from the ontological reception of gift—are immediate. The *eyes* of both the earth creatures are indeed opened, but now the fascination, vulnerability and joy which characterized their relationship (Gen 2:25) is replaced by embarrassment, fear and repulsion. In seeking to *know* the other through the *eyes* of self, rather than a gift of otherness to be received, attraction gives way to antagonism, openness to opposition, harmony to hiddenness. Not only does the desire for a knowledge acquired through human *eyes* violate the otherness of both the physical creation and fellow humanity, but even more devastating it leads to a distancing from the original gift-giver, the Divine Other. If, as fallen humanity now mistakenly believes, knowledge means "control-over" and a grasping of that which is Other, then what prevents their Creator, the Divine Other—the source of all such knowledge—from violating them? With such a distorted perception of *knowledge*, humanity understandably seeks to hide from its own Creator.

In such a reading, fallenness therefore is understood fundamentally as humanity's failure to receive its life as *gift*. Stemming from the mistaken belief that identity is self-constituted, the particularity and uniqueness of the Other is thus denied as both creation itself—the fruit—and the human Other, are literally grasped and *consumed* by the self. In seeking to find

81. Sarna, *Genesis*, 25.

our identity independent of the Other we devour the Other on our terms. The gaze of loving desire between *'ish* and *'ishah* turns to a leer of lust. To mitigate the devastating consequences of this new-found totalizing and exposing knowledge, YHWH, in an act of gracious compassion, makes garments to protect them from further objectification (Gen 3:21). In such a state of distorted *desire*, the Divine Other, becomes reduced to an *idol*; the human Other, an object to be feared or assimilated; and the otherness of creation, something to be utilized and dominated. In contrast to Derrida's gift, that cannot aporetically be acknowledged or received without being annulled, we contend it is the very acknowledgment of the Other, of the gift-giver, which gives the gift its giftedness and therefore prevents it from becoming merely an object that can be assimilated and consumed by the self, independent of relationality. It is the refusal to recognize our own giftedness and the giftedness and therefore particularity and uniqueness of the Other, which represents the triumph of the Cartesian self, and is itself the "original sin."

The consumptive and assimilative nature of the *desire* for a self-constituted knowledge and identity, reaches its nadir in Genesis 4. Here, Cain in his *desire* for an identity constituted independent of others, rather than recognizing his life and all he has as a gift and thus offering the first-fruits back to God in gratitude and response, literally consumes the best of his fruit, and then inhospitably offers his leftovers back to God. His desire for a self-constituted identity climaxes in the murdering of the human other—his brother Abel—and as a sign of his complete ingratitude, his ecological *host*, the ground that had produced his fruit, is now drowned in blood.[82]

However, as with all desire, once whet it becomes more and more difficult to satiate the voracious appetite now aroused. The desire to control, consume and assimilate the Other far from leading to *knowledge*, has the opposite effect, leading one deeper and deeper into deception. Our propensity to see the Other through our own eyes, stimulated by our desire for a self-constituted identity, ultimately leads to our own loss of identity. Like all unhealthy appetites/addictions unable to be *mastered* (Gen 4:7)

82. Such an interpretation overcomes many of the problems associated with this text. Cain's sin is not to be understood as an infraction of an arbitrary divine stipulation—the injunction that one offers one's first-fruits back to God—nor is it an indication that YHWH has a particular predilection for meat rather than vegetables. Rather, Cain's failure to follow the prescribed form of sacrifice is illustrative of his actual "sin": his ingratitude to the Divine Other who has blessed him with the bounty of crops; to the land which is his "host"; and to the broader community who would have shared in the communal "sacrificial" feast. We will expand upon these themes in the next chapter.

this consumptive desire, once devoid of other *others* to prey upon, turns inward and ultimately devours itself.[83] Thus, while the overthrow of the Cartesian self is a major accomplishment of post-structuralist thought, the "non-self" that is offered in replacement of the all-knowing *cogito*, contains the seeds of its own destruction. While post-structuralist thought unmasks the consumptive and assimilative tendency of the Cartesian self, the "non-self" devoid of any fixed or secure identity now turns inwards and in an endless process of deconstruction—divides itself up, consuming itself.

Summary

What are the implications of this doctrine of sin for our understanding of human personhood and identity? While created by the hospitable God, and designed to participate in the communion of the divine persons by receiving and offering the gift of hospitality, as sinful people there appears an inward drive, an inherent bias, to seek to comprehend and control what is Other than ourselves. In doing so, not only do we do damage to the human—and non-human—Other, but we also damage ourselves. But is the human experience to be understood as an unending tension between our desire for experiencing genuine hospitality, and our tendencies to overcome and devour the Other, to assimilate them to the Self? Is all hospitality, as Derrida would tell us, mixed with a little hostility? Is there hope for a new mode of relationality with the Other? Is the embrace of intimacy culminating in a return "home," as depicted in Song of Songs, just a forlorn dream, with our "soul's love" turning out to be a Derridean Messiah who never shows up?[84]

Derrida sees such ongoing tension, this "division," and restless waiting, as preferable to a world of "communion."[85] Likewise, Levinas, faced with the human tendency towards violence, offers a philosophy based on *distance* and *separation* rather than relationship. In contrast, we have contended that *separation-distance* and *division* are not part of the ontological

---

83. 1 Pet 5:8.

84. See Song 3:4.

85. Derrida's preference for this tension and struggle over peaceful communion is stated in an interview, where Derrida remarks: "I don't much like the word community, I am not even sure I like the thing. If by community one implies, as is often the case, a harmonious group, consensus, and fundamental agreement beneath the phenomena of discord or war, then I don't believe in it very much and I sense in it as much threat as promise." Derrida, "'Madness' Must Watch Over Thinking," 355.

fabric of creation but rather, are the result of human brokenness. If, as we have argued, otherness is constitutive of communion, then sin is the human failure to recognize and receive the *gift of otherness*. The failure to recognize our otherness from God cuts us off from the source of communion—from the Divine Other. Unwilling to accept the giftedness of our life from the Divine Other, cut off from the source of divine hospitality, we become "individuals," who seek to control the Other on our own terms. Accordingly, sin is not to be understood morally, as our failure to live up to divine standards, and nor is death therefore to be understood as a punishment from God handed out as a penalty for humanity's moral failings. Rather, death is the ontological consequence of a creation—the other—cut off from its Creator—the Divine Other. In our refusal to accept the gift of otherness we are cut off from the "breath of life," from the loving communion and life-giving embrace of the Trinitarian God. Isolated as individuals our "biological" existence slowly decays and moves towards death.

If division stems from this human inability to live in communion with the Divine Other, and is itself an ontological problem, then the solution lies not, as Levinas and Derrida suggest, in human ethicity, but rather in the realm of ontology. According to Christian belief, this *division* is not overcome by human ethical behavior, but rather through the giving by God, of the ultimate gift—that of his Son. It is the Christian belief that it is in this gift of the incarnation—in the entrance into a world beset with inhospitality and violence of the Divine Other and through the life, death and resurrection of this "stranger" Jesus—that *distance-separation* and *division* is surmounted. It is through our lives being "overtaken" and entering into the welcoming embrace of the Divine Other, and our entrance into the *ecclesia*—the "called out" community—that we find our true identity as persons. It is these themes—Christ as the hidden stranger, the Church as the community of welcome, and the formation of a christological-ecclesial-eschatological identity—which will be the subject of the forthcoming chapters.

≋ *A tête à tête.*

Wrestling with the Other

Getting to Grips with Hostility

(Genesis 29–33)

A FEW CHAPTERS AFTER RECOUNTING THE RELATIONSHIP BETWEEN YHWH and Abraham, the Genesis narrative introduces us to Abraham's grandson, Jacob. From the very beginning of the narrative, in the recounting of Jacob's inter-uterine grappling with his twin brother, the reader is made aware of the *struggle* which will characterize Jacob's life. Having stolen the birthright and father's blessing from his brother Esau, and forced to flee for his life to his Uncle Laban, as Jacob's life progresses it takes on a regular pattern. Despite receiving the blessing of the LORD (28:10–20), for Jacob, unlike Abraham, this experience of divine hospitality is not a reality to be shared with others. Rather, Jacob *desires* to create a self-constituted identity, an identity in which he receives blessing and in which the Other is used for his own benefit. Such a desire results in a series of destructive relationships characterized by deception and manipulation. As the story unfolds, the reader becomes spectator to a litany of broken promises and deceit, watching as Jacob's competitive and combative approach to inter-personal relations begins to permeate all those who come into contact with him—the text exposing all the dirty laundry of a dysfunctional family. Jacob's relationship with his Uncle Laban commences with an exuberant welcome and embrace, but degenerates into an economic power-struggle characterized by treachery and dishonesty, as each seeks to gain ascendency over the other.[1] One also observes the struggle between sisters Leah and Rachel as they fight for the affection of Jacob; and in the supreme example of disrespect of one's family and ancestors, watches with horror as Rachel "fleeces" her own Father's household gods (31:19).

Having out-stayed his welcome in Paddan-aram with Laban, Jacob commences his journey homeward. But where is his "home"? Jacob's life has consisted of receiving blessing and "kisses" of welcome—of his father Isaac (27:26–29), the Angel of the LORD (28:13–15) and Laban and Rachel (29:11–14). Yet, as Jacob nears the end of his journey, he confronts the reality that, while absent for twenty years, his previous sins—towards his brother—are yet to be atoned for, and there is no guarantee he will be welcomed. Genesis 32 is thus the climax of the narrative, as Jacob, in his encounter with the angel of the LORD, comes "face-to-face" with his own life of treachery and struggle.

Having been pointedly omitted from Laban's departure blessing (31:55) and uncertain of the welcome that awaits him on the other side of the river, Jacob pauses at the ford of Jabbok. His life of struggling with and overcoming Others has led him to a point where, despite his economic success, he now stands isolated. His legitimate concerns, over whether his brother Esau after all these years will show "hospitality" towards him, have brought him to a standstill. At the banks of the Jabbok river, Jacob's life, both literally, and metaphorically, stands at a crossroad.

But how are we to understand the complex passage which narrates the struggle between Jacob and the nocturnal visitor? The physical wrestling match with the unknown adversary, like the narrative itself full of "internal doublings and intertextual echoes," is illustrative of the struggle with an inner hostility, the wrestling with identity that the duplicitous

---

1. The episode describing Laban's welcome of his nephew Jacob, like the whole narrative, lends itself to multiple and contrasting readings. Laban's hospitality can be seen as a genuinely warm welcome, highlighted by his exclamation, "Surely you are my bone and my flesh," reminiscent of the praise-speech we have encountered earlier in Gen 2:23, (29:13–14). So too, Jacob's greeting "kiss" of his cousin Rachel and his tears of joy can be interpreted as clear evidence of his delight in encountering kin (29:10–11). But is this necessarily the case? Could it be that Jacob's theatrical display of affection towards his cousin, Rachel, is designed to ingratiate himself to his new "hosts," and that Laban's welcome stems from recognizing the benefits of free family-labor? Is Jacob's overflow of emotion, in meeting his kin—and future wife—Rachel, actually genuine, while Laban's welcome is one of "calculating eagerness," or vice-versa? See Marks, "Biblical Naming," 36n25. The contrasting readings, as we will see, are themselves illustrative of the duplicitous nature of the characters one encounters throughout the narrative and testify to the struggle with hospitality which typifies the fallen human condition.

Jacob himself now confronts.[2] Having spent a whole night wrestling with an unknown stranger, Jacob, following the pattern of his life and motivated by his current state of uncertainty and "homelessness," demands a blessing ("welcome") from his adversary. The response of his adversary—the divine stranger—is to ask Jacob his name. Jacob's subsequent response to this inquiry (32:27) can be read in two ways. Is Jacob's response a declaration of pride?—*"I am Jacob, the supplanter. I have no need of the Other, but rather, as my life testifies, I am the creator of my own identity and destiny."* Or, is it a confession of the origins of his stolen identity (27:18–19) and an attempt to repeal these actions?—*"My name Jacob testifies to my life of seeking to supplant and overcome the Other on my terms, a life which has brought me ultimately to this point of loneliness and 'homelessness'."*

The choice of reading shapes how one understands the actual "struggle" that precedes the conversation between Jacob and his combatant. English translations render verse 25 as "When *the man* saw that he did not prevail against *Jacob*, he (the stranger) struck him (Jacob) on the hip socket." Hebrew pronouns however, are less specific in their reference, and therefore the verse can equally be translated: "When *Jacob* saw that he did not prevail against *the man*, he (the stranger) struck him (that is, Jacob) on the hip socket." In the first reading—usually the one chosen by interpreters—the divine visitor (*'elohim*) is viewed as the "antagonist."[3] But could it be that Jacob is the aggressor? Such a reading is given more weight when one considers the divine stranger's cry for release in the following verse: "Then he [the angel] said, 'Let me go, for the day is breaking.' But Jacob said, 'I will not let you go, unless you bless me.'" [32:26].

These alternate readings—Jacob defending himself from the assault of an unknown assailant or, Jacob the aggressor seeking to overcome another Other—and therefore the ambiguous nature of Jacob's identity, are highlighted further as the narrative moves towards its climax. Having heard Jacob's declaration/confession of his name, *Elohim* now proceeds to rename Jacob, "Israel." Variously translated as "strife"/"strive"/"rule"/"persist," the name can accordingly be interpreted as "El strives [for you]" and therefore be understood as an extension of God's special protection which Jacob has received from YHWH earlier at Bethel (28:13–15). In this reading, the acknowledgement of his name "Jacob," and thus self-confession of his life's struggles is responded to by a divine "renaming," whereby Jacob's life of struggle against the odds, and Others, is seen as either forgiven

---

2. Marks, "Biblical Naming," 34.

3. See, e.g., von Rad, *Genesis*, 315.

or vindicated. Thus, von Rad states, Jacob "is given a new name by the unknown antagonist, a name of honor, in which God will recognize and accept him."[4]

However, the whole episode of wrestling that has preceded this conversation between Jacob and the unknown Other, Herbert Marks suggests, "undermines this pious fiction."[5] Could it be that what we are witnessing is not a renaming—"El strives [for you]"—but rather, in the designation "Israel"—"El strives [against you]"—a redoubling of Jacob's original name? After all, Jacob's aggression in trying to overcome the divine Other—to place him literally in a "head-lock"—simply continues his life-long pattern of seeking to control the Other on his own terms.[6] As Marks notes, even as "the eponym 'Israel' is presented as superseding the birth-name 'Jacob,' with which it is thus somehow at 'strife,' . . . its declared 'prevalence' reconfirms paradoxically the persistence of the displaced 'supplanter.'"[7]

Far from being contrived, this second reading is reinforced by the divine Other's response to Jacob's request for the revealing of his name. Why does Jacob ask for the name of the stranger, when in the act of renaming Jacob, "Isra-*el*," the stranger—*el-ohim*—has already disclosed his hidden identity to his adversary? The stranger, despite Jacob's unequivocal request, refuses to explicitly reveal his own name, perhaps fully aware that anyone prepared to spend an entire night wrestling a stranger, is an individual who is used to having mastery over the Other. Does the stranger fear that in giving up his name, such a foe as he has encountered in Jacob will thus take the opportunity to manipulate and emasculate him through his control of language? Indeed, Jacob's final actions in renaming and thus supplanting Jabbok's ("emptiness") with the name Peniel/Penuel ("presence") testify to Jacob's logocentrism, his desire for a "metaphysics of presence," whereby what is Other can be brought within his comprehension and thus mastered? In contrast to the Sinai theophany, where Moses, though having had the Divine Name revealed to him (Exod 3:14), encounters the "presence" of the forbidden face of YHWH (Exod 33:17–33), at Jabbok,

4. Ibid., 316–17. In a similar vein Sarna writes: "It is the bestowal of the new name that constitutes the essence of the blessing and the climax of the entire episode. Jacob had feared for his posterity; now he is tacitly assured that he will become the patriarch of a nation named Israel." Sarna, *Genesis*, 227.

5. Marks, "Biblical Naming," 40.

6. A further possible translation of "Israel" as "*Let El Rule*" would also imply such a reading, with the new name being a constant reminder to Jacob to allow God, rather than himself, to shape his identity and destiny.

7. Marks, "Biblical Naming," 39.

Jacob's final act of "extraordinary audacity," Marks contends, is to "dispose of this forbidden face—the *pĕnê- 'el*—not waiting for the name which the angel conveys, but seizing its most sacred and paradoxical expression and making it a memorial to his own success."[8]

Even as the narrative draws to its close, the equivocal nature of the text continues to testify to the still unresolved ambiguity of the character Jacob, his ongoing *struggle* regarding his identity, his *wrestling* with an inner *hostility*. Jacob's final speech, which closes the episode—"For I have seen the God face to face, and yet my life is preserved" (32:30)—is illustrative of this ongoing uncertainty. Sarna, commenting on the ambiguous nature of the idioms employed in this verse writes: "To 'see the face' may describe an experience of either cordiality or hostility. 'Face to face,' used only of divine-human encounters, may be an adversary confrontation or an experience of extraordinary intimacy. The deliberate ambiguity simultaneously portrays the perilous and the auspicious nature of the furious struggle."[9]

In the end, the prevaricating tendencies within both the text and the character of Jacob are never resolved. Is the wrestling bout simply another incidence of *self*-defiance—an attempt by Jacob to place God into his own vice-like stranglehold, to subdue the Other and have him on his own terms? Or, is the episode the final battle in which Jacob, after a lifetime of seeking to escape the "embrace" of God, is finally overcome and surrenders; his self-constituted identity replaced with an identity gifted by the Divine Other? The question lingers: Who is the victor—Jacob the supplanter/deceiver, or the divine stranger?

Immediate post-bout events seem to suggest it is indeed the divine "host" who has emerged as the victor and that Jacob has begun to learn the lessons of divine hospitality—that is, that welcome and embrace cannot be demanded, but come as gift. Thus, the following morning Jacob's fears are allayed as his brother Esau's "kiss" (33:4) comes as the final resolution to the bitter events precipitated by Jacob's deceitful "kiss," decades earlier (27:26–27). Indeed, it is this reception by his estranged brother; an act of genuine, gracious and forgiving hospitality—that leads Jacob to declare: "to see your face is like seeing the face of God—since you have received me with such favor" (33:10). Could it be that despite his life of wrestling with Others, and seeking to escape the divine embrace, a "renamed" Jacob finally encounters the face of God, in his acceptance both by, and of, Esau?

8. Ibid., 40–41.
9. Sarna, *Genesis*, 228.

Akin to what Levinas would tell us—"The dimension of the divine opens forth from the human face"[10]—is it through his experiencing of reconciling hospitality with his brother, that Jacob-Israel finally comes to the realization that he has encountered divine hospitality?

While indeed possible, almost immediately the narrative "deconstructs" any such neat resolution. Despite having received a forgiving welcome from his brother Esau, Jacob now proceeds, once again, to mislead his brother. To his brother's suggestion that they should "journey alongside each other," Jacob insists Esau should go ahead to Seir, implying he will arrive later to enjoy his reunited twin's hospitality. No sooner has Esau departed southward for Seir, to prepare for Jacob's "home-coming,"(?) than Jacob changes his course, turns northward and re-crosses the Jabbok, making camp at Succoth. Sarna suggests that Jacob's actions, as he "delicately disengages himself from Esau's presence," stem from "lingering misgivings" he has about "the durability of Esau's amiable mood."[11] But is this the case? Could it be instead that Jacob's actions, in turning his back on Esau's hospitality, and in his re-crossing of the Jabbok, are evidence that the struggle within has not yet subsided?

Jacob's story provides an intriguing counterpoint to our earlier reflection on the life of Abraham. While Abraham, in his obedience to a call, his reception of God's blessing/welcome and the accompanying blessing *by* and *for* Others, serves as an exemplary model of a hospitable life, it is hard not to have a degree of empathy for the character of Jacob. Jacob's faith, "less tractable, more errantly familiar,"[12] and his lifetime of "struggle" seems more akin to our human experience—a life, which while seeking to accept the gift of divine hospitality and to accept the otherness of the Other, is often characterized by injustice and violence, perpetrated either upon us, or by ourselves onto others. But are we, like Jacob, condemned to a lifetime of struggle?

10. Levinas, *Totality and Infinity*, 78.
11. Sarna, *Genesis*, 230.
12. Marks, "Biblical Naming," 37.

5

"LOGOS," "Sacrificial Substitute," and "Eikon"

Christology and the Overcoming of Hostility

God became man that we might be made god.
—Athanasius, *On the Incarnation*

*Welcome one another, therefore, just as Christ has welcomed you,
for the glory of God.*
—Romans 15:7

*I believe in Christianity as I believe that the sun has risen: not only
because I see it, but because by it I see everything else.*
—C. S. Lewis[1]

IN THE PREVIOUS CHAPTER WE OBSERVED THAT THE LEVINASIAN AND
Derridean stress on *différance, division, separation* and *exteriority* exists
only because they seem unable to envisage a peaceful ontology in which
communion and *otherness* mutually coexist. In contrast to these relations
of *différance, division and separation* we have suggested that genuine
hospitality is grounded in relations of love and freedom. Within such
an ontology of communion, relationality is not understood as inevitably
adversarial, in which power is used over the Other, hierarchy implies
domination, "naming" assumes control, and subordination is understood
as subjugation. Rather, within this distinct ontology, "power-over" is replaced with "power-with"; causation is understood as a relational term,
evidence of our ultimate giftedness and therefore otherness; and *distance*

1. Lewis, "Is Theology Poetry?," 165.

and *separation* give way to a mutual sharing, to what Olthuis refers as a "sojourn[ing] together in the wild spaces of love."[2]

However, despite the belief that relationships can be loving and harmonious, we live in a world where every day we are confronted with evidence that this is not the case. The Christian Doctrine of Sin gives an account of this failure of humanity to live "hospitably" with Others. But is there hope to a resolution to this ontological antagonism? How is hostility, the struggle with the Other, both within and exterior to ourselves, to be overcome?

A Christological Response?

Exemplarist and Mediatorial Christologies

Christianity claims that in the person of Jesus Christ—through his life, death and resurrection—the hostility and enmity that besets the world is conquered. Yet how exactly does the life of Jesus end the struggle with the Other that seems to be intrinsic to living in the world? Increasing postmodern sensibilities mean that to speak of the uniqueness of Christ as the savior who overcomes the world's hostility is seen as inappropriate. Indeed, as Kathryn Tanner notes, the contemporary aversion to theological claims of the universal significance of Jesus means that "the Christologies of ancient Antioch return to favour in modern Christologies," and thus "Jesus tends to become nothing more than a human model of compassion, justice seeking, and self-sacrifice, for our imitation."[3]

One can find such a Christology in the work of John Dominic Crossan. Crossan portrays Jesus as a Mediterranean peasant *Jewish* cynic, whose practice of "open commensality" lay at the heart of his program of "building or rebuilding peasant community on radically different principles from those of honor and shame, patronage and clientage."[4] For Crossan, the strategic combination of *free healing* and *common eating* practiced by Jesus and his followers both advocated for and established "a religious and economic egalitarianism that negated alike and at once the hierarchical and patronal normalcies of Jewish religion and Roman power."[5] This Jesus, Crossan believes, saw himself as "neither *broker* nor *mediator*, but

2. Olthuis, "Crossing the Threshold," 37.

3. Tanner, *Jesus, Humanity and the Trinity*, 8.

4. Crossan, *Historical Jesus*, 344.

5. Ibid., 422.

somehow paradoxically, the announcer that neither should exist between humanity and divinity or between humanity and itself."[6] Thus, according to Crossan, the practice of "miracle and parable, healing and eating" that characterized Jesus ministry, were "calculated to force individuals into unmediated physical and spiritual contact with God and unmediated physical and spiritual contact with one another." Jesus, Crossan contends, "announced, in other words, the brokerless Kingdom of God."[7]

Clearly Jesus' life did display a radical ethic—one in which the fear and hatred of the Other was replaced by love, one in which the established roles of hospitality were turned upside down and which operated according to the principles of a different economy. Yet, is his significance to be understood primarily in terms of a new "ethic of hospitality" offered to humanity? Is the historical Jesus simply a good ethical role model, a profound moral teacher, whose teaching and enacting of a radical egalitarian hospitality which confronted the "powers" of his day thus offers inspiration and a strategy for those seeking to respond to a contemporary world of exclusion and inhospitality?

For all their appeal, such Christologies leave a number of significant questions unanswered. How do such *exemplarist* Christologies deal with the underlying emotions of fear, distrust and envy that, as in the narratives of Cain and Abel and Jacob and Esau, seem to be part of our experience of living in the world? In what sense do such Christologies, with their call to an imitation of the radical ethics enacted in the life of Jesus of Nazareth, respond to the genuine yearnings for justice when we have been wronged/violated by the Other? Or, on the other hand, how do they relieve us of the debilitating psychological sense of guilt which so often seems to persist when we, as the perpetrator, violate an Other?

It is these questions of guilt and justice and the accompanying desire for retribution and/or forgiveness which typically figure most prominently in the Christologies of Western theology. In contrast to *exemplarist* Christologies which speak little of "sin," it is this question of how the moral compass of the world is to be righted in a world punctuated by pain, anguish and injustice, which is of the utmost concern in what could be termed *mediatorial* Christologies. According to these Christologies, while there is undeniably a clear exemplary ethical dimension to Jesus' life and ministry, the significance of Jesus cannot be reduced merely to his *life* as an ethical example. Such Christologies argue that Jesus is indeed a "mediator" and

6. Ibid. Emphasis added.

7. Ibid.

that, paradoxically, it is at the place of extreme violence and inhospitality—the cross—that justice is enacted and forgiveness therefore offered. They contend that in Jesus' seemingly inglorious death by crucifixion the hostility that exists between humanity and both the human *Other* and the Divine *Other* is overcome and the hospitality of God is revealed.

While offering a broader soteriology than the ethical *imitatio Christi* of exemplarist Christologies, such mediatorial Christologies still appear somewhat limited in their scope and offer up a new set of awkward questions. While the death of Jesus overcomes the *negative* effects of "sin," what is the *positive* soteriological content of Jesus' death? Does the salvific nature of Christ's work consist merely in redemption from sin? In what way does a mediatorial Christ meet the aspiration for an eternal overcoming of division and therefore reconciliation with what is Other—with the human other, with creation, and with the Divine Other? That is, to what extent do such Christologies offer a secure hope that the hostility that bedevils the world will ultimately cease and that the future will be one composed of an authentic and eternal hospitality?

Often in these mediatorial Christological accounts "death" is understood as the punishment for human sin and disobedience which can be removed once God's justice has been satisfied and the moral law has been upheld by the vicarious death of Jesus. But is "death" best understood as a *punishment* for man's violation or transgression of the divine moral law? We have already suggested that death is perhaps best conceived not as a divine punishment that is imposed, but rather as the existential consequence of our failure to fulfill our designated roles as *imago dei*. That is, sin is not primarily to be construed along juridical lines but rather is to be understood as a *perversion* of the personhood to which we are called, and death is the ontological consequence of this failure of humanity to live as "persons," gift-bearers, offering our createdness back in praise and thanks to the Divine Gift-Giver.[8]

In the face of such an understanding both exemplarist and mediatorial Christologies appear inadequate. While exemplarist Christologies may offer us a new ethic of hospitality to attempt to live by, and mediatorial Christologies may sooth our moral consciousness, neither respond directly to this existential question of death and thus neither tend to speak

---

8. See Zizioulas, *Communion and Otherness*, 228. According to Zizioulas, this understanding, that death is not a divine punishment but rather stems from the perversion of personhood, is particularly evident in Orthodox theology which "sees that the problem of the created is not moral but ontological; it is the problem of the existence (and not the beauty) of the world, the problem of death." Ibid., 261.

explicitly of the *positive* dimension of our hoped-for future. While not denying the negative aspect of Christology in which humanity having fallen from grace requires redemption, Zizioulas reminds us that "Christology should not be confined to redemption from sin but reaches beyond that, to man's destiny as the image of God in creation."[9]

Below, we will develop an incarnational Christology contending that while Christ does indeed offer moral forgiveness and summons those who have received forgiveness to live lives characterized by a new *ethic* of peace and hospitality, these moral and ethical implications are predicated on the ontological significance of Christ. That is, the significance of Jesus' life (ethics) and death (atonement)—stem from the ontological significance of the resurrection. We will claim that Christ's resurrection, in defeating *violence* and *death*, creates a new way for humanity *to be* and thus guarantees for the *created being* its eternal existence and its *particularity*. It is the resurrection of Christ which provides the only genuinely secure foundation, an ethic of unconditional hospitality.

With the help of motifs that feature prominently in the Fourth Gospel and the Letter to the Hebrews—those of *Logos* Christology, the Hidden/Homeless Christ whose life climaxes in an act of "sacrificial substitution," and *Eikon*—we will seek to offer a portrayal of the "hospitable" Christ, in whom humanity finds its true home. As we proceed, we will respond to four specific questions: Firstly: How is it possible for God—who is *uncreated*—to enter into the world of *creation*? Secondly: What is the nature of the Incarnation? Who is Jesus, the Word become flesh, and what are the characteristics of his divine-human life? Thirdly: Can an understanding of Christ's death as "sacrificial" and "substitutionary" provide the basis for a relationality of mutuality and gift-giving or do such metaphors legitimize the myth of redemptive violence and valorize an ethic of self-sacrificial martyrdom? Fourthly: How is this new form of *being*—what we suggest is authentic *personhood*—able to be accessed by humanity?

Christology and Being: The Preexistent Word, Creation and Eschatology

In Johannine thought, the salvific purpose of the Triune God does not commence as an emergency measure to combat the effects of a post-lapsarian world. Rather, salvation history is seen in its broadest possible schema and, although conceived eschatologically, commences prior to

9. Ibid., 237.

the creation of the world. Accordingly, the Prologue of the Fourth Gospel gives us a glimpse into the Godhead, prior to creation. Raymond Brown translates verses one and two thus:

> [1] In the beginning was the Word;
> the Word was in God's presence,
> and the Word was God.
> [2] He was present with God in the beginning.[10]

Consistent with the ontology of *communion* we have outlined, the Prologue speaks of the relationality which characterizes the Triune God. The sense of relational intimacy and closeness Brown attempts to convey is expressed too in A. T. Robertson's translation: "the word was face to face with God."[11] These sentiments are echoed in verse 18, which forms an *inclusio* for the Prologue. In verse one we are told that the "Word *is* God" and in verse eighteen it is "God the only Son, (*[ho] monogenēs theos*) who is close to the Father's heart, who has made him known."[12] The relationality, intimacy and affection of the relationship between the *Logos* and God, the Son and the Father, is expressed in their "face to face" relationship, in which the Son rests in the Father's bosom.[13]

This "face to face" relationship between the Father and the Son is not, however, a self-contained relationship which excludes otherness. Rather, the overflow of love from this relationship of divine affection and mutuality—the *communion* of Father, Son and Spirit—is the act of creation that the Prologue moves on to describe in verses three and four:

> [3] Through him all things came into being,
> and apart from him not a thing came to be.
> [4] That which had come to be in him was life,
> and this life was the light of men.[14]

Influenced by Jewish conceptions of the *Logos*, the Prologue gives a startling account of Christ as the Word who brings *all things* into

---

10. Brown, *John [I–XII]*, 3.

11. A. T. Robertson, *Grammar of the Greek New Testament in the Light of Historical Research* (London, n.d.), 623, quoted in Milne, *John* , 33.

12. Brown, *John [I–XII]*, 17, 36.

13. While Brown translates v. 18 thus: "No one has ever seen God; it is God the only Son, ever at the Father's side, who has revealed Him," he notes that "ever at the Father's side" literally translates as "the one who is in the bosom of the Father," with "bosom" connoting affection. Ibid., 17.

14. Ibid., 3.

existence.[15] In its use of the verb *egeneto* for "came into being" in verse three, the Prologue chooses to employ the word that is used consistently in the LXX of Genesis 1. Verses one to four of the Prologue offer therefore a brief glimpse, one could say a "trace," of the ontology of *communion* that we have been expounding, and demonstrates the interrelationship between the doctrines of the Trinity, Creation, and Christology. Out of the loving embrace, the communion that exists between the Father, Christ the Word, and the Spirit, creation comes as a gift of revelation.

In Johannine Christology, however, creation does not merely find its *origin* through Christ the Word, but also eschatologically finds its *telos* in Christ. Thus, in Revelation John is presented with the vision of Christ as the *Alpha* and *Omega*.[16] The claim that Christ the Word as the agent of creation, is the *Alpha* and *Omega* in which the world finds both its *beginning* and *telos*, is one that is expressed by numerous other early Christian writers. The Apostle Paul speaks of the Father and the Son as joint agents of creation stating:

> . . . for us there is one God, the Father, *from* whom are all things
> (*ta panta*) and *for* whom we exist, and one Lord, Jesus Christ,
> *through* whom are all things (*ta panta*) and *through* whom we
> exist. (1 Cor 8:6)

Elsewhere Paul writes: "For *in* him all things (*ta panta*) in heaven and earth were created, things visible and invisible, whether thrones or dominions or rulers or powers—all things (*ta panta*) have been created *through* him and *for* him" (Col 1:16); "For *from* him and *through* him and *to* him are all things (*ta panta*)" (Rom 11:36); while the writer of Hebrews states that "the Son, whom he appointed heir of all things (*ta panta*), *through* whom he also created the worlds" (Heb 1:2).

From the earliest Christian writings therefore, creation was understood not as an action of a lower, mediatory deity or a Platonic demiurge, but rather as brought about by the agency of Christ, as a *free* expression of the love within the Godhead.[17] The New Testament writers were unani-

---

15. There is still scholarly debate over the cultural and literary background of the Prologue. Regardless of its origins—Hellenistic philosophy, Proto-Gnostic sources, or Jewish ideas—the employment of the *Logos* imagery in the Prologue provides the possibility for a conversation between the worlds of Hellenistic philosophy and Jewish thought, and therefore offers a convergence between our earlier ontological discussions and our focus on Christology in this chapter.

16. Rev 1:8; 21:6; 22:13.

17. This emphasis on the Trinitarian nature of creation is perhaps most keenly expressed in Irenaeus' polemical writings against Gnostic interpretations of creation

mous in their theological claim that the world of *being* finds its origin, sustenance and purpose *in Christ*. As Paul states to the Athenians: "In him [Christ] we live and move and have our being" (Acts 17:28). This understanding of Christ the Word, not merely as the agent of creation, but also as the sustainer of all *being*, and the one in which all *being* finds its *telos*, that is, a Christo-centric *creatio ex nihilo*, has two important implications.

First, the affirmation of a Christo-centric *creatio ex nihilo* reinforces our earlier point that Creation itself is an act of freedom and grace and thus, creation itself is a gift, an act of hospitality. As Zizioulas notes: "To say that the world could just as well not exist means that existence is for us a gift of freedom, a grace. Creation and grace thus coincide."[18]

Second, if *being* itself is not self-existent, but rather is dependent on *communion* and stems from the life that is shared within and ecstatically issues forth from the Godhead, then the *created* world of *being*, when cut off from this *life of communion*, moves inexorably to death and returns to *non-being*. As Zizioulas states: "Being *created* means for us that we are mortal and that we are under threat of total and absolute destruction. The threat of death is the threat of nothingness and 'non-being', in other words of returning to the state of *pre*-creation."[19] As *created beings*, therefore, the only way that our existence can be guaranteed is by being brought into the life and communion of the *uncreated* Triune God. In Zizioulas' words: "*Created* being can only survive when united with something *uncreated*."[20]

Logos Christology

But how can something *uncreated* unite with something *created*? Such thinking is impossible within Greek substantialist ontology, in which each being's identity is determined by its nature and its *otherness* from other beings. In contrast, the opening verses of John's prologue, in revealing a Trinitarian personalist ontology in which otherness and communion is seen as mutually constitutive, states that this uniting of the *uncreated* with the *created* takes place in Christ the Word. Within an incarnational

---

in his *Adversus Haereses* (*Against Heresies*). Irenaeus (ca. 120–202) follows Theophilus of Antioch in arguing that creation was a Trinitarian action involving the two hands of the Father: Logos (the Son) and Sophia (the Spirit).

18. Zizioulas, *Communion and Otherness*, 256.

19. Ibid., 257.

20. Ibid., 260.

Christology, it is Christ, the *Logos* who, rather than being confined by *being* is, as Creator of all *being*, able to enter into the *created* world.

Kathryn Tanner, influenced by the thinking of Karl Barth, argues that it is the radical transcendence/otherness of God—the fact that God is beyond *being*, is not a "kind" of being, but rather is the Creator of *being*—which enables God to enter humanity without loss to divine nature. Tanner states: "Only what is not a kind—and therefore not bound by the usual differences between natures—can bring together in the most intimate unity divinity and humanity. Because divinity is not a kind, God is not bound by apparent contrasts between divine and creaturely qualities; God is therefore free to enter into intimate community with us, without loss to the divine nature, without sacrificing the difference between God and us."[21] For Tanner: "Rather than coming at the expense of divinity, incarnation is the very thing that proves divinity."[22]

The problem with many Christologies founded upon a substantialist ontology is that the Chalcedonian Creed, in which Christ is confessed as both fully God and fully human, without division (*adiairétôs*) and without confusion (*asynchytôs*), becomes nonsensical. One is forced, Tanner suggests, to "divvy up the life of Jesus into divine and human qualities, to figure out where Jesus' humanity ends and his divinity begins."[23] But the hypostatic union at the heart of the Chalcedon Creed has as its basis a relational ontology. As Zizioulas states:

> God and the world are united without losing their otherness only in the person of the divine *Logos*, that is, only *in Christ*. It is a *person* that makes this possible, because it is only a person that can express communion and otherness simultaneously, thanks to its being a *mode* of being, that is, an identity which, unlike substance or energy, is capable of "modifying" its being without losing its ontological uniqueness and otherness. All other, that is, non-personalist, ways of uniting God and the world, while safeguarding otherness, involve either a non-ontological relationship between God and the world (e.g., ethics, psychology, religiosity, etc.) or an undermining of the Incarnation, that is, of the "hypostatic (=personal) union" between created and uncreated being.[24]

---

21. Tanner, *Jesus, Humanity and the Trinity*, 11.

22. Ibid.

23. Ibid., 15.

24. Zizioulas, *Communion and Otherness*, 29.

The *Logos* Christology articulated in John's Prologue provides us, therefore, with the philosophical grammar enabling us to state the significance of Christology to ontology. It is the claim of Christian theology that Christ, the creator of all *things*, is the one who, through his incarnation, saves *all things* from their movement towards death. But in what way does the assuming of humanity by Christ the Word have soteriological consequences? To answer this, our second question, requires us to reflect more deeply on the nature of the incarnation. It is, we will propose, in the event of the Incarnation as the Triune God discloses Himself to the World—a revelation that both unveils while remaining hidden, a revelation that is beyond "grasping and comprehension" and yet simultaneously in its very vulnerability is grasped, violated and suffers—that one discovers the "irreducible structure" of hospitality.

The Incarnation as Struggle, Suffering, and Faithful Obedience

> [5] The light shines on in the darkness,
> For the darkness did not overcome it.
> [8] The true light, which enlightens everyone
> Was coming into the world.
> [10] He was in the world,
> and the world was made by him;
> yet the world did not recognize him.
> [11] To his own he came:
> yet his own people did not accept him.[25]

Christ the Trembling Flame / Dazzling Light

"Aesthetics of sight" and what Brian Robinette refers to as the "contrapuntal interplay of light and darkness" play an important role in the rendering of the salvific story of Christ within the Fourth Gospel.[26] In verse five of the Prologue, the multiple nuances within the Greek verb *katalambanein* hint at the paradoxical nature of the revelation disclosed in the incarnation. On the one hand, *katalambanein* can be translated as "to welcome, receive, accept, appreciate." Thus, the verse would be translated: "The light

---

25. Brown, *John [I–XII]*, 3.
26. Robinette, "Gift to Theology?," 92.

shines in the darkness, yet/for the darkness did not recognize/accept it."
Such a translation parallels verses ten and eleven, which point to the "hidden" nature of God's revelation in Christ:

> Though the world was brought into existence by the Word, his
> presence in the world was not "recognized," though he came "to
> his own home," he was not accepted.[27]

Alternatively, *katalambanein* can be translated as "to overtake,
overcome"; or to "master or absorb."[28] These twin-readings of this verse—
reminiscent of the ambiguity noted in Jacob's struggle with the divine
visitor—testify to John's ironic rendering of this strange revelation that is
disclosed and yet remains hidden in Christ.

This theme of the kenotic nature of Christ who, as a "trembling
candle flame, cornered, assaulted and sabotaged"[29] is nevertheless the
light of the world bringing true illumination and revelation to a world in
darkness, is one to which we will return at the conclusion of this chapter.[30]
Such an emphasis on the self-effacing nature of Christ is evident too in
the juxtaposing of the images of Host and Guest. The "power" of the *Host*,
the Fourth Gospel declares, is displayed in his entrance into the world as
"homeless guest."

Christ as Hidden Host / Homeless Guest

Though having brought the world into *being* by his agency, the entrance
of the true *Host* is not heralded as the arrival of an honored dignitary. As
the Prologue indicates, far from receiving the red carpet treatment and
lavish banquets of a VIP, the entrance of the Word is not merely unrecognized (v. 10), but results in the discovery of closed doors and "keep
out" signs (v. 11). Verse fourteen reinforces both the hostile nature of this
reception and also the sense of vulnerability experienced in the incarnation: "And the Word became flesh (σαρξ—*sarx*) and dwelt among us

---

27. "To his own home" is the NRSV's alternative translation to v. 11: "Who came
to what was *his own.*"

28. For the exegetical background on these alternative readings, see Brown, *John
[I–XII]*, 8.

29. Nutu, *Incarnate Word*, 21.

30. The imagery, introduced in the Prologue, of Christ as "Light of the World,"
(3:19; 8:12; 9:5; 11:9–1; 12:35–36, 46) and yet a Light that is not "recognized" (16:3;
1John 3:1) and not "accepted" (3:11; 12:37) is one that recurs throughout the Fourth
Gospel and Johannine writings.

(σκήνωσεν—*eskenosen*)." The Greek word for *to dwell* (*skēnoun*) is derived from the word for *a tent* (*skēnē*) and the author of the Prologue seems here to be making an allusion to the Old Testament and Israel's building of the Tabernacle. The manifest presence of YHWH, his *shekinah* in the Exodus, (Exod 25:8–9; 33:7–11: 40:34–38), takes place in a temporary structure built by slaves, who, liberated from bondage in Egypt, live as "sojourners" awaiting a new home. As ornate as the Tabernacle / Tent of Meeting was, its location in the desert and its congregation of freed slaves was founded not upon a spirituality of stability and safety, but rather of insecurity and vulnerability.[31] As YHWH had journeyed nomadically with Israel in the harshness of the desert, so Jesus is born into the inhospitable and hostile realities of first-century Palestine, a world steeped in violence and political turmoil.[32]

This vulnerability is not restricted simply to Jesus' birth, but rather, hostility and antagonism appear as the hallmarks of the life and ministry of Jesus of Nazareth. Not only do Jesus' life and actions of radical hospitality raise the ire of the religious and political elites but his very ministry is both misunderstood and disdained by "his own"—both Galileans and his own family.[33] The *Host* who brought the world into existence, exists, as Michael Frost poignantly suggests, as "a shadow person," the "Other" on the margins of society.[34] Indeed, the gospels give witness to a life lived in all its finitude—testifying to a Jesus who suffers from tiredness, hunger, loneliness, rejection, grief, betrayal, humiliation, torture and ultimately, death.

That Jesus' life should involve such struggle and vulnerability is, according to the writers of Hebrews, critical to its salvific import:

---

31. It has been suggested that such tabernacle-tent imagery may also be an allusion to the prophetic message delivered by the herdsman from Judah, Amos, to the covenant-breaking Israel (Amos 9:11–15). See Bouma-Prediger and Walsh, *Beyond Homelessness*, 113–20.

32. This sense of vulnerability and defenselessness—of unwelcome otherness—explicated within the Prologue's testimony to the Incarnation, also is present within the Synoptic Gospels. See Matt 2 and Luke 2:1–20. Such spirituality responds to the Jews whom the Fourth Gospel castigates for their fixation with the Temple, but is also required in our contemporary age where places of worship often resemble impregnable strongholds.

33. For the misunderstanding and rejection of Jesus by townspeople of Nazareth, see Matt 13:54–58; Mark 6:1–6; Luke 4:16–30. For the misunderstanding and criticism from his own family members, see Mark 3:21, 31–35 and John 7:1–9.

34. Michael Frost uses these terms in the video "Becoming the Poor."

> It was fitting that God, for whom and through whom all things exist, in bringing many children to glory, should make the pioneer of their salvation perfect through sufferings. (Heb 2:10)

> For we do not have a high priest who is unable to sympathize with our weaknesses, but we have one who in every respect had been tested as we are, yet without sin. (Heb 4:15)

> Although he was a Son, he learned obedience through what he suffered; and having been made perfect, he became the source of eternal salvation for all who obey him." (Heb 5:8–9)

Indeed, that Jesus needed to enter fully into and assume the "fallen nature" of humanity to overcome the hostility and inhospitality of the human plight, is articulated clearly in the writings of the early Greek Father Gregory of Nyssa, who writes:

> By his intimate union with humanity, [Christ] shared all the marks of our nature. He was born, reared, grew up, and went so far as even to taste death. . . . It was in keeping with his intimate union with our nature that he should be united with us in all our characteristics. . . . That is why, in view of the fact that our life is bound by two extremities (I mean its beginning and end), the power which amends our nature had to reach to both points. It had to touch the beginning and to extend to the end, covering all that lies in between.[35]

Central therefore to the salvific claims of an incarnational Christology is the Anselmian assertion that "only that which is assumed can be saved."[36] The Word's assumption of human flesh involved not the taking on of a *perfect* life, but rather the assumption of humanity in all of its frailty, fragility, and vulnerability. In assuming the human condition in all its infirmity and weakness—a life plagued by the effects of sin—Jesus, like Jacob/Israel, faced a life of *struggle*. Yet, crucially, the life of Jesus differs from the Jacob-like "struggle" of humanity which is characterized by the desire to draw close and yet simultaneously escape the embrace of God and assert our independence. Rather, the life of the Word in human form is characterized by a filial relationship with the Father of deep intimacy and humble obedience. In contrast to fallen humanity, which seeks to find our identity and *personhood* separate from *communion*, the Fourth

35. Gregory of Nyssa, "Address of Religious Instruction," 304, quoted in Tanner, *Jesus, Humanity and the Trinity*, 27.

36. Or, in the words of Gregory of Nazianzus: "The unassumed is the unhealed." Gregory of Nazianzus, *Ep.* 101.7.

Gospel repeatedly points to this intimate relationship that exists between the Father and the incarnate Son. It is the fact that the Father is in the Son and the Son is in the Father, that the Father and the Son are one (10:30; also 14:20; 17:11, 21–23), which means that the Son is always doing and saying what is pleasing to the Father (8:29). His words and actions are not his own, but testify to his being sent by the Father (5:36–38) and are demonstrations of the *communion* shared with the Father (10:37–38; 14:10, 24, 31; 15:10). It is due to this deep sense of intimate *communion* that Jesus is able to live a life of faithful obedience, a life characterized by its *free* submission to the will of the Father.

That this faithful obedience and submission to the Father involves a *struggle* stems therefore not from the seeming failure of Christ's divine nature, but is the inevitable consequence of his assumption of a humanity beset by sin. As Tanner observes:

> The Word's assuming or bearing of all this in Christ means a fight with it, a fight whose success is assured by that very unity of the human with the Word, but a genuine fight nonetheless where success is not immediate but manifests itself only over the course of time.[37]

The Synoptic gospels ensure that their readers are acutely aware of this *struggle* that Jesus experiences. In the Garden at Gethsemane, *wrestling* with the future that awaits him, Jesus, the incarnate Word, experiencing the finitude of human existence, prays both that the cup of suffering "will pass from me" and yet "not what I want but what you want" (Matt 26:36–46; Mark 14:32–42; Luke 22:39–46). Jesus chooses not to hold onto his life, but rather to "lay his life down"; rather than seeking to *possess* the gift, he offers his life as a gift to God for the benefit of others; instead of "exploiting" the Other, he "empties and humbles himself." Such a life of humility and obedience, of looking "not to his own interests, but to the interest of *others*" means, eventually, that "instead of the joy that was set before him he endures the cross."[38] This leads us, to our third question posed earlier, that of the salvific significance of Christ's "sacrificial" and "substitutionary" death on the cross.

---

37. Tanner, *Jesus, Humanity and the Trinity*, 28.
38. John 10:17–18; Phil 2:3–8; Heb 12:2.

The Cross: An Act of "Sacrificial Substitution"?

As well as playing a significant role in the ethical thought of both Levinas and Derrida, the terms "sacrifice" and "substitution," from the earliest days, have played an important role in the attempt of Christian theology to explain the soteriological significance of Christ's life and death. Appearing in scripture and throughout tradition, it is, however, only in Western Christianity after Anselm, that the motifs of "sacrifice" and "substitution" begin to become organized into a cohesive atonement theology.[39]

Increasingly though, many contemporary theologians—particularly feminist, womanist, liberation, and peace theologians—contend that atonement theologies with their grammar of "sacrifice" and "substitution," are inherently violent. Such theories, it is claimed, in socializing violence, turn passive submission and sacrificial suffering into virtues.

One example of such a critique is Mennonite theologian J. Danny Weaver's, *The Nonviolent Atonement*. According to Weaver's analysis, the predominant metaphor of the early church was Christus Victor, in which the cross was interpreted as Christ's victory over principalities and powers. However, the establishment of Constantinian Christendom and thus the church's growing relationship with imperial power meant that over time such imagery became superfluous. Weaver argues that "the narrative-orientated identification of Jesus" gave way to "the ontological definitions of the fourth- and fifth-century statements" of Nicea and Chalcedon, thereby rendering Jesus' ethical actions and teaching—and in particular, what Weaver contends is his ethical rejection of violence—"invisible." Eventually, "narrative Christus Victor disappeared from the picture."[40] Weaver maintains that it is the Church's prioritizing of ontological over ethical questions, its emphasis on the *death* of Christ rather than the *life* and *teaching* of Christ, which leads to the emergence of "satisfaction" theories. Such theories, Weaver argues, at their worst, offer a juridicized, individualized, and de-historicized atonement, in which the atonement is interpreted primarily through a legal paradigm with little emphasis on

39. Broadly speaking, atonement theories can be divided into three main typologies—Christus Victor, moral-influence (Abelardian) and satisfaction (Anselmian). While all three motifs have been evident throughout the history of the church, different motifs have held preeminence during different historical periods and in specific contexts, and also have come to hold sway in particular theological traditions. Generally speaking, Christus Victor tended to be the main motif employed well into the Middle Ages, while the theories of Anselm and Abelard have tended to shape atonement theologies of the last millennium.

40. Weaver, *Nonviolent Atonement*, 88, 95.

ethical transformation; with an over-emphasis on individual salvation and hence an ignoring of systematic and structural sin; and which takes no account of the overall biblical narrative structure of salvation.[41]

Likewise, atonement theories in which the suffering and violence experienced by Jesus seems either to be at the behest of the Father, or, at the least, acceptable to him, are seen as particularly repulsive to many feminist theologians. Joanna Carlson Brown and Rebecca Parker are representative of a number of feminist theologians who argue that atonement theologies turn God the Father into the "Divine Child Abuser," valorize self-sacrifice and suffering, and, therefore, rather than offering liberation, perpetuate degradation and oppression.[42] While the response of Brown and Parker to the inherent "violence" they see within *all* atonement theologies is to jettison atonement theology altogether, Weaver seeks to present an alternative *nonviolent* atonement model, offered as a corrective to what he perceives as the violent soteriology which characterizes *satisfaction* atonement theologies.

While sympathetic to the general thrust of Weaver's nonviolent atonement model, there are ultimately a number of problematic moves Weaver makes in developing his argument. Firstly, in seeking to underscore his point that violence originates with humans and not with God, Weaver asserts that the death of Jesus was neither God's will nor intention and that likewise, Jesus did not *choose* to die.[43] Secondly, in his contention that it is the *life* and *resurrection* of Christ that has soteriological significance, Weaver argues that Jesus' death

> accomplishes nothing for the salvation of sinners, nor does it accomplish anything for the divine economy. Since Jesus' mission was not to die but to make visible the reign of God, it is clear that neither God nor the reign of God needs Jesus' death in the way that his death is irreducibly needed in satisfaction atonement.[44]

41. Weaver's chief assertion that satisfaction atonement theology depends on a God who sanctions violence is made unequivocal when he states: "Make no mistake about it, satisfaction atonement *in any form* depends on divinely sanctioned violence that follows from the assumption that doing justice means to punish." Ibid., 203.

42. Brown and Parker, "For God So Loved the World?," 2, and Brown, "Divine Child Abuse?" Rita Nakashima Brock levels the same charge of "cosmic child abuse" at traditional atonement models in *Journeys by Heart*, 56.

43. Weaver states: "Jesus came not to die but to live, to witness to the reign of God in human history. While he may have known that carrying out that mission would provoke inevitably fatal opposition, his purpose was not to get himself killed." Weaver, *Nonviolent Atonement*, 211.

44. Ibid., 72.

However, such assertions—that Jesus' death was neither willed by God, nor a saving necessity—as Chris Marshall observes, "fly in the face of the accumulated weight of New Testament evidence"[45] and therefore deny the important biblical and historical theological claim that salvation is affected through the self-donation of God/Jesus.

Essentially, the work of Weaver and other atonement critics involves a couple of key, and questionable, assumptions. Firstly, the concepts of "sacrifice" and "substitution," used in all three atonement theories but particularly prominent in Anselmian "satisfaction" theories, are viewed as intrinsically "violent." Consequently, in seeking to distance themselves from this perceived "violence," models of "sacrifice" and "substitution" are completely discounted. Secondly, and connected to this first issue, Weaver, Parker and Brown, and others, railing at what they see as the elevation of ontology over ethics, reverse this pattern and offer Christologies which in focusing on the ethical *life* of Jesus fail to interpret this *life* and *death* within its broader incarnational context and thus within the framework of a Trinitarian ontology. Such Christologies, in which Jesus offers a model for us to emulate and in which the salvation of the world depends on our ethical actions, are, in the end, both unconvincing and more than a little discouraging. Offering no ontological basis for a hope that the violence, enmity and death evidenced in the world has been defeated and will therefore ultimately one day cease to exist, such exemplarist Christologies point rather to some sort of *utopian* future, which, like a Derridean messiah, deep down one knows will never arrive.

Speaking of their "new land" of "Christianity," Brown and Parker state that "peace was not made by the cross. . . . No one was saved by the death of Jesus. . . . Suffering is never redemptive, and suffering cannot be redeemed. . . . God's grief is as ultimate as God's love. . . . Eternally God sings kaddish for the world."[46] Such an assertion, however, seems based on an ontology with strong similarities to the thought of our interlocutors, one in which violence and thus grief seem to be inscribed forever into the fabric of creation and God himself. The essential weakness inherent within such exemplary Christological projects is expressed well by Ivor J. Davidson, who writes: "The determinative effects of his personhood are relativized: what matters is not who *he*—[Christ]—is and what *he* does, but what *we* find *ourselves* inspired to do in response to his historical stimulus. *Our* responsibility, *our* action, forms the real centre of gravity. His

45. Marshall, "Atonement, Violence and the Will of God," 81.
46. Brown and Parker, "For God So Loved the World?," 27.

significance lies in the things he symbolizes, not in the things he secures; he may present us with an existential imperative, but he scarcely confronts us as the person who in himself makes all things new."[47]

But do the underlying assumptions of Weaver and other atonement critics hold true? Are the concepts of "sacrifice" and "substitution" inherently violent, or conversely, can such activities, and therefore the metaphors derived from them, be understood "non-violently"? Is it possible for the concepts of "sacrifice" and "substitution" to still play a legitimate role in a "non-violent" atonement theology?[48] Likewise, rather than being an unhelpful hindrance or the root cause of the myth of redemptive violence, could it be that ontological considerations are essential to a non-violent understanding of the Cross?

In their assumption that "sacrifice" is an act of "sacred violence," many atonement detractors draw extensively on the influential work of René Girard and his thesis that the activity of "sacrifice" both originates in and perpetuates violence.[49] Those seeking to offer "non-violent" readings of the atonement find Girard's thesis—that the Gospels speak of sacrifice only to reject and subvert it—particularly invaluable.[50] However, while bold and insightful, Girard's work has itself come under sustained critique. One of the most telling rejoinders to Girard's theory is that his thesis— that all "sacrifice" is inherently "violent"—does not necessarily correspond with historical or ethnographic examples of "sacrificial" rituals.[51] Far from serving as occasions of bloodlust, aggression and human suffering, the vast majority of historical and anthropological material seems instead to

47. Davidson, "Pondering the Sinlessness of Jesus Christ," 378.

48. Hans Boersma, courageously argues that divine violence is unavoidable in bringing a sinful world into an eschatological state of pure hospitality, offering a defense of "violence" within penal substitutionary and satisfaction theories, albeit, with some modifications. See Boersma, *Violence, Hospitality and the Cross*, and "Penal Substitution and the possibility of unconditional hospitality." Similarly, Miroslav Volf argues that an ethic of Christian non-violence is not dependent on the supposition of a non-violent God. Volf, *Exclusion and Embrace*, 275–306.

49. See Girard, *Violence and the Sacred, Scapegoat*, and *Things Hidden since the Foundation of the World*. There is an irony here in that as Christian theologians become sensitive to a supposed potentiality for violence within concepts such as "sacrifice" and "substitution," these same prominent terms are lauded in the writings of Levinas and Derrida.

50. See esp. Girard, *Things Hidden*, 180–223.

51. Prominent anthropologist Mary Douglas points to the conclusion that rituals of "sacrifice" within human cultures revolve not around violence and scapegoating, but rather are primarily occasions of *sociality and gift-giving*. See *Purity and Danger* and *Leviticus as Literature*.

point to the opposite conclusion: that "sacrificial" rituals in human history were predominantly moments of "festive communion" in which humans brought the best of what they had to their deity and thus joined with the deity and others in a "sacred" and "celebratory meal."[52] Accordingly, the activity and notion of sacrifice is perhaps best appreciated when interpreted as an action of *gift-giving*.[53]

Indeed, throughout the New Testament the language and imagery of "sacrifice" is inextricably connected with the grammar of gift. This sense in which Jesus' life and death is not demanded from him as an obligatory payment to fulfill a contractual obligation, or as recompense for human indebtedness, but rather is offered *freely* as a *sacrificial substitute*, as a gift, a self-donation, is perhaps most clearly articulated in John 10:17–18. As evidence of the love between himself and the Father and in obedience to the "command from my Father," Jesus states: "I lay down my life in order to take it up again. No one *takes* it from me, but I lay it down of my own accord. I have power to lay it down, and I have power to take it up again."

As John Dunnill argues, there are a number of profound consequences stemming from this modern-day aversion to "sacrifice," compounded by the "antisacrificial theory" of Girard and his followers. As well as "a misunderstanding of the Christian roots in the worship of Israel, and of the character of Israel as an ongoing religious community," significant for our argument, such antisacrificial sentiment has, Dunnill asserts, "led to a misunderstanding of Christian redemption insofar as that has been expounded in terms of sacrifice, and necessarily it has led to a misunderstanding of Christ when he is named in sacrificial terms as redeemer, high priest, and final victim."[54]

Such sacrificial terms are integral to the *Letter to Hebrews*, where the death, spilling of blood, and sacrifice of Abel and of Christ are contrasted with one another. However, as we will see, interpreted non-violently as actions of gift-giving, such sacrificial and substitutionary images offer new insights into the salvific nature of Christ's life and death.

---

52. Chilton, *Abraham's Curse*, 26–27. John Dunnill argues persuasively that far from being events designed to satisfy communal blood-lust, Old Testament sacrifices are best understood as activities of "sociality," shared meals of hospitality. Dunnill, "Communicative Bodies and Economies of Grace," 87.

53. In response to his critics, Girard, in his later work, has acknowledged that there may be a positive and therefore legitimate use of the metaphor of sacrifice.

54. Dunnill, "Communicative Bodies and Economies of Grace," 79.

The Typological Relation between Abel and Christ

We noted in the previous chapter, the motivating factor for Abel in offering his "sacrifice" to YHWH stems not from obligation or necessity. Rather, Abel's actions in the narrative are evidence that he operates according to the principles of a gift-economy and his sacrifice is to be seen as an act of praise and thankfulness for the gifts that YHWH has bestowed upon him. In contrast to this gift-economy which Abel functions within, Cain's actions are determined by the principles of competition and the contractual obligations and duties which underlie his economic paradigm. Cain sees his abundant produce not as a gift to be referred back to the Divine Giver in thanksgiving, nor as a gift to be shared with others in a communal feast, but rather as his "gained possession"[55] to be held onto, evidence of his *own* horticultural mastery and economic prowess. Accordingly, he reluctantly and begrudgingly brings to the sacrificial feast not his first-fruits, but his leftovers. Outraged at YHWH's acceptance of Abel's—his competitor's—firstlings and fat and the accompanying Divine response to his ingratitude, Cain's "loss of face" sees him turn his face away from both his brother and YHWH (Gen 4:6). Operating according to the "us or them," win-loss logic of a conflictual-competitive debt economy, what Cain perceives as the "victory" of his younger brother, leads him to what he considers his only logical, though drastic, step: eliminating his opposition. In the first act of fraternal violence, Abel's blood is spilled, and his life, like a puff of breath,[56] is snatched / seized from him.[57]

This connection between internal desire/coveting, the desire to have/to possess what is other, and external violence is one that recurs constantly in the pages of the biblical narrative. In episodes such as Adam and Eve's seizing of fruit, Cain's murdering of Abel, or Jacob's life-time of seeking to gain mastery over others, Scripture testifies to the way in which the desire to seize, hold, and possess that which is other than us, and to bring it under our control leads inexorably to conflict and violence.[58] As the epistle

---

55. While debated, the etymology of the name Cain does seem to be a pun on the Hebrew verb *qana*—to get, acquire or create.

56. Similarly, Abel's name, appears to be a pun on the Hebrew *hebel*, meaning vapor, breath.

57. Our thinking here is influenced by Kathryn Tanner's concept of a "non-competitive" economy. See Tanner, *Jesus, Humanity and the Trinity, Economy of Grace*, and "Kingdom Come: The Trinity and Politics."

58. Other notable examples include Ahab's desire for Naboth's vineyard and Jezebel's murderous scheme to bring this about (1 Kgs 21) and David's desire for Bathsheba which leads to his killing of Uriah (2 Sam 11).

of James states explicitly: "You want something and do not have it; so you commit murder. And you covet something and cannot obtain it; so you engage in disputes and conflicts" (Jas 4:2).

It is against this backdrop—in which Abel's "sacrifice" is understood as an act of *faith*, that is, as an action of *responsive gift-giving* (Heb 11:4)— that the writer of *Hebrews* speaks of "Jesus, the mediator of a new covenant, and the sprinkled blood that speaks a better word than the blood of Abel" (12:24). In contrast to Abel's blood, spilled by the violence of his own brother, his life *seized* from him, Jesus has become our "brother" (Heb 12:11–12, 17), *laying* down his life, offering up his blood *freely*.

Fallen humanity, caught in sin, finds itself trapped within the confines of a distorted and death-dealing economy. Incapable of gratefully accepting gifts from God and allowing these gifts both to be referred back to God and circulated on for the mutual enrichment of others, each holds onto what he or she has and avariciously seeks to take from others. The only place where reciprocity operates within this deformed economy of relations is with regard to the "pay-back" mechanism of violence, where the imposition of violence upon one by the other is followed by the intense desire to strike back. The return of violence upon the other similarly awakens their desire for retaliation, and soon both parties are caught in a never-ending spiral of escalating violence, returning blow for blow, taking an eye for eye, until they give or receive, quite literally, the "gift of death."

Christ, however, in assuming the human condition, does what humanity is incapable of doing. *Firstly*, in choosing to proceed like a lamb to the slaughter, in choosing death over retaliatory violence, in refusing to play by the rules of the death-dealing violence of a "pay-back" economy, Jesus deconstructs the power and logic of evil. In Jesus' non-violence, in his choosing of death over vicious response, the mimetic or "pay-back" dynamic which lies at the heart of sin's power is broken. The pastoral and economic metaphors, evident within the story of Cain and Abel, are echoed when the New Testament speaks of how Jesus responds to and overcomes this fallen tendency to violence. 1 Peter states:

> When he was abused, he did not return abuse;
> When he suffered, he did not threaten;
> But he entrusted himself to the one who judges justly.
> He bore our sins in his body on the cross, so that, free from sins,
>   we might live for righteousness;
> By his wounds you have been healed.
> For you were going astray like sheep, but now you have returned
>   to the shepherd and guardian of your souls. (1 Pet 2:23–25)

Secondly, in contrast to fallen humanity which seeks to *possess* the gift of life bestowed upon them, therefore resulting in the annulling and dissolving of the gift, Christ lives a life of faithful gift-giving. In living and pouring out his life for others, and ultimately, in refusing to hold onto his life, but in offering it back to the Father, Christ becomes our "substitute." Such "substitution" should not be understood in violent terms, as a "vicarious substitute" in which Christ stands in our stead to receive punishment we deserve. Rather, the term "representative" better illustrates Christ's sacrificial action. In his death on the cross it is not a matter of Christ being our "substitute"—that is, *instead of me*, but rather that Christ functions as our representative—that is, *this is me*.[59] Chris Marshall, noting the "*substitutionary dimension* to Christ's death" in the Pauline writings, states: "it is substitutionary not in the sense of one person *replacing* another, like substitutes on a football team, but in the sense of one person *representing* all others, who are thereby made present in the person and experience of their representative. Christ died not so much instead of sinners as on behalf of sinners, as their corporate representative."[60]

Interpreted in light of this Trinitarian dynamic of gift-giving, the cross is thus not to be understood as an action of divine violence—Christ the divine "whipping boy" receiving the wrath of the Father on our behalf. Rather, the violence of the cross stems from the inhospitality of the world, which, operating according to the conflictual-competitive logic of a debt economy is, in the words of the Prologue, unable to "recognize" or accept the Divine Gift. Christ, the Divine Other, viewed as a potential threat to what we "possess" and therefore a risk to the reigning economic paradigm, is seized and sacrificed for the sake of stability. The killing of the

59. See Phillips, "Cross of Christ," and Gunton, *Actuality of the Atonement*.

60. Marshall, *Beyond Retribution*, 61. Despite Marshall's concern regarding sporting analogies there is still a sense in which the term "substitution," as it is most frequently employed in contemporary life—on the sports field—provides an illustration of what we have been seeking to argue. The use of "substitution" in sports takes place when a player is replaced due either to injury or incapacitation, or because the coach recognizes the inability of the existing player to achieve the task required. Good coaches do not vent wrath and anger either at the injured player, the player being replaced, or the "substitute." Rather, the coach views the exiting player with compassion and empathy and the "substitution" is performed in the hope and expectation that the entrance of the new player will allow the team to achieve its primary goal—victory. Christ's "substitution" on our behalf comes not so that he can receive the vitriol and rage of the Father (Coach) but so that he can accomplish the task in which we have failed—of living as *persons* and entering into *communion* with God. As with all analogies there is the inevitable shortcoming, in that in this case, Christ is substituted in for the entire team!

Son, the ultimate gift, is the final attempt of a hostile world to proclaim the precedence and preeminence of its death-dealing economy of conflictual-competitiveness and greed over and against God's economy of freedom and grace. The crucifixion of Jesus is the inevitable outcome of the clash of two distinct economic models.

However, in refusing to hold onto the gift for himself, but in offering his life freely for others, in choosing not to shy away from violence, but rather facing it head on, Christ chooses *freely* to encounter the ultimate enemies of human existence. On the Cross, the death-dealing reciprocal exchange of "pay-back," the cycle of violence, comes to a grinding halt. Violence, sin and death are assumed by the one who cannot be conquered by them. The resurrection of Jesus is the evidence that the power of sin and death cannot overcome the loving hospitable embrace of the Triune God.

Importantly, this also means that the cross is not primarily about the Triune God *suffering* with humanity in an act of solidarity, as Jürgen Moltmann and others suggest.[61] While positive in emphasizing the Trinitarian nature of the Cross, an overemphasis on suffering and, at times, speculative nature of such theologies runs the risk of reducing the atonement to a theodicy. Such theologies, as Colin Gunton suggests, lose sight of the greater biblical truth: "that God does not *suffer* history, he *moves* it."[62] The incarnation and cross are primarily about divine *agency* not divine *suffering*. While Christ's life culminates in a barbaric, torturous and suffering death, it is not in Christ's death and suffering *per se* that hope is found. *Rather, it is the resurrection and therefore Christ's victory over violence and death which provides hope for creation.*

The Cross, therefore, despite its horror and suffering is not, as Brown and Parker maintain, "a sign of tragedy,"[63] but is ultimately a sign of victorious suffering love. Far from giving testimony to a vindictive and punitive God of violence, Christ's death is the clearest evidence of God's abundant, gracious, and non-coercive love. Instead of being understood according to the strict logic of *economic exchange* prevalent in some distorted Anselmian theories, Christ's "sacrifice" is best seen as the reestablishment of the gift-giving economy, the reassertion of an ontology of grace.[64] As the Prologue declares: "From his fullness we have all received, grace upon

---

61. Moltmann, *Crucified God.*

62. Gunton, *Christ and Creation*, 87.

63. Brown and Parker, "For God So Loved the World?," 27.

64. For a further elucidation of the distinction between debt-payment and gift-giving, see Torrance, "Covenant or Contract?"

grace" (John 1:16). The resurrection of Christ testifies to the fact that it is not an economy of *forced* exchange, grounded in law and manifested in contractual obligations, but rather an economy of grace, love and freedom stemming from an ontology of *communion* which is the underlying reality at work in the created world. Understood in light of the gift-giving economy which stems from such a Trinitarian ontology, the cross, as Tanner states, "does not save us from our debts to God by paying them. . . . the cross saves us from the consequences of a debt economy in conflict with God's own economy of grace by cancelling it."[65]

Understood as a Trinitarian act and interpreting the terms "substitution" and "sacrifice" non-violently, Christ's death appears as the climactic expression of hospitality of the gift-giving God. Gunton summarizes our thinking well when he writes:

> Trinitarian biblical talk of the saving action of God draws heavily on the language of sacrifice, and it is this that forms the gateway to the theology of the Trinity here outlined. God the Father "gives up" his only Son, allows him to be delivered into the hands of sinful men. Jesus lays down his life, and, particularly but not only in the theology of the Letter to the Hebrews, offers his humanity, made perfect through suffering to the Father. So it is with the Spirit. As the gift of the Father he is *aparchai*, first fruits, of the perfecting action of God in Christ. Although, under the conditions of the Fall, the sacrifice of Jesus must take the form of the spilling of blood, that aspect is not of the essence of sacrifice, which is rather to be found in the notion of gift. It is the Father's giving of the Son, the Son's giving of himself to the Father and the Spirit's enabling of the creation's giving in response that is at the centre. It is by such a means that we move from the economy to the heart of the being of God. It is as a dynamic of giving and receiving, asymmetrical rather than merely reciprocal, that the communion that is the triune life must be understood.[66]

---

65. Tanner, *Jesus, Humanity and the Trinity*, 88, and *Economy of Grace*, 65. Tanner's assertion that God's salvific purposes operate in accordance with an economy of grace rather than a debt-economy is perhaps best illustrated in Jesus' parable of the unmerciful servant in Matt 18:23–35.

66. Gunton, *One, Three and Many*, 225n19.

Once for All: Infinite Responsibility or Imitative Response?

So what of the accusations that "Christian theology with atonement at the center . . . encourages martyrdom and victimization," that "the cross . . . communicates the message that suffering is redemptive," that those seeking to be a "faithful follower of Jesus" are taught that "suffering for others will save the world."[67] The misplaced charge, that Christ's death valorizes an ethic of martyrdom and suffering, stems from the basic problem that we have been seeking to elucidate. When interpreted purely in *ethical* terms and with a *low* Christology, the life and death of Jesus could indeed be construed as commending an ethic of martyrdom and suffering. However, in contrast to the bifurcating of ethics from ontology apparent in both the thought of our atonement critics and that of our philosophical interlocutors, we have been at pains to assert that in Christian theology, ethics does not precede ontology but rather is inextricably connected to ontological concerns.

It is the assumption of humanity by the Word and his living as our "representative" a "perfect life," a life of faithful obedience, made "perfect through sufferings," which the New Testament emphatically states is a "once for all" sacrifice. It is the ontological nature of Christ's "once for all" life and death which provides the basis for Christian ethics and which clearly distinguishes Christian ethical thought from that of Levinas and Derrida. For, despite the similar grammar employed, the term "substitution," understood Christologically, has a distinctly different tone from its Levinasian usage. In Levinasian thought it is the "I" as a "substitutionary self" with "infinite responsibility" before the face of the Other which is the basis for ethics. In Christian theology it is Jesus Christ who as the "substitutionary (representative) self" has taken on "infinite responsibility" "once for all," who provides the basis for *human ethical response*. In contrast to Levinas' assertion that "I am man holding up the universe 'full of all things,'"[68] the claim of Christian faith is that it is Christ, the one in whom "the fullness of God dwells," who holds up—that is, sustains and redeems—the universe. That is, it is Jesus—the creator of all things, the Messiah who has come—whose death and subsequent resurrection overcomes the hostility of the world, thus reconciling all things. It is not our actions, but God's actions in Christ which reinstates an ontology of peace, reestablishing an economy of loving gift-exchange (Col 1:15–20).

67. Brown and Parker, "For God So Loved the World?," 2–3.
68. Levinas, *Humanism of the Other*, 57.

The "once for all" nature of Christ's death only makes sense and thus can only be construed as a non-valorization of suffering if Christ's significance is understood not *ethically*—as just another "moral teacher" but rather *ontologically*. It is not Jesus' humanity *per se* that has salvific function, but rather the *particularity* of his humanity assumed by the Word, that has salvific import.

According to the writer of *Hebrews*, it is the fact that "we have been sanctified through the offering of the body of Jesus Christ *once for all*" (Heb 10:10), that Christ has "offered *for all time a single sacrifice* for sins" (Heb 10:12), which thus provides the basis for the ethical imperative, to "*provoke* one another to love and good deeds" (Heb 10:24). Likewise, in Romans, the free gift of the grace of the *one man* Jesus Christ, who through his obedience defeats death, leads not to a call to martyrdom and death-dealing, but rather provides the basis for Paul's appeal: "to present your bodies as *living* sacrifices" (Rom 12:1). In these passages and throughout the New Testament, the ethical injunction is neither to continue to engage in death-dealing nor to glory in suffering or other forms of perverse masochist ethic. Instead, the Christian ethic is a call to "lead a life worthy to which we have been called, with all humility and gentleness, with patience, bearing with one another in love, making every effort to maintain the unity of the Spirit in the bond of peace" (Eph 4:1–3).

It is as a result of the ontological change brought about through our incorporation into the resurrected body of Christ that we are called not to the impossibility of "infinite responsibility" but rather to the radical, but nonetheless joy-filled, "imitative response." Hence, the saints in Ephesus are instructed: "be imitators of God, as beloved children, and live in love, as Christ loved us and gave himself up for us, a fragrant offering and sacrifice to God" (Eph 5:1–2).

In Levinas' and Derrida's ethics of deference one seems required to give up any sense of one's own needs and in enacting "infinite responsibility" for the Other one constantly faces the nagging sense of guilt that in preferring one, one has therefore sacrificed an-*other*.[69] In contrast, the Christian ethic is not a call to self-obliteration. Instead, the activity of "imitative response" is a summons to participate in a joyous sharing of reciprocal love. It is the fact that Christ's "substitution" is *once and for all*, that he takes upon himself "infinite responsibility," that paradoxically liberates us from the impossible and potentially paralyzing and guilt-inducing demand of ethics, yet at the same time empowers us, summoning us to take

---

69. See Derrida, *Gift of Death*, 70–71.

"substitutionary" and "responsible" actions *for* the Other. Christ's "once for all" sacrifice does not lead to an antinomianism, a neglect of ethics, but rather provides the very basis for Christian ethical behavior. That the call to "imitative response"—to enact love and good deeds in a world of brokenness—will almost ineluctably involve suffering is not to be denied and is a theme to which we will return in our final chapter.

We have argued that Christ, as our corporate representative, the second Adam, has inaugurated the true form of *personhood*, a life lived in *communion* with the Father, characterized not by violent and conflictual relationality but by radical gift-giving towards the Other. But how does humanity enter into this personhood? If, *in Christ*, the hostility and violence of the world has "once for all" been overcome, how does humanity cross the threshold, so to speak, and begin to participate in this experience of *hospitality?* Our response to this, the fourth of the questions we posed on commencing this chapter, is that it is *not* human ethical action, but rather the response of *faith* to God's initiatory actions which provides the basis for entrance into this new life of hospitality and thus leads to the practice of *hospitality* to the Other. It is our contention that human ethical action— the life of hospitality—is predicated on the *reception* of God's initiatory gift of faith and a *response* of active obedience, and that theological knowledge itself, the very ability to speak of the God who offers such a life, is likewise, dependent on *the gift of faith*. These assertions—that the *response of faith* is prior to ethics and that Christian theology as *gift*, is neither totalizing nor threatened by *otherness*—will be illuminated further in what follows. How such a proposal differs from that of our interlocutors will become clear, as, "face to face" with the readings of Levinas and Derrida, we return to that most disturbing of episodes, the *Akedah*.

The Primacy of Grace and the Optics of Faith

Abraham's Sacrifice and the Call to Faith (Gen 22:1–19)

The biblical character of Abraham, and in particular the climactic episode of the Abrahamic narrative, the *Akedah*, have long been the attention of theological, philosophical and ethical discussion, and as we have already observed, play a significant role in the ethical thought of both Levinas and Derrida. Levinas recognizes that one cannot engage with the troubling *Akedah* narrative without reflecting upon Kierkegaard's musings on this episode so strikingly presented in *Fear and Trembling*.[70] While respectful

70. Kierkegaard, *Fear and Trembling*.

of Kierkegaard, Levinas finds his "teleological suspension of the ethical" deeply troubling and expresses astonishment not only at Kierkegaard's move of putting "God above the ethical order!" but also at the very obedience of Abraham to God's call to sacrifice Isaac.[71] For Levinas, the key to the story is the fact that Abraham kept himself "at a sufficient distance" from this obedience to hear the second, and more important call from the voice of the angel, commanding Abraham to stay his hand.[72] According to Levinas—who throughout his writings repeatedly distances his philosophy from ecstatic religion or forms of mysticism, instead advocating an ethical praxis of the Torah as true *mysticism*—the *Akedah* is not, as Kierkegaard would suggest, the "suspension of the ethical," but rather is the *beginning* of the ethical. Contrary to Kierkegaard's interpretation "where subjectivity rises to the level of the religious," Levinas claims it is "Abraham's attentiveness to the voice that led him back to the ethical order" which "is the highest point in the drama."[73]

Similarly, in *The Gift of Death*, Derrida offers an extended commentary on the *Akedah* and Kierkegaard's thought. Derrida argues that each of us, like Abraham, faces the dilemma of Mt Moriah each and every moment we make an ethical decision. He writes: "Day and night, at every instant, on all the Mount Moriahs of this world, I am doing that, raising my knife over what I love and must love, over those to whom I owe absolute fidelity, incommensurability."[74] For Derrida, every decision to respond to an Other involves therefore a sacrifice or betrayal of other others to whom we also owe responsibility and thus, "[this] land of Moriah . . . is our habitat every second of every day."[75] Derrida thus takes the *leap* to interpret the *Akedah*—and Kierkegaard's reading of it—as fundamentally about *ethics*, and in doing so, turns the very singularity of this moment of decision by Abraham into a universal paradigm. But in doing so, does Derrida not, as Dominic Moran asks, "risk banalizing that momentous event, divesting it of its exemplarity/singularity?"[76] Is the narrative of the *Akedah*—and for that matter, Kierkegaard's reflection upon it—primarily concerned with the question of ethics? A closer reading of the *Akedah* text

71. Levinas, *Proper Names*, 74.
72. Ibid., 77.
73. Ibid.
74. Derrida, *Gift of Death*, 68.
75. Ibid., 68–69.
76. Moran, "Decisions, Decisions," 118.

itself, with particular attention to the interplay between visual and aural imagery, suggests otherwise.

A recent fashion for commentators seeking to offer a fresh perspective on this long-discussed narrative is to offer Levinasian-inspired readings of the text, giving particular emphasis to the optical motifs within the text.[77] Influenced by midrash commentary on the narrative and by Levinas' own assertions—that "the epiphany of the face is ethical"; "the dimension of the divine opens forth from the human face"; that there is "authority in the face"; that "the face says to me: 'You shall not kill'"—such *new* readings place great emphasis on *the face* of Isaac.[78] Thus, Claire Elise Katz, seeking to explain what it is that allows Abraham "sufficient distance" to hear the second voice preventing the sacrifice from being followed through, claims:

> Something had to take place in order for Abraham to be receptive to this voice: he had *seen* the face of Isaac. . . . The staying of the hand was the continuation, or affirmation, of an action that was already set into motion; Abraham had already begun to abort the sacrifice. That is, he has turned from *sheer obedience to the ethical.*[79]

Likewise, James Mensch suggests that: "In a Levinasian reading of the story of Abraham, God appears in the face of Isaac. The voice of God, commanding Abraham not to kill Isaac, is an appeal issuing from Isaac's own face. The face exhibits, to those who can recognize it, the authority without power that marks God's presence."[80]

But are such readings, in which primacy is given to the optical signifiers, *faithful* to the narrative? While there are certainly optical signifiers within the *Akedah* story, the aural motifs that appear throughout the text appear to be at least as, if not more, important for interpreting the narrative.[81] Just as there are three explicit optical motifs, so too there are three

---

77. Optical imagery is indeed critical to the narrative, appearing explicitly three times in the passage: "Abraham *looked* up and *saw*" (22:4); "Abraham *looked* up and *saw* a ram" (22:13); and Abraham called that place "The LORD will provide/will *see*. On the mount of the LORD it shall be provided / he shall be *seen*" (22:14) NRSV.

78. For these Levinasian assertions regarding the Face, see Wright et al., "Paradox of Morality," 169; Levinas, *Totality and Infinity*, 199, 78; Levinas and Kearney, "Dialogue with Emmanuel Levinas," 24; and Levinas, *Ethics and Infinity*, 86–87.

79. Katz, "Voice of God." Emphasis added.

80. Mensch, "Abraham and Isaac," 193.

81. Indeed, even Levinas, though ignoring the first voice—God's command for Abraham to sacrifice Isaac—asserts that the critical point of the story is Abraham's *hearing* of the second voice of the Angel.

aural occurrences where Abraham *hears*—and significantly—*responds obediently* to a voice of the Other. To the address of each of these voices— God (v. 1), Isaac (v. 7), and the angel of the LORD (v. 11)—Abraham answers with the declaration of his availability: "Here I am" (*hineni*). Indeed, a defining feature of Abraham's faithfulness is *his obedience to what he hears*, not merely in this episode, but throughout the Abrahamic narrative. While those offering "Levinasian readings" speculate on what Abraham *saw*, thus enabling him to *hear* the voice of the Angel, the text actually reverses this order. Hearing the voice of the angel (v. 11), Abraham pauses his knife mid-point and then *responds obediently* to the Angel's command to stay his hand. It is after this *aural reception and subsequent obedient response* that the text explicitly states that "Abraham looked up and saw" not, as midrash writers and post-modern readings of the text posit, Isaac's face, but rather, the face of "a ram" (v. 13).

The text suggests then, that it is not the human ethical encounter with the Other, that is, the *seeing* of the face of Isaac, which is the primary moment within the episode. Rather, the very ability to *see* Isaac's face stems from Abraham's *faithful obedience* to the voice of God. It is not, as Levinasian thought asserts, the immanence of human ethical behavior which is the transcendent moment, but rather an encounter with the transcendent Angel of the Lord, and one's availability (*hineni*) and *obedience* to his command which thus determines the morality of one's actions.[82]

Even if one does follow a "Levinasian-reading" and give particular emphasis to the optical imagery that appears within the passage, such a reading still runs counter to the conclusion that the narrative is primarily concerned with ethics. Indeed, it is in testimony to the faithfulness of God—the preeminence of God's *sight* and God's activity of graciously providing a ram to sacrifice—that Abraham proceeds to name the place of sacrifice, *Jehovah Jireh*, stating: "The LORD will provide/*will see*." On the mount of the LORD it shall be provided / *he shall be seen*" (v. 14). Abraham's enigmatic name conferral here consists of a pun on the basic word of "see." The first half of the pun is active: God *sees*; the second clause is passive: God is *seen*. Thus, in echoing the description of his mistress Hagar, who earlier had named the angel of the Lord she had encountered, "El-roi," that is, "The God of *seeing* has *seen* me" (Gen 16:13), Abraham makes a profound pronouncement. He confesses that his *seeing* of God— that is, his knowledge of / relationship with YHWH—does not stem from

---

82. As will become clearer as we proceed, none of this is to suggest a simplistic "divine command theory" approach to ethics.

his initiative, but rather has its origin in God's primary action of *seeing* and *calling* him. Likewise, his ethical actions stem not from his own determination of appropriate ethical behavior but rather are actions of obedience to the address of the Divine Other who calls and commands.[83]

Thus, even if engaging in a "Levinasian-reading," one were to concur with Mensch that God appears in the face of Isaac, such a reading does not inevitably lead to the prioritizing of ethics over *faith*. That the face exhibits "the authority without power that marks God's presence," Mensch acknowledges, is not transparent to all, but rather only "*to those who can recognize it.*"[84] It is our contention that such recognition, the ability to *see* the presence of God in the face of Other requires a transformation of our optics. Such optical transformation finds its basis not in human action. Rather, the *eyes of faith* that allow such *recognition* are themselves, a gift of grace.

It is this prioritizing of grace over ethics which is the central theme of Kierkegaard's ruminations on Abraham and the *Akedah*, expressed via his pseudonym Johannes De Silentio, in *Fear and Trembling*. Far from interpreting the *Akedah* as a passage concerned with ethical dilemmas, Kierkegaard, as Ronald Green states: "uses a *surface* discussion of ethical questions to present his more basic soteriological concerns."[85] The point behind Kierkegaard's use of Abraham as a "figure" or "type" in *Fear and Trembling* is, as Green notes, "to establish a Christian ontology in which the order of merit—of ethics, 'the law,' or 'works righteousness'—is subordinated to the realm of grace. The 'teleological suspension of the ethical' is introduced not to defend a form of conduct but to point the way, in the face of persistent human moral failure, to God's redeeming grace."[86] As Green puts it:

---

83. Having already predetermined that the narrative is concerned with "ethics" and that God's initial command is unethical, Levinas, in only giving credence to the second of the voices, thus implies a disregard or disobedience to the first primary command of God. Such a distinguishing between the two addresses not only seems to run contrary to Levinas' very notion that addressed by the Other we are called to responsibility and obedience, but also begs the question on what grounds one establishes what is *ethical*. If faced and addressed by the Other we are called to infinite responsibility, then how does one determine whether the command of this face is *ethical* or *unethical* and thus to be obeyed?

84. Mensch, "Abraham and Isaac," 193.

85. Green, "Enough Is Enough," 192–93.

86. Ibid., 199.

Fear and Trembling is not a defense of the possibility of murder at God's command, nor is it, despite the commentators, a celebration of Abraham's *moral* heroism. Quite the contrary, it is a tribute to the one who first adopted the stance to which all his spiritual descendents are called; the stance of living "beyond ethics" in absolute dependency on God's grace. To sinners, it is the stance symbolized by the name of the place of Abraham's sacrifice, Jehovah-jireh: "God will provide."[87]

It is here, in this offering of an ontology in which ethics is subordinated to grace, that we therefore see some unexpected yet clear parallels between the thought of atonement critics discussed above, and Levinasian-Derridean thought. Both Levinas and Derrida in their belief that the *Akedah* narrative is primarily concerned with *general* ethical questions, find the passage—and particularly Kierkegaard's interpretation of the passage—troubling. Brown and Parker and other atonement critics repeat this same error. In viewing the cross fundamentally as about *ethics* they presume that Jesus' death is offered to us as a *general* ethical model to emulate. It is the failure of such advocates of exemplarist Christologies to recognize the *particularity* and *singularity*, the "once for all" nature of Jesus' life and death, which leads them to suggest that Christ's death valorizes an ethic of self-sacrifice and suffering and perpetuates an economy of sacrifice. However, in contrast to both Levinas' and Derrida's ethical reading, Kierkegaard's *Fear and Trembling* asserts that the central theme of the *Akedah* narrative is not a summons to return to *ethics*, but rather a call to enter a journey of *faith*.

And what is the nature and who is the *object* of this faith? Hebrews having outlined a long line of those who have lived by faith—including Abel and Abraham—states that these ancestors though "commended for their faith did not receive what was promised, since God had provided something better so that they would not, apart from us, be made perfect" (Heb 11:39–40). The writer of Hebrews states instead that it is Jesus who as "the pioneer and perfecter of our faith"—its *origin* and *telos*—we are to "fix our eyes on."[88]

Yet, doesn't fixing our eyes on the face of the Other, bringing them within the sphere of our consciousness, as our philosophical interlocutors have argued, involve totalizing and violating them, robbing them of their otherness? To return to questions we posed at the beginning of section

---

87. Ibid., 204.
88. Heb 12:2, NRSV. "Fix our eyes" from NIV.

two: Does not the activity of "doing theology" consist of a Jacob-like attempt to wrestle the Divine into the confines of language, therefore reducing Him to an *object* which can be assimilated and brought under our domination? For Levinas and Derrida any attempt to speak of God, risks doing violence to God's transcendence and, as argued by Feuerbach, turns God into an idol. But is this necessarily the case for Christian theology?

Christ the Dazzling Eikon and the Non-Violating Nature of Christian Theology

> [12] But all those who did accept him
> he empowered to become God's children
> That is, those who believed in his name—
> [13] those who were begotten,
> not by blood, nor by carnal desire, nor by man's desire,
> but by God.
> [14] And the Word became flesh
> and made his dwelling among us.
> And we have seen his glory,
> The glory of an only Son coming from the Father,
> filled with enduring love.
>
> [16] And of his fullness
> we have all had a share—
> love in place of love.
> [17] For while the Law was a gift through Moses, this enduring
> love came
> through Jesus Christ.
> [18] No one has ever seen God; it is God the only
> Son, ever at the Father's side, who has revealed Him.[89]

Jean-Luc Marion, sympathetic to the Levinasian and Derridean critique of onto-theology, attempts to construct his own post-metaphysical theology upon the development and elaboration of the concept of the "saturated phenomenon." For Marion, the "saturated phenomenon" refers to "the impossibility of attaining knowledge of an object, comprehension in the strict sense," not "from a deficiency in the giving intuition, but from its surplus, which neither concept, signification, nor intention can forsee, organize, or contain."[90] For Marion, it is the Christ event which is

---

89. Brown, *John [I–XII]*, 3–4.
90. Marion, "In the Name," 39–40.

the "saturated phenomenon" *par excellence*. With unmistakable echoes of the Prologue, Marion speaks of the incarnation as:

> a phenomenon saturated to the point that the world could not accept it. Having come among its own, they did not recognize it; having come into phenomenality, the absolutely saturated phenomenon could find no room for its display. But this opening denial, and thus this disfiguration, still remains a manifestation.[91]

Reiterating the theme of this section on the primacy of grace and the optics of faith, Marion contends that Christ's face is not an object that, *seen* by the self, is thus made captive to human consciousness, grasped and comprehended as a totality. Rather, it is the face of Christ, who as the active agent places the viewer in his gaze. Drawing on the juxtaposition of light and darkness within Johannine thought and the mystical theology of Psuedo-Dionysius, Marion argues that revelation does not consist in us finding God, but rather God finding *us*.[92] The face of Christ is not *seen* and thus absorbed, but rather produces "bedazzlement" for sight.[93] Christ is not reducible to an idol, but rather is an *eikon*, the One who gives us a glimpse of the Divine *communion*, yet never able to be totally captured by thought. As the Prologue to the Fourth Gospel states, "No one has ever seen God; it is God the only Son, ever at the Father's side, who has revealed Him." That is, *seeing* the face of God in Christ, and likewise the ability to see the image of God in the human Other, is dependent on the prior event of God *bedazzling* us and giving us *eyes of faith* to *see* God's own self-revelation. Our acceptance, our welcoming of the Word, and thus our adoption "to become God's children" stems not from human initiative, but rather is a response of faith, a response that is itself dependent on an external "empowering." The human action of "believing in his name" is simply a response to the prior *desire* of God. Those who see Jesus, who are illuminated by the "light of the world," are those who, according to the gospel, have been born from above. Dazzled by our encounter with the light that shines forth from the crucified yet resurrected face of Christ, we become the objects who through "fixing our eyes" upon the iconic face of Christ, undergo a process of transformation. As our eyes become adjusted to the blaze of dazzling light, so our vision is transformed, enabling us to catch, in the vulnerable faces of others, glimpses of the face of God.

91. Marion, *Excess*, 208.
92. Marion, *God Without Being*, 100–102.
93. Marion, *Being Given*, 237.

The primacy of *faith* in the realm of soteriology holds true too for the practice of theology itself. Just as human salvation stems not from human ethical actions, but rather from the initiative God has taken in Christ, so too, the action of theologizing—speaking about God—finds its basis not in human intellectual insights, but rather in the prior speech of God. Christian theology, put simply, is the attempt to put into words that which through the Word has first been spoken to us.

Accordingly, this means that the activity of *doing theology*, of speaking about God, is likewise dependent on taking a stance of faith—that is, receiving God's gift of grace which therefore opens our eyes to see. Unlike the pragmatic agnosticism of our interlocutors in which the distinction between the human Other and the Divine Other is blurred, and ethics is given priority over grace, Christianity is a summons to faith not in the incomprehensibility of the unknown Other, but rather in Jesus, the Word made flesh. While agreeing with Levinas' assertion that "the dimension of the divine opens forth from the human face" (*TI* 78), it is the Christian claim that the fullest revelation of the divine is manifest in the human-divine face of Jesus Christ, and the ability to see the trace of the divine in the Other is dependent upon a transforming of our *sight*, the receiving of the gift of *eyes of faith*. Such *faith* is not a well-meaning *faith* in the "natural" human inclination of empathy towards the fellow human. Rather, biblical *faith* is a trust in God's faithfulness to fulfill his promises and overcome human brokenness and then a life of empowered obedience lived in response to God's initiatory actions in ending *hostility*. Such faith does not lead, as Levinas and Derrida fear, to ethical inaction. Their charge—undoubtedly influenced by their observation of the behavior of the Church in Germany and Algeria—that "a metaphysical relation with God" is often accompanied by an "ignorance of men and things" is one that fails to ring true of authentic Christian faith. Rather, as so vividly displayed in the life of both Abraham and Jesus, faith involves a hearing of the address of the Transcendent Other, accompanied by a response of obedience. As we will explore in our next chapter, the primary evidence of this life of faith, is one's response of obedience to the command "to love one another."

Summary

In this chapter we have traced the outline of a Christology and soteriology in which Christ is understood as the universal solution to the inhospitality and hostility present in our world. Using motifs drawn from the Prologue of the Fourth Gospel and the book of Hebrews—Christ the *Logos* as creator, sustainer and redeemer of *being*; trembling flame-dazzling light; hidden host-homeless guest; substitutionary sacrifice, and *Eikon*—and, drawing on resonances with the Old Testament characters of Abel, Abraham, and Jacob, we have argued that it is in Christ and in the singularity and particularity of his incarnation that humanity finds the basis for authentic personhood. The significance of the entirety of this life—a life characterized by an intimate relationship with the Father and one of radical obedience and due to the fallen nature of the world, suffering—is not, we have argued, primarily one of providing a moral or ethical example. Rather, it is the ontological change brought about by Christ's assumption of fallen humanity and his resurrection triumph over sin, violence and death, which establishes the only secure foundation for the practice of a radical hospitality to the *Other*.

Christian theology claims that those who are *seen* by Christ and who through *faith* are incorporated into the body of the resurrected Christ, are set free from slavery to mimetic violence and therefore to the fear of death. They become, through the indwelling of the Spirit of Christ, new gift-giving *persons*. The shape of this new Christologically-formed personhood, which, having received the hospitality of God, is called and empowered to act hospitably through its new life in the *ecclesia*, is the focus of our final two chapters.

~~ *A tête à tête.*

Seen by the Other

The Call to Faith

(John 1:35–51)

THE MOTIF OF CHRIST AS *EIKON* AND THE TRANSFORMATION THAT OC-
curs as we look to the face of Christ is one employed by British theologian
David F. Ford in his book *Self and Salvation*. Ford, in a Christology shaped
by a close interaction with the thought of Levinas, suggests that "being
faced by God" and "turning to face Jesus Christ in faith" are among the
defining characteristics of Christianity.[1]

While innovative, Ford's concept of a "worshipping self" *generated*
by its facing of the face of Jesus, does seem to revert to an exemplarist
Christology. John Webster expresses disquiet at Ford's employment of
"the face" as primary soteriological metaphor—a metaphor "tending to be
static rather than dramatic, [of] Christ as image rather than agent."[2]

But does using the "face of Christ" as one's primary soteriological
metaphor, inevitably lead to an exemplarist Christology and a Pelagian
soteriology? A close reading of Scripture reveals that the concept of Christ
as *eikon*, rather than being construed as "static," can still be understood
as underscoring the dramatic agency of God *in Christ*. Both Levinas and
Jean-Luc Marion—who adopts, though not uncritically, Levinas' conception of the Face—suggest that an encounter with the Other, far from

1. Ford, *Self and Salvation*, 24–25.
2. Webster, review of *Self and Salvation*," 548–59.

reducing the Other to an idol which is grasped and totalized, rather leads to "a dazzling, where the eye holds more than it can hold."[3] In an encounter with the Divine Other, the face of Christ cannot be reduced to an idol, but rather our gazing at the Other is reversed by the gaze of the divine icon who envisages us.[4] It is not our sight that has primacy, but rather our very *seeing* of Christ is dependent on his own self-revelation to us. That is, *seeing* the face of Christ is dependent on the prior event of God *seeing us*, of God revealing Himself and giving us, through the gift of faith, eyes to *see*.

This claim that our identity and salvation stems not from our initiative—whether ethical actions or intellectual insight—but originates in the active *seeing*, *calling*, and *naming* of the Divine Other, is strikingly made in the Fourth Gospel. In narrating the episode which marks the beginning of the discipleship of Andrew, Simon Peter, Philip, and Nathanael, the Fourth Gospel eloquently connects this theme of *seeing* with that of hospitality.

With striking parallels to the *Akedah* narrative, the Fourth Gospel records that John the Baptist, on being approached by Jesus, declares: "*Look!* Here is the Lamb of God who takes away the world's sin" (1:29), and again later, John the Baptist declares to two of his disciples: "*Look*, here is the Lamb of God!"(1:36).[5] In response to John the Baptist's bold Christological declaration, two disciples—Andrew and John—begin to follow. It is Jesus though, who takes the initiative and speaks for the first time in the Fourth Gospel. The question "What are you looking for?"(1:38), as Raymond Brown observes: "touches on the basic need of man that causes him to turn to God, and the answer of the disciples must be interpreted on the same theological level. Man wishes to stay (*menein*: 'dwell, abide') with God; he is constantly seeking to escape temporality, change, and death, seeking to find something that is lasting."[6]

The disciples' reply to Jesus' initiatory question with their own query: "Where are you staying?" Their active and energetic response to Jesus' invitation to "Come and see" (1:39) testifies to their desire for a place of permanence and intimacy, a place to *dwell* and *abide* in safety and security.

Andrew's immediate action after spending time with Jesus is to find his brother Simon and to announce not that he has spent time with a *Rabbi*, but to boldly declare that he has *found* the *Messiah*. Taking his

---

3. Levinas, *Of God Who Comes to Mind*, 67.

4. Marion, *God Without Being*, 21.

5. Brown, *John [I–XII]*, 55.

6. Ibid., 78–79. The verb *menein*—to dwell, to lodge, to abide—which appears three times in 1:38–39, is a motif developed throughout the Fourth Gospel.

brother along to meet this Messiah, Jesus "*looked*" at him and said, 'You are Simon, son of John; your name shall be Cephas' (which is rendered as 'Peter')" (1:42). Caught in the gaze of a face—a gaze not of violence but full of love—Simon, restless and shifting, discovers a new identity, his new name Peter—Rock, testifying to the solidity and stability that ensues from being *seen*, *named* by, and *found/founded* in Christ.

In a parallel story, the Fourth Gospel then continues with a recitation of Jesus' encounter with Philip and Nathanael (1:43–51). As with the previous episode, it is Jesus who takes the initiative, travelling to Galilee and *finding* Philip. Like Andrew, Philip responds to his being *found* by then seeking out another—in this case Nathanael—to be brought to *see* and be *found* by Jesus. And, replicating Andrew's "*Messiah*" declaration, Philip, confident in the *new-found* ability to *see* clearly, announces boldly to Nathanael: "We have found the very one described in the Mosaic Law and the prophets" (1:45). Despite Nathanael's initial doubt—"Nazareth! Can anything good come from there?"—Philip persists, instructing Nathanael: "Come and *see* for yourself" (1:46).

As with Simon Peter, so with Nathanael: Jesus *sees* Nathanael approaching and declares: "*Look!* Here is a genuine Israelite; there is no guile in him" (1:47). To Nathanael's puzzled enquiry: "How do you know me?" Jesus states, that prior even to Philip's invitation to Nathanael to "Come and see," he had already been *seen*.

Indeed, in contrast to Jacob, who as the first "Israel" sought to *see* God on his own terms, Nathanael, true to his name—"God has given /gift of God"—becomes aware that his *seeing* is ultimately conditional on his first being *seen*. Unlike Jacob/Israel, whose *vigorous wrestling* with God is testament to his constant attempt to comprehend God, Nathanael's posture of *passive-responsivity*, is characteristic of genuine *faith*. Nathanael's reception of the *gift* of faith, his receiving of God's goodness and grace, leads to an *active response*. In an outpouring of "praise speech" he offers the climactic Christological declaration of the titles offered in these episodes. "*Lamb of God*"; "*Rabbi*"; "*Messiah*"; the One "*whom Moses in the law and the Prophets testify to*," indeed, but even more so, Nathanael declares: Jesus is the "Son of God," the "King of Israel" (1:49). Nathanael's reception of the gift and his accompanying annunciation of faith lead Jesus to announce that through such eyes of faith "you will *see* heaven opened and the angels of God ascending and descending upon the Son of Man" (1:51).

---

7. The verb "looked"—*embelepein*—Brown states: "means to fix one's gaze on someone and thus to look with penetration and insight." Ibid., 74.

Thus, as Luke T. Johnson notes, "in a single deft allusion John has Jesus identify himself as the Holy Place where humans encounter God, the one who has descended from God and returns to him, and the 'gate' through which others can go to God."[8] For those who receive the gift of faith, and whose eyes are opened to *see*, Jesus appears as the new House of God— *Bethel*—the locus of God's hospitality.[9]

8. Johnson, *Writings of the New Testament*, 482.
9. See Gen 28:10–22.

6

Dwelling in Christ and the In-Dwelling Other

Forming the Ecclesial and Eschatological Self

Community is a terrible place. It is the place where our limitations and our egoism are revealed to us. When we begin to live full-time with others, we discover our poverty and our weaknesses, our inability to get on with people, our mental and emotional blocks, our affective or sexual disturbances, our seemingly insatiable desires, our frustrations and jealousies, our hatred and our wish to destroy. While we were alone, we could believe we loved everyone. Now that we are with others, we realise how incapable we are of loving, how much we deny life to others.

—Jean Vanier[1]

PREVIOUSLY, WE HAVE ARGUED THAT ALL OF CREATION, AND HUMANITY itself, is brought into being as a gift, its origins lying in the hospitable and *ecstatic* actions of the loving Triune God. However, distorted by our own *desire* to live *distantly* and *separately* and therefore cut off from the life of this divine *communion*, humanity becomes fearful of *otherness*. The Other is no longer perceived as one who comes offering joy, enrichment and mutual beneficence, but rather as a threat to our existence, one to be struggled against and overcome. Fear erupts into violence, hospitality gives way to hostility.

Stemming from the infinite love shared between Father, Son and Spirit and their *desire* that humanity should enter into the joy of *communion*, humanity is not left in this state of *hostility* and *homelessness*. Rather, in the event of the incarnation, the Son comes and enters the totality of

1. Vanier, *Community and Growth*, 17.

the human predicament. Although there are vestigial moments of joy, intimacy and love, it is, ultimately, betrayal, suffering and death which come to the fore as a *hostile* humanity enmeshed in a self-serving, death-dealing economy of violence reveals its unpreparedness to receive the ultimate gift of the true *Host*.

It is, however, the audacious claim of Christian faith that the assumption of humanity by Jesus the Word, his subsequent *face to face* encounter with human violence and his *overcoming* of death brings resolution to the antagonism and aggression that besets the world and provides the basis for humanity's ontological and therefore ethical transformation. The nonviolent, non-coercive overcoming of the *inhospitality* of the world—the inauguration of a *new way of being*, of authentic *personhood*—is grounded therefore not in human ethical effort or *desire*. Rather, rooted in the actions of God on our behalf, it stems from God's *desire* for humanity. *But, how does the self enter into this new way of being and participate in the authentic form of personhood found in Christ? What are the processes that bring about the transformation from a hostile to hospitable self? And, what are the contours and characteristics of this new hospitable self?*

In this chapter our focus will be primarily pneumatological and anthropological as in describing the transforming work of the Spirit within the self we set forth an alternative account of identity than that offered by our philosophical interlocutors. Continuing with the themes of *dwelling* and *inhabitation*, we will reflect on the way in which *dwelling* in Christ entails the presence of the Paraclete, the *disturbing Other*, within the baptized self. It is this indwelling Other, who, through the activities of *reclothing, prosecuting, disturbing, expanding* and *renovating* actualizes the new post-baptismal existence and transforms the affections and desires of the fearful and hostile self. What begins to emerge, as the self participates in this work of the Spirit, is the forming of a self with new contours and a new character. "Keep out" signs are replaced by "welcome" doormats, barricaded boundaries give way to opening doors. In the words of John Zizioulas, *biological existence* is replaced by a new *ecclesial existence*.[2] Or, as we have suggested, the "hostile self" begins to make way for a new "hospitable self."

---

2. See Zizioulas, *Being as Communion*, 49–62.

The Forming of the Hospitable Self

Baptism: The Crucified, Resurrected, and Re-clothed Self

Earlier, in reflecting upon Jesus' *call* of the first disciples, we gave particular attention to the motif of Christ as *dwelling* place. We argued that it is in being *seen* by Christ, in responding to his initiatory *call* and in *dwelling with* and *in* him, that one finds authentic personhood. Throughout the New Testament these images of *dwelling and inhabitation* are central to the attempt to articulate the ontological transformation that takes place as humanity enters into and participates in the life of Christ. As one enters through *faith* into *union* with Christ, the Spirit, who raised Christ from the dead, enters and *indwells* the believer. To be found *in Christ* involves the entrance of the Spirit of Christ into the self and the incorporating of this new Self into the Body of Christ—the welcoming of the self into God's new community being formed in the world.

From the earliest days of the church it was the rite of baptism which both marked one's entrance into the *Ecclesia*, and also played a significant role in the Church's understanding of the transformation of the self that occurs as one confessed faith in Christ. For New Testament writers, baptism was not viewed as a "purely external rite," serving as a "mere symbol," or "as a rite that effects what it symbolizes."[3] Rather, baptism was understood as an ontological event in which the new believer entered into union with Christ. The Apostle Paul employs a number of striking motifs to elucidate this ontological transformation that takes place within believers as they pass through the waters of baptism.

Firstly, baptism was understood as a participation in Christ's death and resurrection. In sinking under the water, the believer was ontologically *united* with Christ in his death, and in being raised up out of the water was incorporated into a new life found *in* Christ. Thus, Paul states:

"For to me, living is Christ and dying is gain." (Phil 1:21)

"So if you have been raised with Christ, seek the things that are above, where Christ is, seated at the right hand of God. Set your minds on things that are above, not on things that are on earth, *for you have died, and your life is hidden with Christ in God.* When Christ who is your life is revealed, then you also will be revealed with him in glory." (Col 3:3–4)

---

3. Beasley-Murray, "Baptism," 61.

"For through the law I died to the law, so that I might live to God. *I have been crucified with Christ; and it is no longer I who live, but it is Christ who lives in me.* And the life I now live in the flesh I live by faith in the Son of God, who loved me and gave himself for me." (Gal 2:19–20, emphasis added)

Paul's employment of life and death vocabulary in these passages does not primarily refer to the possibility of such life and death experiences occurring now that the new disciple has chosen to *imitate* the moral example of Christ. While the imitation of Christ does stem from participation in Christ, and the practice of radical *unconditional* hospitality contains the very real possibility of suffering and potentially biological death, here, Paul is concerned with making an ontological statement about what has *already taken place*. Paul's conception of the self is that those who respond to Christ's *call* and embrace the gift of *faith* enter ontologically into *union* with Christ, and thus participate in the death and resurrection of Christ.[4]

Secondly, elsewhere, Paul employs imagery of one being reclothed and prepared for a banquet. Drawing on the actual practice of the baptism ritual during the apostolic period—that of stripping off old clothes and being baptized in the nude, before putting on new garments—Paul again stresses the transformation that occurs as one enters, through faith, into *union* with Christ, and the ensuing ethical behavior that flows from this new ontological reality. Thus, in *Galatians*, Paul states that, to be "baptized into Christ is to have *clothed* yourselves with Christ" (Gal 3:27).

The language employed here is evocative, suggestive of the Spirit as the chief designer and wardrobe assistant who fashions new clothing and then re-dresses the self. Such imagery is particularly striking in our contemporary consumer age with its fascination with image and the projected appearance of the self. Yet, unlike the postmodern self which is lauded for its chameleonic nature, its malleability and the ability to constantly reinvent itself—a self in which appearance is simply a simulacrum and where identity is closely linked to one's entity as a consumer—the baptized self, is being dressed in new, long-lasting "imperishable" apparel.[5] In contrast to the contours of the postmodern self, which, projected onto the billboards, Web pages, television screens and magazines, constantly changes and is redrawn according to the dictates of "fashion," the self inhabited by the Spirit finds itself being conformed to the image of a different *eikon*.[6]

4. Rom 6:3–11.
5. 1 Cor 15:35–58.
6. The imagery of Christ as transforming *eikon* is also expressed in 2 Cor 3:17–19.

The corollary of this ontological transformation is the commencing of a process of transformed character and ethical behavior. In contrast to the models and fashion-designers of "reality" television programs such as *Next Top Model* and *Project Runway*, whose behind the scenes bickering, envy and petty jealousies betray the poised and glamorous personas portrayed on stage, Paul calls for a different behavior. Paul urges believers to rid themselves of "anger, wrath, malice, slander, and abusive language," and calls on them to cease lying to one another . . . "seeing that you have *stripped off the old self* with its practices and have *clothed yourself with the new self*." In Paul's logic it is the new post-baptismal reality which dictates that members of this new community, "chosen . . . holy and beloved" should now "*clothe* yourselves with compassion, kindness, humility, meekness and patience. . . . and above all, *clothe* yourselves with love" (Col 3:8–14).

Thirdly, elsewhere Paul mixes metaphors, combining these motifs of death, burial, and reclothing with imagery drawn from the Jewish rite of circumcision. Thus, in his letter to the church at Colossae, Paul writes: "In him [Christ] also you were circumcised with a spiritual circumcision, by putting off the body of the flesh in the circumcision of Christ; when you were buried with him in baptism, you were also raised with him through faith in the power of God, who raised him from the dead" (Col 2:11–12).

In summary, for Paul, faith in Christ, dramatically evidenced in the rite of baptism, entails an ontological transformation as the old self, full of hostility and violence, is, like old clothing, cast aside, put to death *in Christ*. In its place emerges a new resurrected self, which "comes to fullness" *in Christ*, the one in whom the "fullness of the Godhead dwells" (Col 2:9–10).[7] To be found *in Christ*, means the beginning of a process of preparing for the final eschatological banquet. Suitable attire is required for participants attending such a significant and auspicious occasion, and though humanity, confined to the limits of its own wardrobe is incapable of dressing itself in the appropriate garb, the Spirit of Christ, the authentic fashion designer with access to all the *fullness* of Christ, is in the process of replacing our rags for riches, substituting our torn and stained garments with that which cannot rust or rot.[8]

---

7. As Zizioulas puts it: "baptism leads to a new mode of existence, to a regeneration (1 Pet 1:3, 23), and consequently to a new 'hypostasis.'" Zizioulas, *Being as Communion*, 53.

8. Matt 6:19–20, Jas 5:2.

The Paraclete: Presence of the Absent Christ, Disturbing Comforter

While using different vocabulary from that utilized in the Pauline writings, Johannine thought also employs a number of evocative images to describe the process by which the self *dwelling* in Christ and *indwelt* by the Spirit undergoes a transformation from *hostility* to that of a *hospitable self.* In Johannine thought, the *dwelling* of God within his disciples takes place through the work of the Paraclete. The multiple and contrasting nuances of the Greek term *paraklētos*—derived from the verb *parakaleō*, literally, "to call beside"—far from being problematic, instead can be seen to offer a broad and rich palette for depicting the work of the Spirit.[9] Below, we will suggest that it is the seemingly paradoxical, yet actually mutually reinforcing motifs of the Paraclete/Spirit as *Presence in Absence* and *Disturbing/ Prosecuting Comforter*, which provide a striking account of the Spirit's transformation of the self.

It is no coincidence that discussion of the Paraclete in the Fourth Gospel occurs during Jesus' final discourse to his disciples, in the context of a pre-Passover shared meal.[10] In the intimate surrounds of their final meal together Jesus explicitly speaks of the hospitality of God about to be made manifest in his glorification, and the subsequent formation of a new community—a community comprised of those who through *faith in* Christ will be indwelt by the Spirit. The initial intimacy of this Last Supper shared between the Rabbi and his disciples—evident in the role-reversal as Jesus washes his disciples feet—is soon dissipated by a misunderstood prediction of Judas' betrayal (13:21–30), Jesus' announcement of his imminent departure (13:33), and his sharp rebuff of Peter's bravado (13:36–38). As the conviviality, familiarity and trust gives way to a new atmosphere of uncertainty and fear, Jesus speaks words of reassurance to the troubled disciples:

> Do not let your hearts be troubled. Believe in God, believe also in me. In my Father's house there are many dwelling-places. If it were not so, would I have told you that I go to prepare a place for you? And if I go and prepare a place for you, I will come again

9. Four main interpretations for the term *paraklētos* are offered by scholars—*comforter/consoler, advocate/attorney, intercessor/mediator/spokesperson,* and *exhorter/ encourager/witness*—with interpreters differing mainly over whether the term should be understood actively or passively, forensically or non-forensically.

10. John 13–17.

and will take you to myself, so that where I am, there you may
be also. (John 14:1–3)

Central to Jesus' reassurance to his now fearful and anxious disciples
is the paradoxical explanation that his imminent departure will inaugu-
rate a new experience of radical hospitality, that the ushering in of the *eschaton* of hospitality and peace is dependent on his forthcoming *absence*.
Using imagery of the host who goes ahead to prepare for a banquet feast
Jesus announces that his intention is not to leave his disciples languishing
as orphans. He reassures them that his departure will only be temporary
and ultimately his *absence* will result in his ongoing *presence* and *union*
with his disciples. His declaration: "I will come again and will take you to
myself, so that where I am, there you may be also" (14:3) is reiterated three
times through this Last Supper discourse: The Spirit will come and "abide"
and "be in you" (14:16–17); Jesus will return to dwell with his disciples
(14:18–21); and the Father and I "will come to them and make our home
with them" (14:23–24). The outcome of Jesus' glorification on the cross
and his triumph over human hostility, will be the *dwelling* of God within a
newly constituted humanity; a humanity that in *seeing* and *receiving* Jesus,
has therefore *seen*, *believed* in, and received the hospitality of the Father.

In an unexpected resonance with the insights of our post-structuralist interlocutors, Johannine thought therefore speaks of a paradoxical
relationship between *presence* and *absence*. The *presence* of the Spirit is
dependent on the *absence* of Christ, with Jesus himself stating: "it is to
your advantage that I go away, for if I do not go away, the Advocate will
not come to you; but if I go, I will send him to you" (16:7). In Johannine
thought, the newly constituted humanity, brought into existence after the
glorification—death and resurrection of Jesus—is not to be characterized by a "metaphysics of presence," evident in Philip's Jacob-like request
"Lord, show us the Father, and we will be satisfied" (14:8). Rather, it is the
very *absence* of Jesus which is the precondition for the new community of
faith becoming the *presence* of Christ in the world, as the Spirit enters this
community and acts as revealer and teacher to them (14:26, 16:13). This
new humanity will be known for its faith even in *absence* (20:29) and for
the radical love shared between them (13:35).

This aporetic association between *presence* and *absence* extends too,
to the contrasting roles of the Paraclete as both *comforter/consoler* and
Prosecutor. John 16:8–11 employs courtroom imagery characterizing the
Spirit-Paraclete as *Prosecutor* who comes to testify against and "to convict the world of sin, righteousness and judgment" (16:8). The Paraclete's

role here as Prosecutor is not however one of convincing the world of its sin, for, like the other Paraclete, Jesus, whom the world could not *see* or *accept*, the Spirit of Truth is unable to be *seen* or *known* and therefore *received* by a world living in illusion and lies (14:17). Indeed, as Max Turner notes, rather than offering "independent witness," the Paraclete's task of prosecuting (16:8–11) is inextricably linked to its function as teacher and revealer to the new community of *faith* (16:12:15).[11] It is in "guiding the new community into all truth" by "declaring the things that are to come" (16:13) that the Spirit points to the glorification and victorious triumph of Jesus over the hostility of the world. As teacher and revealer the Spirit reminds the disciples of the sin of the world in refusing to accept the gift of Jesus, demonstrates the injustice of the world's justice that adjudges guilty the only One truly innocent and just, and reinforces the point that the world in condemning Jesus, has judged itself. In doing so, the Spirit therefore reveals to the disciples the way in which Jesus' death stems from an inhospitable world trapped within the confines of a scapegoat system, a system in which the Other is perceived not as gift, but threat.[12]

This revelation by the Spirit, bearing witness to Christ's victory over death and therefore the overcoming of the hostility of the world, while comforting and consoling, is also, by its very nature, discomforting. The presence of the Spirit of Truth within the self in its revelation of what has taken place in the death and resurrection of Jesus by corollary exposes to the self the assumptions, illusions and downright deceit under which the self continues to operate. In speaking truthfully of the hostility of a world, bent on violence and control of the Other and by announcing that such a system has been defeated *in* Christ, the Spirit exposes the powerful ideologies still at work in the self which function to exclude us from the Other.[13] The Paraclete's work of consoling and comforting as it *dwells* within this newly constituted humanity does not, therefore, consist of a reassurance of the *Same*, a smoothing over and soothing of tension and *difference*. Rather, the Spirit is one who *unsettles* the self, or, to use Anthony Gittins' parlance, is *a presence that disturbs*.[14]

This imagery of the Spirit as the Prosecuting *Other*—of the self interrogated, accused, in one sense, even held *hostage* by this *Disturbing*

11. Turner, "Holy Spirit," 350.

12. See Brown, *John [XIII–XXI]*, 711–14.

13. On the essential connectedness between the practise of hospitality and honoring of the truth, see Hütter, "Hospitality and Truth," and Hauerwas, *Peaceable Kingdom*, 142–46.

14. Gittins, *Presence That Disturbs*.

Other—is evocative of language employed by Levinas. Nevertheless, there is a clear contrast between Levinasian thought and that which we propound. The disturbing presence of the Spirit—unsettling the self, revealing the self's participation in the system of *sameness* which therefore excludes and victimizes the Other—ultimately summons the self not to an endless Levinasian examination of one's ethical actions. Rather, the self is called again to accept and *participate* in the new life brought about by the once-for-all redemptive actions of Christ.

The Contours of the Emerging Hospitable Self

A Bounded and Centered Self?

Thus far we have outlined an account of how the Spirit as the *presence* of Christ, working within the believer, makes available the benefits of Christ's overcoming of the inhospitality of the world. Through the waters of baptism the old biological self is crucified and a new self emerges. The in-dwelling Spirit of Christ actively actualizes this new self through the process of reclothing the self in new *imperishable* clothing appropriate for the final homecoming and union with the Divine Other. At the same time, by *prosecuting/disturbing* the self, the Spirit exposes to the self the lies and ideologies which function as a discourse of hostility distancing the self from others. *But what are the contours of this new self that emerges from the baptismal waters? How does one conceptualize this hospitable self, united with Christ and indwelt by the Spirit? Does the Spirit as the disturbing Other inhabiting the believer overpower or efface the self? And, can one, in light of the post-structuralist critique of the notion of self-identity, even speak of a self, distinct from Others? Is it possible, in an age of deconstruction, to conceive of a "centered self," one able to be inhabited by an Other?*

Miroslav Volf responds to these probing questions by tackling head-on the post-structuralist conception of the self. Volf notes insightfully that despite Derrida's aversion towards "hegemonic centrality"[15] his understanding that difference is internal to the self presupposes the existence of some kind of centre. Indeed, as Volf observes, "when talking about identity one cannot do without a center; otherwise, the talk of difference and its being internal to oneself makes no sense."[16]

---

15. Derrida, *Other Heading*, 38.
16. Volf and Gundry-Volf, *Spacious Heart*, 46.

Instead of being considered hegemonic and therefore exclusionary of otherness, Volf argues that "personal centeredness must be preserved for the sake of difference"[17] and, in contrast to a Derridean centre, which seemingly acts as "merely a container of the difference,"[18] Volf proposes an understanding of the self with a "de-centered center."[19]

Integral to Volf's "distance-belonging" schema, which he offers as a model for understanding human identity, is his reflection upon the doctrine of the Trinity. For Volf, the perichoretic dynamic which exists within the Trinity "describes the kind of unity in which the plurality is preserved rather than erased,"[20] and therefore offers an important resource for a conception in which self-identity is constituted by the Other interior to the self, while also affirming the distinctiveness and uniqueness of the self. Volf, arguing that human identity is created in the image of this Trinitarian God, makes two claims regarding *identity*. Firstly, that "*identity is non-reducible*," that is, that in contrast to Buber's thought, a person cannot be reduced to their relations. For Volf, the person "is always already outside of the relations in which he or she is immersed"[21] and therefore by implication the notion of a self-identity involves some sense of *boundaries*. Secondly however, Volf believes that "*identity is not self-enclosed*" and contends that such "boundaries of the self are porous and shifting."[22] Drawing on the work of Gunton, Volf states:

> The self is itself only by being in a state of flux stemming from "incursions" of the other into the self and of the self into the other. The self is shaped by making space for the other and by giving space to the other, by being enriched when it inhabits the other and by sharing of its plenitude when it is inhabited by the other, by re-examining itself when the other closes his or her doors and challenging the other by knocking at the doors.[23]

In imagery which resonates with our description of the Spirit as a *prosecuting* and *disturbing* presence, Volf posits that it is as a result of the

17. Ibid.

18. Ibid.

19. Volf, *Exclusion and Embrace*, 71.

20. Volf, "Trinity Is Our Social Programme," 110.

21. Ibid., 111.

22. Ibid., 112.

23. Ibid. Gunton, noting the spatial imagery within the Trinitarian notion of *perichoresis* argues that the term is best understood not as "dancing around" but as "making room." Gunton, *One, Three and Many*, 163–66.

new birth in and by the Spirit, that a "fissure" is formed in each believer "through which others can come in."[24] Differing from the *divided* and *fractured* post-modern self, which is constantly undergoing deconstruction and demolition, this understanding of the self recognizes the way in which the self is constituted by the presence of the Other, but also affirms that hospitality is dependent on a metaphysical *home*, that the welcome of otherness is dependent itself upon some form of "boundary maintenance."[25] Following Volf here, we endorse the idea of boundaries that distinguish the self from the Other. While affirming the insights of post-structuralist thought that the self is "constituted in relationality,"[26] is open to, and shaped by *otherness*, like Volf, we maintain that such openness to difference is only possible if one can conceive of some *a priori* sense of identity, a self composed of a de-centered *center*.

Such a model of identity, of the self as a *home* with walls which create a safe haven where the self can be nurtured and yet with doors and windows which open to the Other, is evident too in the thought of Catholic writer Henri Nouwen. For Nouwen, the solution to a world of loneliness and inhospitality comes not from "creating a milieu without limiting boundaries."[27] Echoing the sentiments of Volf, Nouwen believes that "openness loses its meaning when there is no ability to be closed."[28] Instead Nouwen asserts that

> real openness to each other also means a real closedness because only he who can hold a secret can safely share his knowledge. When we do not protect with great care our own inner mystery, we will never be able to form community. It is this inner mystery that attracts us to each other and allows us to establish friendships and develop lasting relationships of love. An intimate relationship between people not only asks for mutual openness but also asks for mutual respectful protection of each other's uniqueness.[29]

24. Volf, *Exclusion and Embrace*, 51.

25. Volf, "Trinity Is Our Social Programme," 111.

26. Butler, *Giving an Account of Oneself*, 64.

27. Nouwen, *Reaching Out*, 33.

28. Ibid.

29. Ibid., 32. The basic necessity of boundaries for ongoing existence and health is most apparent in the world of cellular biology. Caroline Westerhoff writes: "Like a cell membrane, a boundary must be semi-permeable: admitting and containing only what is necessary for sustaining and enriching life, discharging and excluding anything that does not belong within its borders. A membrane that allows for anything and everything to enter and leave is a membrane that is no longer functioning. The cell—the

Nouwen contends for a conception of self in which "the painful contours of our hostility" are overcome by the gradual creating of a "free, fearless and friendly space."[30]

In the model of self-identity offered by Volf and Nouwen, the self consists of a "de-centered center" with porous boundaries which both safeguard one's particularity and uniqueness and yet, containing apertures, also gives the Other access to the self. Yet, a critical question arises: Is it the "god of the self" or the triune God who "is the doorkeeper deciding about the fate of the otherness at the doorsteps of the self"?[31] An excellent illustration of such a model of self-identity, which recognizes the way in which the self is constituted in *communion with* others and gives attention to the identity of the "doorkeeper," is found in the parable Jesus tells in John 10 where he characterizes himself as both "sheep-gate" and "shepherd."

Centered Catholicity (John 10:1–21)

Critical to understanding Jesus' parable in John 10 is an awareness of shepherding practices employed during Jesus' time—practices which have continued almost unchanged through to contemporary Palestine.[32] In a first-century Palestine context, sheep belonged to small family-owned flocks and over many years an intimate relationship would develop between the livestock and their shepherd. Palestinian shepherds knew all their sheep individually, often by name, and led their small flocks from in front, with the sheep following in response to the reassuring and known voice of their shepherd. During the day, sheep belonging to various families would intermingle in the pastures and at night they would return, for their safety, not to a sealed or secured barn or building, but rather to an enclosed courtyard, under the watchful eye of a *gatekeeper* (*thyroros*). The following morning, the child agreed upon by a number of families to shepherd their collective sheep would arrive and the sheep would respond to the distinctive call or whistle (often a flute) and leave the sanctuary of the pen for another day in the pastures. During the summer months shepherds often would not return to the village courtyard but would utilize make-shift pens that dotted the hill pastures, often constructed of rock walls and topped with thorn-bushes, to protect the sheep from wild

system—is now dead or dying." Westerhoff, *Good Fences*, 83.

30. Nouwen, *Reaching Out*, 68, 63.

31. Volf, *Exclusion and Embrace*, 71.

32. What follows draws on Bailey, "Shepherd Poems of John 10."

animals. In this case, the shepherd would sleep in the entrance to the pen, thereby becoming the gate.

While Jesus' parable, as Raymond Brown rightfully posits, acts as a figurative attack on the Pharisees,[33] it also illustrates well the notion of the self and personal identity that we have been developing. While the sheep maintain their own individual and particular identity—known intimately by name and owned by specific families—their identity is not constituted by a radical separation from sheep of other folds. Rather, the key determinant in the establishing of the identity of each sheep is their *proximity* to, and *intimacy* with, the shepherd. However, centering one's life around Jesus, the parable contends, does not necessarily guarantee safety. Indeed, while the imagery of the gate-keeper elicits a sense of safety and protection, Jesus' statement "I am the gate" and his emphasis on the movement of "coming in" and "going out" develops this image in a surprising and disturbing way. The image, Rodney Whitacre notes, "is not that of a door as a barrier for protection, but of a door as a passageway."[34]

Such an understanding of identity is brought into even sharper focus using the categorizations of missiologist Paul Hiebert, upon whose work Volf also draws. In contrast to *bounded sets* which operate on a binary logic, i.e., either/or, us/them, or, *fuzzy sets*, in which boundaries are effaced or blurred, Hiebert suggests that identity is best understood as a *centered set*. In a centered set model, identity is defined in terms of (1) a *centre*, that is a unifying principle of unity or source of loyalty/object of allegiance, and (2) the *relationship* one (or one's group) has with that centre. Within such a model there is (3) *variational* movement, i.e., proximity or distance from the centre which therefore creates (4) a *dynamic* quality to the relationship.[35] These four key characteristics of a *centered set* conception of identity: *centered*, *relational*, *variational* and *dynamic*, are all evident within the parable of the Good Shepherd. In the parable, the key determinant regarding the identity of the sheep is their *relationship* with the *central* figure—the Shepherd (Christ)—a relationship of intimacy in which the sheep *know* the Shepherd's voice and are *known* individually by name. However, the sheep are not confined or captured but rather move freely from this centre and their self-identity is also co-constituted by their engagement with, and difference from, sheep of *other* folds.

---

33. Brown, *John [I–XII]*, 383.

34. Whitacre, *John*, 258.

35. Hiebert, "Category 'Christian' in the Mission Task."

Ultimately, the Christian conception of the *hospitable* self that we have developed is therefore not an *essentialist* conception of identity, one based upon rigid boundaries and a clear demarcation between the self and the Other. Neither though does it subscribe to an *instrumentalist/constructionist* model of identity, which sees the self as containing no *essence*, but as simply an assemblage of its relationships, one in which the self is constantly undergoing a process of "recycling."[36] Rather, the conception of self-identity we have developed, refusing the bifurcating logic inherent in other models, recognizes the uniqueness and particularity of the self, but also gives due credence to the way in which the identity of the self is constituted by both *others* and the *Divine Other*. The hospitable self is a catholic identity constituted by being *in* Christ and being incorporated with others into the life of communion within the *Ecclesia*.

The Expanded and Renovated Self

Such an understanding of the corporate or catholic nature of identity distinguishes this Christian concept of the *hospitable self* from the conceptions of the self offered by both Levinas and Derrida. Sharing the Foucauldian presupposition, that knowledge is power and that all relations are inherently relations of power *over* the other, both Derrida and Levinas, as we have observed, have a deep suspicion of the concept of *community*, preferring instead to advocate a relation between the self and the Other based upon *distance* and *separation*. But inevitably, such an ontology means that despite the advances beyond the autonomous and self-grounding self of Cartesian thought, the post-structuralist self still appears as a lonely and alienated "I." As Richard Rorty, perceptively notes, there is "no 'we' to be found in Foucault's writings, nor in those of many of his French contemporaries."[37]

But can one really speak of a self, and therefore of an ethic of hospitality, without a "we"; that is, without the notion of community? If, as Stanley Hauerwas and Alasdair MacInytre contend, our ethical behavior and the character and virtues that shape such behavior are formed by narratives of meaning and being which emerge from within the shared experiences of a community and their tradition, then the Levinasian and Derridean suspicion and distrust of both community and tradition/dogma becomes deeply problematic. Can an isolated and estranged "I," divorced from the

36. Bauman, *Life in Fragments*, 80–82.
37. Rorty, "Habermas and Lyotard on Postmodernity," 174.

identity-shaping structures of community and tradition, devoid of a narrative of being or meaning, without a metaphysical "home," really offer hospitality to the Other?

In contrast to this post-modern self, central to our Christian account of the self is the belief that the baptized self, indwelt by the Spirit of Christ, is not a rootless and centre-less wanderer, *separate* and *distant* from the Other. Rather, through baptism, the self becomes a newly constituted person, incorporated into a new community, the Body of Christ. Gunton succinctly expresses this distinction stating that "a person is different from an individual, in the sense that the latter is defined in terms of *separation from* other individuals, the person in terms of *relations with* other persons."[38] Or, as Volf puts it: "The Spirit sets a person on the road toward becoming what one might call a 'catholic personality,' a personal microcosm of the eschatological new creation. Catholic personality is a personality enriched by otherness, a personality that is what it is only because all differentiated otherness of the new creation has been reflected in it in a particular way."[39]

Once again the New Testament uses a number of different images to express this new ecclesial reality, to describe a self which is united with Christ and indwelt by the Spirit and thus joined ontologically with Others who are *in* Christ. Perhaps the most evocative image is the corporeal imagery of the Body of Christ, which Paul uses in his first letter to the believers at Corinth (1 Cor 12:12–31).

For Paul, the human body, while comprised of *different* and *particular* parts (hands, eyes, ear, noses) distinguishable from one another, remains nevertheless, *one* body. Paul both affirms the *differences* that exist—Jews, Greek, slaves, free—but stresses that such *differences* are grounded not upon an ontology of *separation* and *division*. Drawing on banqueting and hospitality imagery, Paul contends that identity is found not as separated individuals but rather is constituted as *one* Spirit inhabits *all* and *all* drink from the same Spirit. Unlike our philosophical interlocutors who see *difference* and *communion* as antithetical, arguing that *communion* is simply a disguise for *sameness*, the Christian conception of the body of Christ affirms that particularity, difference and uniqueness is not threatened by communion and mutuality. Rather than difference being dissolved and dissipated into a totalitarian *Same* it is the Christian claim that in *communion* the particularity and uniqueness of each self is honored and celebrated.

38. Gunton, *Promise of Trinitarian Theology*, 11.
39. Volf and Gundry-Volf, *Spacious Heart*, 43.

As well as this corporeal imagery of the Body of Christ, with Christ as the crowning glory, the head (Eph 1:22–23, 4:15–16, Col 1:18), Paul also employs architectural and "home-making" metaphors to describe the new community that, post-resurrection, has emerged in the world. The *ecclesia*, the called-out community, Paul asserts, is God's building (1 Cor 3:9) being built upon a sure foundation with Christ as its cornerstone (1 Cor 3:11; Eph 2:20). It is, the members of this new community, "joined together" *in* Christ, who are being grown into a "holy temple," "built together in the Spirit into a *dwelling* place for God" (Eph 2:21–22; 1 Cor 3:16). This new community of hospitality, founded upon and participating in the radical hospitality of the Triune God offered in and through Christ is, Paul contends, "a new humanity." The violence and hostility that formerly existed between those of different ethnic identities—Jews and Gentiles—Paul states, has been put to death in Christ whose death and resurrection has restored the original primordial peace (1 Cor 3:9, 11, 16; Eph 2:11–22).[40]

In the same way, Peter employs architectural images of the temple in Jerusalem, calling for his listeners to come to Christ "the living stone" and to allow themselves to "be built into a spiritual house, to be a holy priesthood, to offer spiritual sacrifices acceptable to God through Jesus Christ" (1 Pet 2:4–10). Again, the imagery employed here speaks not of a totalitarian *sameness*. The imagery here is not of the architecture which characterized modernity—static and sterile monoliths of monotonous uniformity and sameness—but rather of a building constructed from naturally-hewn stone. While each stone has its own unique features—shapes, shades, hues—it is the combining of these *different* stones which, rather than detracting from each stone's distinctive qualities, has the opposite effect: enhancing and enriching the visual appeal of each particular stone, and creating a structure that both functionally provides shelter and is also pleasing to the eye.[41]

Such architectural language, in which the new baptized self is understood as one being renovated and expanded, offers therefore a further striking image of the Spirit. In Christ's absence it is the Spirit's presence, the Spirit operating as a *master builder*, who is refurbishing the self, "making room" within it, preparing it for inhabitation by the Other. Such a

---

40. On the peace-making and home-making connotations contained in Ephesians 2:12–22 see Bouma-Prediger and Walsh, *Beyond Homelessness*, 206–7, 279–80.

41. Hence the significance of John's vision of the New Jerusalem in Revelation 21:9–21, in which the walls of the new dwelling of God presents an imagery of almost unspeakable beauty.

metaphor is both appropriate and particularly poignant in contemporary Western culture, where the fascination with the redesigning and renovation of houses is evidenced in the abundance of home-improvement and do-it-yourself television "reality" shows. In these reality shows renovations are hurriedly undertaken in a race against the clock, culminating at the end of the set time-frame—either sixty minutes or a weekend—with back-slapping, high-fives and made-for-television smiles. In contrast, the Spirit's transforming work is more akin to the arduous and long-term journey of joy and sorrow, delight and despair that those involved in genuine construction projects experience. This analogy of understanding the work of the Spirit within the self as a long-term and difficult building process affirms the processes of *deconstruction, renovation* and *restoration*, and also the creation of all "new" spaces.

The Spirit's transformation of the self, while restoring aspects of our personality damaged by sin, is not a return to the past but rather creates a new hospitable identity. The space created within the self for the Other is inextricably linked to the ultimate purpose of preparing the self for its ultimate home-coming, for its union with the Triune God, when as the dwelling-place for God, the Bride will walk in the radiating light of the Lamb (Rev 21:23–24) and God will be "all in all" (1 Cor 15:28).

As we have noted, central to the new life of this new ecclesial self, as it is incorporated into a new community and formed into a new dwelling, is the development of and adherence to a new pattern of behavior. Of critical importance however, is the understanding that this new behavior stems not from duty or obligation, but rather flows from the inward transformation being experienced within the self. So it is that Paul, in his damning critique of the banqueting etiquette of the church at Corinth (1 Cor 11:17–34), sees the increasing disharmony and lack of respect being shown between members—the return to the hierarchical, paternalistic and oppressive relational patterns of 1st Century Greco-Roman society— as simply symptomatic of the underlying problem: a loss of emphasis upon and experience of the most critical gift—love (1 Cor 13–14). Paul's letters to the new emerging communities of believers are full of commendations, where he urges his listeners to remain true to the ontological transformation that has taken place within them and to follow a new set of *household* codes characterized by love and mutual submission. He recognizes however, that the capacity for these communities to live as a new humanity of welcome is utterly dependent on the extent to which they remain connected to the life-giving love of Christ which courses through the veins of the living organism.[42] This awareness, that ethical behavior is not primarily something "we do," but rather stems from something being "done to us"; of hospitality not as a mode of *doing*, but rather a mode of *being*; that love for others is only possible as one participates in the dynamic of love which those *in* Christ find themselves caught up in, are recurring themes within Johannine thought.

The Loving and Desiring Self

In Johannine thought, the touchstone of one's love for Jesus and therefore for the Father is obedience to their commandment. This commandment, Jesus states, is: "that you love one another as I have loved you" (John 15:12; 1 John 3:23–24).

Read *deontologically*, the Fourth Gospel and 1 John could be construed as arguing that one's *duty* and appropriate response to God's love is to keep his commandments, or, following the logic of Levinas, that love for the other *is* love for God. Such a reading is, however, rendered nonsensical by the metaphor of the vine that Jesus employs while speaking to his disciples in John 15. Obedience to Jesus' commandments—love for God and for others—is not perceived as an ethical duty, nor even as an ethical *return* to God's initiative, but rather is described as an unavoidable ontological reality. Thus Jesus states:

> Abide in me as I abide in you. Just as the branch cannot bear fruit by itself unless it abides in the vine, neither can you unless you abide in me. I am the vine, you are the branches. Those who abide in me and I in them bear much fruit, because apart from me you can do nothing. (John 15:4–5)

The inexorable connection between the self abiding in the love of Christ and therefore being transformed into a lover of others, likewise, is the repeated refrain in the Johannine epistles. As in Matthew's gospel (Matt 22:37–39), John sees the two commandments of the Torah: the love of God (Deut 6:5) and the love of one's neighbor (Lev 19:18) as inextricably connected.[43] John is adamant that far from offering a new commandment, the only change is that through Christ dwelling within and transforming the self, obedience to these commands has now become possible (1 John 2:7–8). The evidence "that they have come to know him" (1 John 2:4), the

42. Note Paul's employment of the body metaphor in Eph 4:15–16.

43. On the relationship between the two commandments, the "double aspect of the moral life," see O'Donovan, *Resurrection and Moral Order*, 226–44.

proof, that the self abiding in Christ has "passed from death to life" (1 John 3:14), that they have "eternal life abiding in them," (1 John 3:15) that they have been "born of God and know God" (1 John 4:7) is, John unequivocally states, their obedience to his commandment—that they love one another (1 John 3:14, 23).

With allusions back to the grapevine imagery used in the Fourth Gospel (John 15), John declares that those "born of God," in whom the seed of God abides, cannot bear tainted fruit (1 John 3:9). The clearest expression of such tainted fruit, a sign that rather than being exposed to the light that brings life, one "is still in the darkness," is hatred for the other (1John 2:9–11; 3:18–21). Such hatred, John suggests, stems from fear of the other produced when we live according to the *desires* of this world. In his instructions to believers, John writes:

> Do not love the world or the things in the world. The love of the Father is not in those who love the world; for all that is in the world—the desire of the flesh, the desire of the eyes, the pride in riches—comes not from the Father but from the world. And the world and its desire are passing away, but those who do the will of God live forever. (1 John 2:15–17)

The influence of René Girard—at least with regard to how his earlier writings have been interpreted—has led to common misconception that the mimetic drive and therefore both *desire* and *imitation* are inherently negative.[44] But it is not *desire* per se that is wrong. Numerous philosophers, including Levinas, note that *desire* is one of the core constituting elements that makes us human. For Augustine, as well as other early church Fathers, *desire* was understood positively. *Desire*, aroused by, and inflamed by the Father's love for us, functions in drawing us back towards the loving God who alone can answer our deepest longings and meet our need for communion.[45] In the famous words of St. Augustine's *Confessions*: "You arouse

44. In *Things Hidden* Girard hints at a non-violent *imitation* and a positive conception of *desire*, yet this is never developed explicitly in his writings. As with our other French interlocutors, it is in an interview that light is shed on Girard's seeming ambiguity. Girard acknowledges that *desire* is constitutive of what it means to be human and thus impossible to give up and explains that he is advocating the giving up of *appropriative desire*. See Adams, "Violence, Difference, Sacrifice," 11–33. It has been up to Girardian scholars, particularly those developing his work along explicitly theological lines, to expound a more positive notion of *mimetic desire* and *imitation*. See, e.g., Swartley, "Discipleship and Imitation," 218–45.

45. For a stunning exposition, shaped by a close reading of Gregory of Nyssa, of how God awakens within us an "infinite inflaming of desire" thus drawing us into a pilgrimage "always discovering and entering into greater dimensions of this beauty," see Hart, *Beauty of the Infinite*, 187–210.

us so that praising you may bring us joy, because you have made us and drawn us to yourself, and our heart is restless until it rests in you."[46]

Elsewhere, Augustine explicitly connects the love gifted to us through the indwelling Spirit and therefore the arousal of our desire for the Divine Gift-giver, stating: "the gift of the Holy Spirit, by whom charity is poured forth in our hearts, that we may be drawn to God by a desire and yearning for Him, and reaching Him may find rest, and want nothing besides."[47]

In contrast to this positive form of *desire*, 1 John speaks of three negative features that characterize the *desire* that stems not from the Father but from the world (*kosmos*): (1) "*the desire of the flesh*," that is, the desire to gain personhood without entering into *communion* with otherness; (2) in an allusion to Gen 3:6, "*the desire of the eyes*," the seeking to seize and lay hold of God's freely offered gifts; and, (3) "*the pride in riches*," the hoarding of these resources for oneself rather than sharing with others. For John, these are all aspects of the world's love, in which the Other is understood as a threat to the self and therefore one to be feared. Conversely, "there is no fear in love, but perfect love casts out fear" (1 John 4:18). Ultimately, it is John's assertion that these *desires* of the world (*kosmos*) are merely transitory, having been overcome once and for all through Christ's death and resurrection. History is a catalogue of this negative, acquisitive and appropriative *desire*, in which fear of the other eventually develops into an open hatred and aversion, and separation from the other is often accompanied by later explicit attempts to control the one different from oneself.[48] In contrast, the non-acquisitive and non-appropriative *desire*—the way of Christ—is fanned into flame by the breath of the in-dwelling Spirit of Christ. Participating *in* Christ, the self is inexorably drawn into a mimetic imitation of the way of Christ. Participation leads to imitation and, as James Alison contends, through such imitation of Christ, Christians, "learn to receive their identities as human beings through an entirely nonrivalrous, nonenvious, nongrasping practice of life."[49]

For those "born of God," who abide in the secure dwelling of Christ and who thus experience—in ever-deepening measures—the intoxicating reality of the height, depth and breadth of the love of God, there is an accompanying rechanneling of the desire within the self. The rearousal of

46. Augustine, *Confessions*, I.i, 39.

47. Augustine, *Literal Meaning of Genesis*, 114.

48. The Holocaust, and the system of apartheid which held sway in South Africa during the 20th century, are simply the most obvious examples of many that could be given.

49. Alison, *Joy of Being Wrong*, 168.

the dormant *desire* for genuine life-giving love, once released, launches the self onto a life-time journey of faith, one in which the gift of love received is passed onto others. Such *loved* and therefore *loving* selves see the Other not as a dangerous threat—an adversary potentially able to take possession of the items acquired and appropriated for oneself and therefore to be feared—but rather, as one coming to bless, or, as one requiring blessing. In a Christian conception of desire the Divine Other is understood as the origin/cause of *desire*, the Other who moves towards us (in the event of the Incarnation), and as the *telos*, the end-point of that *desire*. Within such a schema the self is thus conceived of as a *sojourning* self. Aroused by its desire for the Other, the self, in receiving its life as a gift, journeys alongside others as they together seek the final revealing of their full identities.

Again, such an understanding of the self differs from that of our post-structuralist philosophers. For both Levinas and Derrida there is no *telos* or eventual rest to desire. As Levinas states: "the Other is not a term: he does not stop the movement of Desire. The other that Desire desires is again Desire."[50] Not only does such an account of desire appear utterly exhausting[51]—but a self which desires without rest or *telos*, reminiscent of Taylor's "careless wanderer,"[52] is, as we have already suggested, the anthropological foundation for the over-consumptive tendencies of "late" capitalism.

This connection between the contemporary practice of over-consumption and post-modern philosophical accounts of identity with their loss of *telos* and their emphasis on *distance* and *separation*, is also observed by William T. Cavanaugh. In *Being Consumed: Economics and Christian Desire*, Cavanaugh persuasively argues that, contrary to popular sentiment, greed is not *attachment*, but rather *detachment*.[53] It is the fact that we perceive ourselves as *detached*—that is *separate* and *distant*—from what is Other (whether human or non-human) that provides the basis for the acquiring of consumer items and/or relationships, their subsequent

50. Levinas, *Totality and Infinity*, 269. Elsewhere Levinas writes: "The negativity of the *In-* of the Infinite—otherwise than being, divine comedy—hollows out a desire that could not be filled, one nourished from its own increase, exalted as Desire—one that withdraws from its satisfaction as it draws near to the Desireable. This is a Desire for what is beyond satisfaction, and which does not identify, as need does, a term or an end. A desire without end, from beyond Being: dis-inter*estedness*, transcendence—desire for the Good." Levinas, *Of God Who Comes to Mind*, 67.

51. As Zizioulas, referring to Levinas' desire without end, suggests, an "interminable motion is inconceivable." Zizioulas, *Communion and Otherness*, 51.

52. Taylor, *Erring*, 157.

53. Cavanaugh, *Being Consumed*.

use, and then their disposal—freeing us up for acquisition of the next commodity. Cavanaugh writes:

> In consumer culture, dissatisfaction and satisfaction cease to be opposites, for pleasure is not so much in the possession of things as in their pursuit. There is a pleasure in the pursuit of novelty, and the pleasure resides not so much in having as in wanting. Once we have obtained an item, it brings desire to a temporary halt, and the item loses some of its appeal. Possession kills desire; familiarity breeds contempt. That is why shopping, not buying itself, is the heart of consumerism. The consumerist spirit is a restless spirit, typified by detachment, because desire must be constantly kept on the move.[54]

Cavanaugh's insight into the way in which consumerism is grounded not in attachment but detachment also helps explain the compelling and yet tragic nature of many of those who, seeking to escape from the contemporary culture of consumerism, embrace a form of asceticism, detaching themselves from both material possessions and relationships. Such a way of life, in which detachment from people, place and possessions is often synthesized with a romanticism of nature, rather than responding to the underlying problem, simply perpetuates the restlessness and drivenness of the modern individual. The disastrous consequence of such asceticism is evident in John Krakauer's moving account of the life and death of Chris McCandless: *Into the Wild*. McCandless, an intense and idealistic recent college graduate, seeking to discover his true self and live an authentic existence, gives up his existing identity—money, possessions and name— and spends two years hitch-hiking around the States, before eventually, tragically, starving to death, alone, in the Alaskan wilderness. It is both poignant and sobering that McCandless, reading Boris Pasternak's *Doctor Zhivago* as he approaches death, underlines the following passage, which echoes many of the themes we have reflected upon.

> Now what is history? It is the centuries of systematic exploration of the riddle of death, with a view to overcoming death. That's why people discover mathematical infinity and electro-magnetic waves, that's why they write symphonies. Now, you can't advance in this direction without a certain faith. You can't make such discoveries without spiritual equipment. And the basic elements of this equipment are in the Gospels. What are they? To begin with, love of one's neighbor, which is the supreme form of

54. Ibid., 47.

vital energy. Once it fills the heart of man it has to overflow and spend itself. And then the two basic ideals of modern man—without them he is unthinkable—the idea of free personality and the idea of life as sacrifice.[55]

A desiring self, restless, always on the move, never at rest, acquiring and appropriating possessions and yet driven by fear away from others, resembles the troubled characters of Cain and Jacob. In stark contrast is the Patriarch Abraham, whose travel is not directionless, but rather is a journey, originating in the gift of faith from the Divine Other; who heads towards a final destination, the promised land of *rest*, and whose arrival in this new land is characterized by the building of relationships of mutuality with the inhabitants.

The Eschatological Self

This Christian understanding of the eschatological nature of the self distinguishes it from the restless self of post-structuralist thought, ever on the move, consuming otherness to fill the vacuum of identity. However, though baptized into Christ and incorporated into a new community, nevertheless the self continues to live in the in-between, in the *now-but-not-yet*. The face of the Divine Other has been revealed to us, and in seeing Christ we have seen the Father and have become aware of the final resting place, and the road we must journey along to reach this final destination (John 12:45–46; 14:1–7). And yet, even while seeing the face of Christ, such vision does not encompass or capture the face. As we noted earlier, the face of Christ the Other is not something we can reduce to an idol. Rather, the face of the resurrected Christ is an *eikon*, a brief glimpse of totality, and yet infinite and beyond total comprehension. An encounter with the resurrected Christ serves, therefore, not as an end-point. In contrast to our Jacob/Israel-like tendency to grasp at and contain the divine, an encounter with the risen Christ actually summons us to an ongoing journey of discovery, a voyage in which Christ's presence, by his Spirit, is assured, and yet, is often unrecognized.[56]

55. Krakauer, *Into the Wild*, 187.

56. A classic example of this tendency to seek to "hold" onto and domesticate ecstatic moments of divine visitation is found in gospel accounts of the Transfiguration. While dazzled by the face of Christ, Peter's immediate reaction is to seek to erect shelters for Jesus, Moses and Elijah. This desire to "stand-still" and capture the moment for perpetuity, far from being unique to Peter, is one that all on the journey of discipleship encounter. Like Peter, we need reminding that the road to resurrection glory—which

While our identity has begun to be disclosed, it also remains "hidden" (Col 3:3), awaiting its final unveiling. It is with Christ's return that our full identity will be revealed, when the opacity that blurs our eyes will finally be lifted and we shall see Christ "face to face." It is in the final *eschaton* that "knowledge" as an attempt to totalize, categorize and grasp the Other, will finally and completely be overcome by the "knowledge" of love (1 Cor 13:12; 1 John 3:2). Finally, liberated completely from fear and hostility, we will enter into the intimate and loving embrace of the Divine Other, the Triune God. Our entrance into the fullness of God's hospitality and thus the revealing of our full identity will be symbolized in the receiving of a "new name" (Rev 2:17). The Triune God who walked in the garden with Adam and Eve in the beginning will come and set up his "home," dwelling in his restored creation, establishing a garden city. The trees within the city will bear abundant fruit which rather than being hoarded for oneself, or offered deceptively to the Other, will be given and received freely and joyfully as gifts. This city, of great beauty and diversity, its inhabitants drawn from every nation, tribe, people and language, while surrounded by walls, has gates which are always open and is a city which welcomes other sojourners drawn to the healing waters and dazzling light that emanate from within (Rev 7:9; 21:1—22:5).

Such a vision, of eternal light, of the peace and tranquility of a garden, not of a *restlessness without end*, but rather, an *endless rest*, leads Augustine in *The City of God* to write: "the seventh day . . . our Sabbath, whose end will not be an evening . . . the eternal rest not only of the Spirit, but of the body also. There we shall rest and we shall see, see and love, love and praise. Behold what it will be, in the end to which there shall be no end!"[57]

In such an account, the term *eschaton* does not mean, as Levinas fears, "a finality, an end (*fin*)," in which the seizure or appropriation "of God as a *telos* . . . degrade[s] the infinite relation with the other to a finite fusion."[58] Rather, the Christian *eschaton* speaks of the hope for an *endless rest* in which the self maintains its particular and unique identity—gender, language, ethnicity, personality—and yet lives in communion *with* others, one in which the closer the self is drawn to the infinite beauty, the source of all light and love, the Wholly *Other*, the more the self is aware that it has only just begun its pilgrimage of discovery.

---

the Transfiguration prefigures—involves taking the path of suffering—the way of the Cross.

57. Augustine, "City of God against the Pagans," 1182.

58. Levinas, "Ethics of the Infinite," 66.

Summary

In this chapter we have outlined the development of the "hospitable self," noting both similarities but also clear divergences from the concept of identity offered by Levinas and Derrida. Our central argument has been that hospitality is not firstly something *we do*, but rather something that *we are*. That is, the love of God—the Wholly Other—and the love of Others is not something which finds its origin in the self, but neither is it pre-ontological, beyond being, and therefore unable to be explained. Rather, as the Fourth Gospel declares, any love we have for the Other is simply fruit that is produced as the love of the hospitable God fills and expands the self. As John states: "We love because he first loved us" (1 John 4:19).

In contrast to an emphasis on *difference* which therefore conceives of a relationship with the Other based on *distance* and *separation*—one in which there is always an element of hostility—our account of the self builds upon an explicit ontology of *communion*. The self, we have contended, is not a deconstructed individual, meaningless and purposeless, ever on the move. Rather, the self is better conceived of as a catholic self, in which true identity is unveiled as we are indwelt by the Divine Other and incorporated into the new existence of the *ecclesia*. While the breath of God gives biological life (Gen 2:7), it is as one abides *in Christ* that the life-giving Spirit (1 Cor 15:45) breaths fresh air into our dusty and musty interiors. As these dark and dank attics and basements of the self, full of hidden hurts and festering fears—with the potential over time to develop into open hostility and hatred—are exposed to the light and swept clean, so room is made within the self for others.

The relationship between christology, pneumatology and self-identity that we have traced here, and the ontological transformation that takes place within the *self* as it *dwells* in Christ and is *in-dwelt* by the comforting, yet disturbing Spirit, is clearly articulated in the work of second century theologian Irenaeus of Lyons. For Irenaeus, it is the incarnation and Christ's identification and *union* with humanity which has made possible the capacity for humanity to enter into *union* through Christ with God. As Irenaeus states: "How shall man pass into God, unless God has [first] passed into man?"[59] This new humanity, established in Christ, is then passed onto humanity as the Spirit of Christ comes and dwells in the lives of humanity. Irenaeus writes:

---

59. AH 4.33.4.

These things, therefore, He recapitulated in Himself: by uniting man to the Spirit, and causing the Spirit to dwell in man. He is himself made the head of the Spirit, and gives the Spirit to be the head of man: for through Him (the Spirit) we see, and hear, and speak.[60]

Irenaeus posits that it is the inhabitation of the Spirit within the believer making possible the self's identification and union with Christ, which leads to a new-found ability to *see*, *hear* and *speak*. Through the Spirit, the eyes of controlling *desire* which seek to possess the Other are salved and opened to recognize the Other not as threat but gift; ears, deaf to the call of the Other, are unblocked; the mouth, prone to violent outburst, now issues forth praise. This new life of welcome stemming from those transformed by the Spirit and incorporated into the ecclesia will be the focus in our final chapter.

60. *AH* 5.20.2.

≋ *A tête à tête.*

A Drink with the Other

Gift-Exchange and Transformed Identity

(John 4:1–42)

SO WHAT IS THE NATURE OF THE RELATIONSHIP WITH THE OTHER SHAPED
not by hostility? We have already noted Derrida's skepticism regarding
whether "pure" hospitality/genuine gift-giving can function in the economy of human relations. For Derrida:

> Now the gift, *if there is any*, would no doubt be related to econ-
> omy. One cannot treat the gift, this goes without saying, without
> treating this relation to economy, even to the money economy.
> But is not the gift, if there is any, also that which interrupts
> economy? That which, in suspending economic calculation, no
> longer gives rise to exchange? That which opens the circle so
> as to defy reciprocity or symmetry, the common measure, and
> so as to turn aside the return in view of the no-return? If there
> is gift, the *given* of the gift must not come back to the giving. It
> must not circulate, it must not be exchanged . . . [1]

But must gift-giving operate outside of an economy of reciprocity?
In contrast to Derrida's "pure" unilateral gift, an episode recounted in the
Fourth Gospel suggests that it is by the very exchanging of gifts with the
Other that hostility is overcome. That is, it is in the action of giving to *and*

1. Derrida, *Given Time*, 7.

receiving from the Other, in participating in moments of *hospitality*, that our own inner hostility towards *otherness* is surmounted.

Jesus, returning from Judea, chooses to make his way via the shorter but less-travelled route through Samaria. Travel-weary, thirsty, seeking shelter from the heat of the day, Jesus stops at the well of Sychar, and in so doing encounters a Samaritan woman. An *Other*, *scapegoated* and *distanced* from her own community, the woman is forced to come to the well in isolation. As with his calling of the first disciples, it is Jesus who takes the initiative, making a request to the woman to: "Give me a drink" (v. 7). The woman's response to Jesus' initial and subsequent requests highlights the degree of antagonism and hostility, developed over the centuries, existing between the Jews and Samaritans. Her retort to this Other who dares to contravene the established norms for relational interactions: "Who do you think you are! You, a male Jew, speaking not only with a Samaritan, but with a female Samaritan at that!" (v. 9).

Commentators often point to the use of irony in this passage and to the role that misunderstanding plays as a literary technique, suggesting that while Jesus is speaking of the "living water" as a spiritual reality (see John 7:38–39), the woman is concerned only with the physical realm. But does such a clear demarcation really exist? In the verbal sparring that takes place it is clear that both Jesus and the woman see the conversation as fundamentally concerned with questions of economy, identity and one's relation with the Other.

In response to the woman's initial antipathy, Jesus begins to speak of a new economy of gift-exchange—"the gift of God"—in which the woman could participate. To Jesus' suggestion that it is he who can provide "living water," the woman not only bluntly points out the practical impediment to Jesus providing such a "gift"—"You have no bucket and the well is deep" (v. 11)—but also through her rhetorical question—"Are you really greater than *our* [Samaritan] ancestor Jacob?" (v. 12)—seeks to establish and consolidate her claim to the well. Despite being an "outsider" to her own community—a fact that due to her presence, alone, in the middle of the day, Jesus undoubtedly would have deduced—the woman seeks to make clear that it is she, not he, who is at "home" and thus as "host," the one to be offering gifts.

Alternatively, the woman's response can be understood according to a broader, more inclusive reading of *our*. Thus the woman's rejoinder, "Are you really greater than *our* [joint] ancestor Jacob?" can be paraphrased: "What is the ridiculous economy of the gift which you speak of? Do you really believe in the reality of an economy which steps outside the history

of *hostility* and the economy of *struggle* which epitomizes *our* joint ancestor, Jacob?" (v. 12). While growing slightly more comfortable in the
presence of this male Jew, potentially becoming open to the possibility of
sharing the well, the woman wants to remind Jesus that ethical behavior
and actions are not singular abstracted moments, but are always shaped by
cultural history and memories. Challenging Jesus' naive idealism in which
a Samaritan woman and a Jewish male could share a drink, the woman
makes it clear that Jesus' gift-giving economy, while a nice concept, is an
impossibility, one unable to emerge given the history of mutual ethnic
hatred.

Despite the woman's rudeness, defensiveness, and outright antagonism, Jesus perseveres. He highlights that in contrast to this historical
economy of *struggle*, the new economy of gift of which he speaks is characterized not by *competition* but by *mutuality*, nor by limit and scarcity
but rather by an abundant excess. Those who choose to accept the "gift
of God" and enter into this new existence "will never be thirsty again.
The water that I give will become in them a spring of water gushing up to
eternal life" (v. 14).

Jesus' persistence pays off. The animosity of the woman to this unexpected "guest" who breaks the prevailing conventions of social interaction slowly gives way to curiosity; her interest aroused by the mention of
"living water" which, in endlessly quenching her thirst, would therefore
free her of the lonely trek each day to the well (v. 15). Her admission, that
she *desires* such water for *herself*, to reduce her own sense of *isolation* and
otherness, momentarily ends the verbal joust and the conversation moves
to a deeper, more intimate level. Jesus' next request of her: "Go, call your
husband, and come back" (v. 16), cuts to the heart of the matter, touch-
ing on the raw nerve from which stems some of her retaliatory rancor.
Entrapped, like her ancestor Jacob, in her own history of destructive and
broken relationships, the woman seeks healing water to sooth her inner
wounds. Shunned, alone, and vulnerable, the woman's sense of identity
and self-worth have been shaped by the centuries-old, well-established,
and dominating ideologies: *women are second-class citizens, Jews are the
enemies, unmarried women with a track record of divorce are impure*. The
woman's aggressiveness towards Jesus is simply an outworking of these
prevailing prejudices towards the Other which she has incorporated,
her virulence, a manifestation—an "imitative response" as it were—of
the ostracism she has experienced at the hands of her own inhospitable
community.

As quickly as the conversation moves to a deeper level of engagement, the woman, aware of the chink in her armor now exposed, turns the conversation away from the *particular*—the subject of her own brokenness— and back to the *general*—the familiar territory of the *enmity* that exists between Jew and Samaritan: "*Our* ancestors worshiped on this mountain, but *you* say that the place where people must worship is Jerusalem"(v. 20). While the woman turns the discussion back to the questions of ethnic hostility, reminding Jesus of the *differences* that *divide* them, again Jesus' response is to point her to his new alternative economy. It is not geographical location nor ethnic background but rather one's knowledge and acceptance of "the gift of God" and thus one's entrance into the new alternative economy of the kingdom, that will determine one's identity (v. 21). In this new existence which is the authentic form of *personhood*, *otherness* does not *divide* but rather is constitutive of *communion*. Those who through the Spirit have had their own inner brokenness revealed and are led into "truth" will, with this *hostility* conquered, join with others in worship of the Wholly Other and participate in a new economy of mutual gift-exchange.

It is at this stage of proceedings that the disciples who had "gone to the city to *buy* food" (v. 8), now return. While "astonished" to see Jesus contravening established norms by speaking not only with a Samaritan, but with a *woman* to boot, the disciples remain silent.[2] The fact that the disciples "do not criticize Jesus' behaviour," Rudolf Schnackenburg attributes to "the reverent attitude of the disciples towards Jesus."[3] But does this give too much credit to the disciples? While silence can often be a sign of reverence and respect, it can also testify to an extreme awkwardness and discomfort. To ask their rabbi who the woman is would require an acknowledgment of her *presence*, but the disciples are trapped themselves within the same economy of hostility, in which the *differences* between women and men, Samaritans and Jews, are ones that *divide*. Their optics shaped by the prevailing ideologies, in the eyes of the disciples, the woman is a nobody, a faceless, barely visible, Other.

---

2. Rudolf Schnackenburg suggests the astonishment of the disciples stems not from Jesus' "disregarding the barriers of race" but rather, "They are thinking of the reserve imposed on all Jews, and a rabbi in particular, with regard to the female sex." Schnackenburg, *Gospel according to St. John*, 443. The typical attitude towards women in first-century rabbinic thought is expressed by Aboth Rabbe Nathan: "One does not speak with a woman on the street, not even his own wife, and certainly not with another woman, on account of gossip." Quoted in Haenchen, *John*, 224.

3. Schnackenburg, *John*, 443.

Likewise, Schnackenburg sees the evangelist's comment in verse 8 ("His disciples had gone to the city to *buy* food") as "an afterthought" and commenting on the hasty departure of the woman states: "that there is no need to see anything in the abandonment of the water-jar except that she wants to reach home quickly and unimpeded, to return with the people" (see v28).[4] However, it seems much more likely that these detailed editorial asides are in fact crucial to understanding the central emphasis of the narrative. For, it is the contrasting behavior of the Samaritan woman and the disciples which provides the backdrop for understanding the second section of the story.

Declining the food that his now returned disciples have *purchased*[5] in the village, Jesus continues to expound on the topic begun with the now absent woman: that of human relations and economics. The disciples, while willing to *purchase* food from Samaritan "retailers," still regard the Samaritan woman as an inferior and impure Other. Their attitude towards Samaritans in general is one of barely veiled disdain, one in which relations exist only under circumstances of dire necessity—their need for food—and even then to be pursued along purely formal and contractual lines. In contrast, the behavior of the Samaritan woman in leaving behind her water jar is testimony to her breach with such an economy of *hostility* and her acceptance of, and entrance into, Jesus' new gift-giving economy. Disregarding the cultic laws which prevent the sharing of drinking and eating vessels, the woman leaves her jar, so that Jesus may indeed use it to draw water *freely* from the well.

Jesus—employing the "unclean" vessel to draw water from the well—thus enacts before the eyes of his disciples the alternative economy which he has been expounding. Making use of the transforming and destabilizing power of sight, Jesus now redirects the inward gaze of the disciples outwards, stating: "*Look around you*, and see how the fields are ready for harvesting" (v. 35). While for the disciples Samaria is a barren wasteland to be moved through as quickly as possible, to Jesus, they are golden fields, full of abundant life. Their current context is an ideal location to declare and enact the new economy of the kingdom—an economy characterized not by competition but rather by an appreciation of one's differences, one where sower and reaper "rejoice together," sharing in the delight of mutual gift-exchange (v. 36). In declaring to the disciples that "I sent you to reap

4. Ibid., 424, 443.

5. As with verse 8, the evangelist's utilization of an editorial aside in verse 9 to remind the reader of this point, has the paradoxical effect of highlighting the importance of this detail to the overall narrative.

what you have not worked for. Others have done the hard work, and you have reaped the benefits of their labor" (v. 38),[6] Jesus indicates that others have already gone before them into this harvest field—the Samaritan woman!—and invites them to join her in this missionary task. Using the apostolic language of sending (*apesteila*), Jesus portrays the Samaritan woman not as a faceless Other to be ignored, but rather as a model of apostolic activity.[7]

And, such is the witnessing power of this Samaritan missionary, her desire that others may discover this "Gift," that the formerly discordant community, believing in her testimony, return to the well in the heat of the day, for their own thirst-quenching drink with the "Messiah." The ensuing transformation of the village inhabitants, their entrance into the new economy of the "gift" and thus the overcoming of inter-community tension and intra-ethnic hostility is evidenced in their immediate actions. The transactional relationality borne out of mistrust and prejudice, in which the Other is ignored while commodities are *purchased* for individual consumption, now gives way to an opening of their homes to Jesus and his disciples. The former Others are now welcomed into the village and the Samaritans provide hospitality to the "gift of God," supping intimately with He who "is truly the Savior of the world" (v. 42), the one who, in overcoming division, inaugurates in Himself a new economy.

6. *New International Version*

7. See Thiessen, "Jesus and Women in the Gospel of John," 52–64.

7

Performing a Different Script

Participation in the Practice of Ecclesial Hospitality

As long as there are fears and prejudices in the human heart, there will be war and bitter injustice. It is only when hearts are healed that the great political problems will be solved. Community is a place where people can be human beings, where they can be healed and strengthened in their deepest emotions, and where they can walk towards unity and interior freedom. As fears and prejudices diminish and trust in God and others grows, the community can radiate a witness to a style and quality of life which will bring a solution to the troubles of our world. The response to war is to live like brothers and sisters. The response to injustice is to share. The response to despair is a limitless trust and hope. The response to prejudice and hatred is forgiveness. To work for community is to work for humanity. To work for peace is to work for a true political solution; it is to work for the kingdom of God. It is to work to enable everyone to live and taste the secret joys of the human person united to the eternal.

—Jean Vanier[1]

IN CONTRAST TO OUR POST-STRUCTURALIST PHILOSOPHERS WHO HAVE a strong aversion to the idea of *community*, we have contended that it is only in *communion* with Christ, and thus in community *with* others that the self finds its true identity. While it is God's desire that all of creation should be brought into the *joy* of the Divine embrace, humanity, in its "sinful" desire for *communion* without *otherness*, construes the Other

---

1. Vanier, *Community and Growth*, 45.

not as one to delight in, but rather as one to be feared, struggled against, vanquished. This hostility towards both the human Other and the Wholly Other however has been overcome through Christ. Jesus, as the representative of humanity, in living a life of obedience, of genuine sacrifice/ gift-giving, prevails over the ontological obstacle to *communion*, death. Refusing to abide by the death-dealing logic of an economy based on debt and violence, but rather offering his life *freely* back to God, Christ, the second Adam, reestablishes the original peaceful pattern of relationality, reconstituting an economy of grace and freedom.

In the last chapter we traced the outline of the "hospitable self." We noted how those who respond to the call of Christ and are *united* with him in his death and resurrection, receive "eternal life," and enter into this new form of authentic personhood. Being found *in Christ* involves, through the work of the in-dwelling Spirit, a transformation of one's affections and *desires* and the incorporation into a new form of life, the sociality of the *ecclesia*. This community of covenant people constituted not by their own efforts but by God's gift, and drawn to participate in the hospitality of the Triune God, are empowered to live lives which welcome rather than distance *Others*.

Our belief, that Christian faith is not reducible to a universal ethic and that the biblical story is not a primarily concerned with offering injunctions and suggestions to assist individuals to become more "ethical," should, by now, be obvious. Rather, Christian faith is an alternative account of the world, its being, and its ultimate purpose. In particular, it is an account of God's formation of a covenant people, who, to the extent that they continue to *dwell in Christ* and therefore participate in the hospitality of the Triune God, give witness to God's gracious and loving actions of creating, sustaining and redeeming the world. As Richard Hays puts it:

> . . . the primary sphere of moral concern is not the character of the individual, but the corporate obedience of the church. Paul's formulation in Romans 12:1–2 encapsulates the vision: "Present your bodies (*somata*, plural) as a living sacrifice (*thysian*, singular), holy and pleasing to God. And do not be conformed to this age, but be transformed by the renewing of your mind . . ." The community, in its corporate life, is called to embody an alternative order that stands as a sign of God's redemptive purposes in the world.[2]

2. Hays, "Ecclesiology and Ethics in 1 Corinthians," 33.

But, what does this "alternative order," witnessing as "a sign to God's redemptive purposes," look like? What shape does the relationship between the self and the Other take when based not on fear or toleration, but on love? What are the significant features one should see as evidence of the ecclesial community's new "hospitable way of living," as it exists in and through the life-giving breath of the Spirit of Christ? And, what are the practices, rituals and rites which sustain this alternative way of living within a world in which hostility and enmity continue to exist?

This chapter will respond to these questions. In drawing together themes already touched on we will endeavor to bring into clearer focus how the relationality of the ecclesial person differs from the modes of relationality envisaged by either the contemporary discourse of the market or that offered by our post-structuralist interlocutors. In contrast to either the formalized contractual relationship of the market-place or the unilateral relationship of the "pure-gift," most often manifested in forms of "charitable giving," we will suggest that the Christian narrative posits a relationship between the self and the Other of asymmetrical mutual gift-exchange, one founded upon love, joy and freedom.

The Ecclesia: Relations of Purified Exchange and the Telos of Mutuality

"Gift of Death" or Resurrection Joy?

In August 1944, imprisoned in Tegel prison and facing death, Dietrich Bonhoeffer, jotted notes for the outline of a book in which he proposed to set out "the real meaning of Christian faith."[3] He wrote: "The church is the church only when it exists *for* others."[4] Confronted by the church in Germany which had lost sight of its responsibility to the other, in particular to the Jews, Bonhoeffer contended that true faith is an: "Encounter with Jesus Christ." Further notes augment this theme:

> The experience that a transformation of all human life is given in the fact that "Jesus is there only for others." His "being there for others" is the experience of transcendence. It is only this "being there for others," maintained till death, that is the ground of his omnipotence, omniscience, and omnipresence. Faith is participation in this being of Jesus (incarnation, cross,

3. Bonhoeffer, *Letters and Papers*, 382.

4. Ibid. Emphasis added.

and resurrection). Our relation to God is not a "religious" relationship to the highest, most powerful, and best Being imaginable—that is not authentic transcendence—but our relation to God is a new life in "existence for others," through participation in the being of Jesus. The transcendental is not infinite and unattainable tasks, but the neighbour who is within reach in any given situation. God in human form . . . "the man for others," and therefore the Crucified, the man who lives out of the transcendent.[5]

Bonhoeffer's writing here has an almost Levinasian tone to it, with its emphasis "our relation to God is a new life in 'existence for others.'" However, critical to understanding Bonhoeffer's thought is the phrase: "*through participation in the being of Jesus.*" In a divergence from Levinas' and Derrida's *infinite responsibility*,[6] Bonhoeffer states that "no one is responsible for all the injustice and suffering in the world,"[7] and rather, posits that the believer's ethical *imitation* of Christ, that is, one's "existence for others" stems from, and is utterly dependent upon, one's "*participation in the being of Jesus.*" Such "participation in the being of Jesus," as we noted earlier, involves, through the sacrament of baptism, the death of the self-centered individual. Indeed, as Bonhoeffer so powerfully articulates in *The Cost of Discipleship*: "When Christ calls a man, he bids him come and die."[8] Critically however, and in contrast to our post-structuralist interlocutors, this death of the self is not the ultimate *telos*. Christian ethics is not grounded upon the death of the self, but rather stems from the new resurrection life inaugurated in Christ, into which the newly baptized self enters. Bonhoeffer elucidates this important distinction with his comparison of Socrates and Jesus:

> Socrates mastered the art of dying; Christ overcame death as "the last enemy" (1 Cor 15:26). There is a real difference between the two things; the one is within the scope of human possibilities,

---

5. Ibid., 381–82.

6. Levinas is fond of quoting a passage from Dostoyevsky's *Brothers Karamazov*: "Each of us is guilty before everyone for everyone, and I more than the others." Levinas, *Otherwise than Being*, 146; see also Levinas, *Outside the Subject*, 44. Elsewhere Levinas states: "One is never without debt with regard to another." Levinas, *Ethics and Infinity*, 11. Derrida concurs stating: "This guilt is originary, original sin. Before any fault is determined, I am guilty inasmuch as I am responsible. . . . Guilt is inherent in responsibility because responsibility is always unequal to itself: one is never responsible enough." Derrida, *Gift of Death*, 51.

7. Bonhoeffer, *Letters and Papers*, 13.

8. Bonhoeffer, *Cost of Discipleship*, 73.

the other means resurrection. It is not from *ars moriendi*, the art of dying, but from the resurrection of Christ that a new and purifying wind can blow through our present world. . . . If a few people really believed that and acted on it in their daily lives, a great deal would be changed. To live in the light of the Resurrection—that is what Easter means.[9]

Central to the Christian account of hospitality we have expounded, and fundamental to the distinction of such an account from that offered by our post-structuralist interlocutors, is this emphasis upon the resurrection. As Oliver O'Donovan emphatically declares: "Christian ethics depends upon the resurrection of Jesus Christ from the dead."[10] The determinative role in our account of both ontology and teleology are understood in light of this resurrection, that is, they are of an eschatological nature. In contrast to a unilateral relational structure in which the *telos* appears to be the self-sacrificial *death* of the self, the *telos* to which the *ecclesia* looks forward and which shapes its ethical action is not the death of the self, but rather the joy of mutuality. "Being there *for* others" is therefore not an *end* in itself but rather is the *means* to the end, the summoning of the Other to participate in the new economy of gift-exchange, in which gifts of *love* are *freely given and received*.

Indeed without this distinctive *telos*, an ethos of "being there *for* others," while preferable to a relational model of the self *over* the other, continues to perpetuate unhealthy relational patterns. The unilateral nature of "being there *for* the other"—often manifest in "charitable giving" from a distance—has a number of problematic consequences for both the donor and the recipient. In such a mode of relationality there is the risk of developing patronizing and paternalistic attitudes which disempower and dehumanize the recipient. Also, as well as missing out on the richness and nourishment that the Other may offer in response, the *distance* that often accompanies such "charitable giving" can mean that the donor, no longer exposed to the immediacy and challenge of the Other, avoids the call to repentance. Being there *for* the Other can thus lead either to a new form of ethical smugness in which the self receives a psychological reward for its beneficence to the Other or, conversely, to entrapment in the never-ending demands of the Other, thus creating a form of dependency detrimental to both donor and recipient.

---

9. Bonhoeffer, *Letters and Papers*, 240.

10. O'Donovan, *Resurrection and Moral Order*, 13.

Ultimately, therefore, an "ethic of hospitality" that is divorced from an ontological account of how hostility and death have been overcome inevitably becomes distorted and regresses to a human ethic of law and duty emptied of its liberating and life-giving dynamic. In his *Theology and Joy*, Jürgen Moltmann, reflecting on the renewed emphasis on ethics within Christian theology post World War Two, warns of the perils of an ethic divorced from the joy of resurrection life. Christian ethics without an account of joy, Moltmann believes, leads inexorably to a new law of bondage and slavery. In an extract striking for its use of what we have come to see as Levinas' signature phrase—"infinite responsibility"—Moltmann writes:

> Our social and political tasks, if we take them seriously, loom larger than life. Yet *infinite responsibility destroys a human being because he is only man and not god.* I have an idea that laughter is able to mediate between the infinite magnitude of our tasks and the limitations of our strength. Many people, who really get down to work, are saying—and rightly so: "Unless we do a lot of joking, we have to cry and cannot get anything done."[11]

Moltmann summarizes well the key theme we have here sought to explicate, stating:

> . . . being-there-for-others is not the final answer, nor is it an end and not even freedom itself. It is a way, although the only way, which leads to *being-there-with-others*. Christ's death *for us* has its end and future in that he is *with us* and that we shall be living, laughing and ruling *with him*. Being-there-for-others in vicarious love has as its end to be *with others* in liberty. Giving bread to the world's hungry has as its end to break our bread *with all mankind*. If this is not our end, our care for others merely becomes a new kind of domination. *Church for others* may easily lead us back to the old paternalism, unless its ultimate end is that kingdom where no one needs to speak up for the other any more but where each person rejoices with his neighbor and all men enjoy themselves together. *Being-there-for-others* is the way to the redemption of this life. *Being-there-with-others* is the form which the redeemed and liberated life itself has taken. The church therefore must not regard itself as just a means to an end, but it must demonstrate already in its present existence this free and redeeming being-with-others which it seeks to serve. In this sense—and only in this sense—the church is already an end in

11. Moltmann, *Theology and Joy*, 46. Emphasis added.

itself, not as *church* complete with hierarchy and bureaucracy but as the *congregation of the liberated.*[12]

Egalitarian yet Asymmetrical Relations

In contrast therefore to the unilateral relationship with the Other envisaged by our post-structuralist interlocutors, in which the "gift of death" is the ultimate gift one can give, the ecclesia, living in light of the resurrection and facing towards the hope of the final eschaton, is summoned and empowered to live a new form of life. We have already noted how the Apostle Paul, describing this new humanity as the Body of Christ, contrasts the relational patterns of this alternative form of personhood with the hierarchical, paternalistic and oppressive relational patterns of 1st Century Greco-Roman society. Membership within this new welcoming community is not based on a status according to ethnicity, gender, or wealth. Rather, as Paul notes, such status distinctions that the world draws are relativized (Gal 3:26–29). Using banqueting imagery, Paul argues that unlike the seating arrangements of the surrounding Greco-Roman society, where those of higher status were afforded seats closer to the host, "God has so arranged the body, giving greater honor to the inferior member, that there may be no dissension within the body, but the members may have *the same care for one another*" (1 Cor 12:24–25).

However, while with regard to status there is equality within this new community, the experience of each individual as they make their way through life is not necessarily equitable. Paul, recognizing that members of this new community still suffer the vagaries of the human condition—some experiencing suffering, others joy, some with abundance, others having little—does not therefore advocate for an *equality of gifts*—"the *same gift* for one another"—but rather for "the *same care* for one another," a "mutual affection." Paul explicates this further in his letter to the Philippians, where he urges that Christians' experience of "encouragement in Christ" and "sharing in the Spirit" should shape their treatment of each and every other. Paul writes: "Do nothing from selfish ambition or conceit, but in humility regard others as better than yourselves. Let each of you look not to our own interests, but to the interests of others. Let the same mind be in you that was in Christ Jesus" (Phil 2:3–5).

12. Ibid., 86–87.

In Paul's thinking, the new post-resurrection community of the ecclesia now operates according to a new ethos. Having received the gift of Christ—a genuine gift, not earned, but offered freely—the ecclesia consists of a community whose self-centered *desires* have been put to death and in whom new desires and affections are emerging as a result of the work of the indwelling Spirit. The attitude of the members of this community, Paul contends, should not be one of self-interest, nor one of "pure" disinterest, but rather, sharing the mind of Christ, each should seek each other's interest. Rather than espousing an ethic of self-obliteration, in which the prioritizing of the other corresponds with a loss of the self, Paul, suggests that as each looks to the interests of the other their interests will also be met by others acting according to the same principle.[13] Instead of the win-loss logic which undergirds a unilateral, self-sacrificial model of ethics, the new "household of God" is to be characterized by a win-win logic, based upon a principle of mutuality.

Terminology employed by John Milbank helps delineate further the nature of the relationality of the ecclesia and that of our interlocutors. Critical of the ethical philosophies offered by Levinas and Derrida, Milbank claims at the heart of their project is a "refusal of reciprocity."[14] In response to the thought of both Derrida and his former pupil, Marion, Milbank argues that Christianity offers a metaphysic not of "pure gift," but of *"purified gift-exchange."*[15] And, unlike Levinas, who "never really considers whether reciprocity could be itself asymmetrical,"[16] Milbank advocates for a relational model of *"asymmetrical reciprocity."*[17]

While Derrida, in his analysis of the gift, argues that any form of reciprocity or return of a gift traps the gift into an exchange economy, therefore annulling it of its giftedness[18], Milbank, drawing on the work of Pierre Bourdieu, suggests that that there are two features which distinguish a gift from that of a binding contract. Firstly, the gift, rather than being returned immediately—which "implies a *lack* of gratitude, a desire to discharge a *debt* as soon as possible"—usually involves a *"delay of return."*[19]

13. Paul's statement is, of course the antithesis to Adam Smith's belief that self-interest will bring mutual beneficence.

14. Milbank, "Reciprocity, Part One," 376–77. See also, Milbank, "Can a Gift Be Given?"

15. Milbank, "Can a Gift Be Given?," 131.

16. Milbank, "Reciprocity, Part One," 342.

17. Milbank, "Reciprocity, Part Two," 486.

18. Derrida, *Given Time*, 7.

19. Milbank, "Can a Gift Be Given?," 125.

And, secondly, the gift given back is *almost* always different, that is, there is a "*non-identical repetition* between the gift and counter-gift."[20]

To understand Milbank's argument here it is worth applying his analysis of gift-giving to our contemporary world and the experience of participating in the so-called "hospitality industry." Arriving at a cafe or restaurant, we order, receive our drink and/or meal, and then, at the conclusion, pay a price that has been agreed in advance—either through a verbal agreement such as bartering, or, more generally the case in a Western context, through an implicit agreement, in which having noted the menu prices and in choosing to order we enter into a contract. At the end of our meal, not only are we "obliged" to pay *immediately*—indeed, to leave without paying would constitute "theft"—but likewise, the price to pay, the "gift-return" so to speak, is, except in exceptional circumstances, not open to renegotiation, but rather follows an *identical repetition*. Obviously there are occasional exceptions to this contractually agreed price. Such as when a customer feels the service delivered does not justify the payment about to be rendered and upon lodging a complaint have their outstanding bill reduced. Or, on the occasions when the customers are so delighted in the "gifts" they have received, that they seek to offer a further gratuity. However, the general rule is that what one customer pays for a cup of coffee is the *identical* price that all customers pay for a cup of coffee. Thus, while such a relational engagement is perhaps evidence of an underlying desire for relations of reciprocity, such contractual transactions are not genuine "gift-giving." Each participant's "gift" and behavior, rather than following the random paths evident in the *free expression* of love and joy, follow a preordained and predetermined procedure.[21]

None of this is to suggest that one cannot experience "hospitality" while engaging in a relationship originally established along contractual lines. To adopt again the example of the restaurant: regular patronage at a specific restaurant over a long period of time often leads to a deepening of relationships between the owner and the guest and the initially formal relationship of service-provider and consumer develops into one of friendship. Instead, our point is that genuine relationships of hospitality

---

20. Ibid.

21. Even the ritual of offering a *gift* above and beyond the expected and obligated return—"tipping"—in some contexts has been robbed of its gift-like character. In the United States, the practice of "tipping" is an expectation and to fail to do so is seen either as a criticism of the service received or, evidence of one's "scrooge-like" character. In many situations a percentage of the final total is automatically added to the bill as the customer's "tip."

and love with the Other must move beyond the purely formalized nature of contractual relationality.[22]

The problem, Milbank contends, with Marion's and Derrida's an-economic "pure gift" and the unilateral relational structure advanced in Derrida's and Levinas' work, is that such a notion, rather than offering an alternative to the contractual relationality that characterizes the economic system of capitalism, is instead grounded upon the same conception of the world: a world of isolated individuals and a refusal of reciprocity. Thus, Milbank writes: "capitalist contracts which bind inexorably and impersonally are in theory the result of entirely willed, voluntary emissions from isolated egos capable only of either inflexible demand or else absolute free gift."[23]

In contrast to either unilateral or contractual relationships, perhaps the clearest illustration of a relational mutuality—one composed of an "asymmetrical reciprocity" in which each agent engages in a dynamic of "purified gift-exchange," a gift-exchange following a pattern not of *identical repetition* but rather of "free expression"—is the sexual gift-giving that takes place in life-long, monogamous relationships, such as marriage. In healthy relationships, the offering of gifts is based not upon *distance* and *separation* but rather on intimacy and proximity, and the *self*, rather than having power over the Other, extends itself to the Other, sharing in a mutual dance of desire, joy and delight. Within such relationships the return of counter-gifts stems not from a forced *duty* or *obligation*, nor, out of *necessity*, but rather, is a joyous offering of pleasure back to the Other, a desire to participate in a celebration of mutual gift-giving. Indeed, sexual relationships in which one partner holds power over the Other and the Other is *forced/obligated* to respond are almost universally recognized as a violation of the others' freedom and constitute rape, while sexual relationships where the response from one partner simply stems from an agreed contractual transaction are characteristic of "the oldest profession" known: prostitution. Both incidences are a distortion of the mutual joy, delight, intimacy and sharing of love that are essential to authentic human sexuality.[24] It is no coincidence, therefore, that instructions on marriage

22. Such development of relationships of mutuality and respect are of course not confined to the "hospitality industry" but rather have the potential to develop in all human vocational interactions.

23. Milbank, "Reciprocity, Part Two," 486.

24. C. S. Lewis also points to the example of the marriage relationship in making the same points: that self-denial is not an end in itself, and that neither does a return, or the "promise of reward," make "the Christian life a mercenary affair." See Lewis, "Weight of Glory," esp. 94–95.

feature so prominently in the "household codes" of Paul and other early church writers. Not only is it the case that such monogamous relationships of fidelity and love provide the sound basis for families and societies as a whole, but the loyalty, faithfulness, and the giving and receiving of gifts envisaged in such relationships is also seen as analogous to the relationship that Christ seeks to build with his church.[25]

Within a Christian account therefore, the practice of hospitality, the giving of gifts to the Other, does not stem from a slavish adherence to the infinite demand of ethics, nor follow a prescribed and formalized pattern. Rather, such gift-giving is a free joyful response to God's grace, an action that stems from the self's participation in a new law: the dynamic of love. As Moltmann writes: "The so-called *new obedience* is *new* only when it is no longer obedience but free, imaginative and loving action. The so-called *new law* is *new* only when it is no longer a law but the play of love which does the right whenever it does as it will."[26]

The enactment of such gift-giving, the practise of "imaginative and loving action" requires first and foremost, therefore, not legal or political changes, but *our* ontological transformation. To engage in the "play of love" is dependent not on our ethical actions but rather upon our death. Surrendering to the grace of God, entering into God's drama, division and separation gives way to communion and otherness, and our inner *hostility* is replaced by *hospitality*. As John Zizioulas puts it: "communion and otherness are supposed to permeate our lives in their entirety. They are to become an *attitude*, and *ethos* rather than an ethic and a set of principles."[27]

However, if authentic hospitality is not an *ethic* but an *ethos*, and is not the programmatic following of a predetermined set of responses but rather is more akin to what Samuel Wells refers to as *improvisation*,[28] is there a discernible pattern or shape to such *free expression*? Are there some defining characteristics and qualities of "purified gift-exchange"? That is, despite the multiple variations that stem from differences in personalities, cultures, and context, are there particular universal features that one should expect to see as the called-out community of the Ecclesia participates in the divine life of hospitable gift-giving?

25. The marital analogy of YHWH as husband to an often unfaithful, wife, Israel, (Isa 54:5, 62:5), is utilized by Jesus who refers to himself as the bridegroom coming for this bride (Matt 9:15; 25:1–13; John 3:29) and is also employed in other New Testament writings. See Eph 5:22–33 and Rev 19:7; 21:2; 22:17.

26. Moltmann, *Theology and Joy*, 67.

27. Zizioulas, *Communion and Otherness*, 81.

28. Wells, *Improvisation*.

Features of Ecclesial Hospitality (2 Cor 8:1–15; 9:1–15)

Seeking to raise funds for the church in Jerusalem undergoing famine, Paul, writing to the believers in Corinth, commends the example of the believers in Macedonia, who he sees as a prime illustration of this new ethos of mutuality and "purified gift-exchange" in action. Drawing on Paul's example of the Macedonians, below we will offer five features that we contend are evidence of a community whose practice of hospitality stems from, and is nourished by, its participation in the divine drama. Ecclesial hospitality, we will argue, is characterized by: (1) the cheerfulness and joyous disposition of those who are giving; (2) a radical generosity, that is, a giving which is profligate, excessive and abundant; (3) the universal and unconditional nature of such gift-giving; (4) a conscious and deliberate choice to enter into relationships of close proximity with strangers; and, (5) the willingness of the giver to accept and endure suffering.

The Cheerfulness and Voluntary Nature of Hospitable Giving

We have all undoubtedly endured the experience where the disposition of the hosts jars with the very offering of hospitality, where the atmosphere is anything but "welcoming." Situations where, as an unexpected Other, we turn up unknowingly at the most inappropriate and inopportune moments, and while the host greets us and summons us to enter, their grim disposition betrays a barely veiled sense of displeasure at this unwanted imposition. Then there are the occasions when we sense the eyes of the host watching apprehensively as we clumsily navigate ourselves around precariously balanced family heirlooms; observe the horror on the host's face when, rather than following accepted social convention and refusing the first offer of "seconds," a guest immediately heartily fills their empty plate; or the scarcely disguised gasps of dismay as a guest, oblivious to social etiquette, commits unbeknown to themselves, another social *faux pas*.

Such performances of "hospitality" are often motivated by an adherence to social norms or ethical duties, a "gift-giving" arising from self-interest in which one seeks to raise one's status through giving, or engages in giving to prevent the "loss of face." In contrast is the cheerful and joyful demeanor of those whose gifts are an overflow of love stemming from their participation in Christ. Decrying gift-giving/hospitality motivated by *obligation* or *compulsion*, Paul commends the example of the believers in Macedonia, whose generous gifts are not *extorted* (9:5) from them *reluctantly* (9:7), but rather, are given "voluntarily" with *cheerfulness* and joy (8:3; 9:7). While in the midst of "a severe ordeal of affliction, their abundant joy and their extreme poverty have overflowed in a wealth of generosity on their part," and further, Paul observes, the giving, far from being "reluctant," is characterized by keenness, the benefactors "begging us earnestly for the privilege of sharing in this ministry to the saints" (8:1–4). For Paul, therefore, the mien of the donor is a tell-tale sign of the motivating factor for one's actions of hospitality and gift-giving.

Why Paul regards motivation as so critical is expressed in his aphorism: "the one who sows sparingly will also reap sparingly, and the one who sows bountifully will also reap bountifully" (9:6). Prosperity preachers and tele-evangelists are right in recognizing that Paul offers here a core principle of a new economy, but are sadly mistaken in their understanding of that principle. Far from advocating a giving stemming from self-interest—the more one gives the more one will get in return—Paul is simply reiterating the principle which undergirds Jesus' alternative economy of the kingdom of God proclaimed in Luke 6:37–38. In God's economy of grace it is those having experienced God's grace who are freed from judgment and condemnation and are now enabled to offer such forgiveness and unconditional giving to others. In contrast, once giving ceases being cheerful, but becomes a matter of determining debts incurred and accounts owed, and is motivated by ethical duty and obligation, then one has begun to cut oneself off from the life-giving grace of God and, quite literally, has annulled the gift.[29]

For both Jesus and Paul, as for Derrida and Kant, the motivation of the giver is critically important. However, whereas Kant and his neo-Kantian successors seek to purge the gift of its agonistic tendencies, Paul holds not to the concept of a "pure" disinterested giver, but rather believes that the interests and desires of the self are transformed as one participates in Christ. In the Christian account, therefore, genuine giving is not an obligation imposed upon us, but, rather an inevitable outward expression of the transformation taking place within the self. As Volf states:

> Inscribed in the very heart of God's grace is the rule that *we can be recipients only if we do not resist being made into its agents.*

29. Such is the message of the parable of the Unforgiving Servant (Matt 18:23–35), in which the actions of a servant in demanding the day's wages he is owed by a fellow servant is set in stark contrast to the cancellation by the King of his own enormous outstanding debt—fifteen years' wages. While acting legitimately within the parameters of the law in demanding what he is owed, the action of the servant is evidence of his failure to have experienced the true freedom of grace.

> In a precisely defined way that guards the distinction between
> God and human beings, *human beings themselves are made
> participants in the divine activity and therefore are inspired, and
> powered, and obliged to imitate it.*[30]

The Extravagance of Aneconomic Hospitality

The second feature we should not be surprised to see amongst those whose actions are "inspired" and "powered" by their participation in the character-forming divine drama, is an *extravagance* and *excessive* quality to their hospitality. As with the Macedonians' "wealth of generosity" (8:2), such excessive and profligate giving stems from a radical reorientation and transformed conception of resources and therefore economics.

At the heart of human economics is, Daniel M. Bell Jr. argues, an ontology of poverty. That is, human economics is grounded upon a basic description of the world in which humanity competes for *scarce* resources.[31] In contrast to such an ontology based upon the core principles of *scarcity* and *lack*, in which human relations are therefore understood, at best, as "a tamed version of Hobbes's state of nature,"[32] is the Christian ontology we have outlined. Entering into the Christian narrative is to have our lives reshaped according to a new script and in our performing of this new script we are given the privilege of participating in God's new economy.

God, the giver of all gifts, does not give miserly nor manipulatively (Jas 1:17, Matt 7:7–11), but the reception of his gifts does entail our transformation. To respond to the call of Christ, to be incorporated into the Body of Christ, is to be initiated into a new way of being, one where the hoarding of resources for oneself is transformed into a faith in God's daily sustaining of *our* corporate needs. Like the provision of manna to the Israelites in the wilderness, the ecclesial life is one of daily dependence on God's grace. Those participating within this new divine economy do not therefore give out of their surplus, offering what they have left over after sustaining their own needs. Rather, akin to Levinas' claim that "to give is to take bread out of one's own mouth, to nourish the hunger of another

---

30. Volf, "Theology for a Way of Life," 255. Emphasis added.

31. Bell offers a quotation from Lionel Robbins as the standard definition of the discipline of economics: "Economics is the science which studies human behavior as a relationship between ends and *scarce* means which have alternative uses." Robbins, *Essay on the Nature and Significance of Economic Science*, 16, quoted in Bell, "Forgiveness and the End of Economy," 327.

32. Ibid., 327.

with one's own fasting"[33] Christians are to give out of their weakness and poverty. Such hospitality, dependent not on our own resources, is a movement of faith, a demonstration of one's confidence that *"God is able to provide you with every blessing in abundance"* (9:8), but more than this, an assurance that God will provide not merely *one's own* "daily bread," but will also provide sufficient bread to share with *others*. Thus Paul, in imagery reminiscent of Jesus' own words in the Sermon on the Mount (Matt 6:25–34) speaks of God as the supplier of seed and provider of bread, who gives enough *"so that by always having enough of everything, you may share abundantly in every good work"* (9:8).

Participation in God's new economy which operates according to the aneconomic principles of excess and abundance is therefore typified by the radical and extravagant nature of giving. As Stanley Hauerwas puts it: "Only by being initiated into the Christian tradition concerning the economy called 'trinity' does one have a chance of being freed from the necessities called 'economics.' For Christians know that the love displayed in God's life is not a zero-sum game but one of overflowing plenitude."[34]

Critical once again, however, is the understanding that the *end* of such giving out of poverty, is not the starvation of oneself *for* the Other, but rather the enacting of a new economy of mutuality. Paul therefore explicitly states that the trusting of oneself to God's steadfast faithfulness and one's participation in this new economy does not "mean that there should be a relief for others and pressure on you." Rather, the desired *end* of such giving is one of a "fair balance" (8:13–14).

Our repeated emphasis here is that while self-sacrifice, suffering, and potentially even death may serve as the *means*, the ultimate *end* envisaged in the action of hospitality practised by the Church is not one of masochism, but rather the joy of a shared life of mutuality and communion. It is, to paraphrase Jesus, "in losing our lives—of self-interest—that we therefore find and enter into true living."[35] Such an emphasis forces a radical rereading of some of the biblical passages most often cited with regard to giving; passages most often interpreted as commending and exhorting a life of self-sacrificial giving as an *end* in and of itself.[36]

33. Levinas, *Otherwise than Being*, 56.

34. Hauerwas, *Sanctify Them in the Truth*, 222.

35. Matt 10:39; 16:25; Mark 8:35; Luke 9:24.

36. See for instance Addison G. Wright's compelling rereading of the story of the Widow's Mite, recounted in Mark and Luke's gospels (Mark 12:41–44 and Luke 21:1–4). Wright argues, that read in context, the story told by Jesus, far from being an approbation of the Widow's gift, is rather, "a downright disapproval." Wright, "Widow's

Universal and Unconditional Giving

The third defining feature of the hospitality of the *Ecclesia*, evidence of their participation in the new divine economy, is the *universal* and *unconditional* nature of their giving. Within a world of inequalities, injustice and need, and with finite resources at one's disposal, donors are often called upon to give an account of their giving, to offer some rationale for why and how they determined who should receive their offered hospitality and gifts of aid—to provide some sort of "cost-benefit" analysis. Within such circumstances, often beneath the surface, lies a notion of a "deserving" and "undeserving" Other. Yet, the very notion of a "deserving" or "undeserving" stranger is rendered nonsensical in light of the Christian doctrine of sin. God's gift offered to us is a free gift, one that is dependent not on the achievement of certain moral standards, nor on an ability to live ethical lives. As Jesus states: "the Father . . . makes his sun rise on the evil and the good, and sends rain on the righteous and the unrighteous" (Matt 5:45). Indeed, as we have argued throughout, it is not moral transformation or ethical behavior that entitles us to reception of God's free gift, but rather the converse; it is the reception of the free gift offered in Christ which provides the basis for our ontological and therefore moral and ethical transformation.

Likewise, the Christian understanding of the eschatological nature of identity—the fact that the true and full identity of the Other awaits a final unveiling and disclosure—once again speaks against any attempt to classify or categorize the Other. As Zizioulas states: "It is not on the basis of someone's past or present that we should identify and accept him or her, but on the basis of their *future*. And since the future lies only in the hands of God, our approach to the other must be free from passing judgement on him or her. Every 'other' is in the Spirit a potential saint, even if he or she appears to have been or continues to be a sinner."[37]

Despite our divergence from Derrida's thought, nonetheless, Derrida's desire for a hospitality which operates beyond the constraints of law and principles resonates with the argument we have put forth here. Derrida writes:

> To the extent that we are looking for criteria, for conditions, for passports, border and so on, we are limiting hospitality. . . . But if we want to understand what hospitality means, we have to think

Mite: Praise or Lament?," 262.

37. Zizioulas, *Communion and Otherness*, 6.

of unconditional hospitality, that is, openness to whomever, to any newcomer. And of course, if I want to know in advance who is the good one, who is the bad one—in advance!—if I want to have an available criterion to distinguish between the good immigrant and the bad immigrant, then I would have no relation with the other as such. So to welcome the other, you have to suspend the use of criteria. I would not recommend giving up all criteria, all knowledge and politics. I would simply say that if I want to improve hospitality . . . the politics of hospitality, I have to refer to pure hospitality . . . if only to control the distance between in-hospitality, less hospitality, and more hospitality.[38]

Derrida perceptively recognizes that any attempt to have criterion available by which we evaluate and distinguish the "good" immigrant from the "bad" immigrant, the "deserving" stranger from the "undeserving" stranger has the effect of extinguishing our relation with the *other*. Indeed, that the establishing of ethical principles, that is the "categorization of what *ought* and what *ought not* to be done" goes hand in hand with a moral categorization of the *other*, is a point made insightfully by Zizioulas, who states: ". . . the other is not identifiable ontologically in moral terms, for he or she would cease to be truly Other if placed in a class or category applicable to more than one entity. By being a person, the Other is by definition unique and therefore unclassifiable. Only in this way can one remain truly and absolutely, that is, ontologically, Other."[39]

In the world of "professionalized charities" with giving often reduced to a set of ethical principles the Other is often in danger of being categorized and classified. While not necessarily adhering to crude classifications according to moral attributes, donors often following strict economic principles are required to determine whether the Other demonstrates the nous and wherewithal to purposefully utilize the gifts and thus is "deserving" of the precious resources being bestowed upon them. Such an attempt to determine whether the Other will be a "success story" and thus worthy of time, effort and resources, is, in one sense, no less an act of ethical classification.[40]

38. Derrida, "Discussion with Richard Kearney," 133.

39. Zizioulas, *Communion and Otherness*, 81. Zizioulas posits that an "ethos of ethical apophaticism" should characterize the Church. Ibid., 111–12.

40. None of this is to deny the importance of wisdom in the distribution (stewardship) of gifts and nor is it to ignore Jesus' adage of not "throwing pearls before swine" (Matt 7:6). Our point here, is that such wise "stewardship" is to be determined not according to the logic of human economics—the funding only of prospective "winners"—but rather by the radical nature of the gospel, which operates according to a

The gospels provide multiple episodes which illustrate this distinction between the tendency to classify and categorize the Other and the contrasting *ethos* of *ethical apophaticism*. Another striking example of is contained in Victor Hugo's classic, *Les Misérables*. In one of the most memorable scenes of the novel, the protagonist of Hugo's story, Jean Valjean, having been turned away or ejected from all the other dwellings in a village, arrives as night falls, on the doorstep of the local bishop, Monseignuer Bienvenu.[41] Such has been the power of the discourse of ethical categorization and classification to which he has been exposed, that as the door opens and before the bishop is able to speak, Jean Valjean by way of introduction, gives a catalogue of his own moral background, failings and tribulations:

> See here! My name is Jean Valjean. I am a convict; I have been nineteen years in the galleys. Four days ago I was set free. . . . When I reached this place this evening I went to an inn, and they sent me away on account of my yellow passport, which I had shown at the mayor's office, as was necessary. I went to another inn; they said: "Get out!" It was the same with one as with another; nobody would have me. I went to the prison, and the turnkey would not let me in. I crept into a dog-kennel, the dog bit me, and drove me away as if he had been a man; you would have said that he knew who I was. I went into the fields to sleep beneath the stars: there were no stars; I thought it would rain, and there was no God to stop the drops, so I came back into town to get the shelter of some doorway. There in the square I lay down upon a stone; a good woman showed me your house, and said: "Knock there!" I have knocked. What is this place? Are you an inn? I have money; my savings, one hundred and nine francs and fifteen sous which I have earned in the galleys, by way of my work for nineteen years. I will pay. What do I care? I have money. I am very tired . . . and I am hungry. Can I stay?[42]

After nineteen years of exposure to the discourse of social exclusion, Jean Valjean, despite being freed on parole, identifies himself according to the moral label attached to him by society—"I am a convict." Aware of the prejudice that exists, and having himself taken on the tag of "undeserving,"

---

different "wisdom" in which God chooses the "foolish," "weak," "lowly" and "despised" to be the recipients of his gifts (1 Cor 1:26–29).

41. The bishop's name is itself highly significant: "Bienvenu" being French for "welcome." For this episode see II.iii—*The heroism of passive obedience* in Victor Hugo, *Les Misérables*, 51–54.

42. Ibid., 51–52.

Jean Valjean seeks to reassure his host that while he may be an unworthy recipient of "welcome," he does possess money and therefore is able to *pay* for any hospitality provided. The bishop's welcoming response: "Madame Magloire, put on another plate," suggests to Jean Valjean a misunderstanding and thus he reiterates his introductory refrain: "Stop! Not that, did you understand me? I am a galley-slave—a convict—I am just from the galleys" and presents his yellow passport of parole as corroborating evidence of his untrustworthy character. While on the second response from the bishop: "Monsieur, sit down and warm yourself: we are going to take supper presently, and your bed will be made ready while you sup," the new reality being offered begins to dawn on Jean Valjean,[43] even then his predisposition leads him to stress again that he can *pay* for his lodgings.

Elsewhere in this work we have alluded to the belief that central to the redemptive nature of hospitality and the overcoming of the ideological power of exclusion is the offering of, the reception, and the vocalizing of, a new name and title. Such a claim is similarly observable in Hugo's thought with the bishop's referring to Jean Valjean as *monsieur*. Hugo states:

> Every time he said this monsieur, with his gently solemn, and heartily hospitable voice, the man's countenance lighted up. *Monsieur* to a convict, is a glass of water to a man dying of thirst at sea. Ignominy thirsts for respect.[44]

In contrast to ethical categorization, in which the Other is labeled according to his or her qualities—physical, social, moral—and hence classified as a "terrorist," a "fundamentalist," or a "pervert," is the identity-shaping nature of authentic naming. Ethical classification which takes place outside of relationship is a form of self-fulfilling prophecy. The self, interpreting the actions of the Other in accordance with the limits and parameters of the category which they have imposed, is blinded to the

---

43. Hugo writes: "At last the man quite understood; his face, the expression of which till then had been gloomy and hard, now expressed stupefaction, doubt, and joy, and became absolutely wonderful. He began to stutter like a madman." Ibid., 52.

44. Those familiar with the story of *Les Misérables* either from Claude-Michel Schönberg and Alain Boublil's musical, or from adaptations brought to film, miss out on one of the earlier scenes—I.x.: *The bishop in the presence of an unknown light* which details the *disturbance* of the bishop through his experience of receiving the hospitality of a dying conventionist. This scene in Hugo's novel provides the background for the development of the bishop's own radical ethical apophaticism and its expression in unconditional hospitality, and reinforces the point we have stressed throughout—that the offering of radical unconditional hospitality to the Other is inextricably connected to our willingness to receive hospitality from this same Other. Ibid., 25–33.

true reality of the Other. Yet, as we have observed earlier, the investiture of names upon the Other, taking place in the context of relationships of trust and love, constitutes the true identity of the Other, summoning them to actualize their authentic identity, to live out the truth of their bestowed name.

Near and Distant Neighbors: Proximity to the Other, Pilgrimage to the Periphery

Thus far we have suggested that the hospitality practiced by the ecclesial community that has received and continues to participate within God's free and gracious hospitality will be characterized by joyfulness, cheerfulness, and extravagant generosity, and will be universal and unconditional by nature. Nevertheless, the practical question still remains: Who is the Other to whom we are summoned to extend this radical hospitality? How, in a world of "infinite need" do we decide who to offer assistance to? Questions of discerning to whom, and how, with the finite daily resources we have at our disposal we respond to the needs of the Other have always existed. However, living in the contemporary globalised world with a milieu of media and bombarded daily by the "needs" of a multitude of others and thus unable to claim ignorance of the plight of the Other, such ethical questions take on an even greater complexity. In such a globalised world, even when the motivation may not be one of seeking to justify ourselves, we nevertheless find ourselves uttering the same question as a young lawyer in an encounter with Jesus: "Who is my neighbor?" (Luke 10:29).

Miroslav Volf, responding to this difficult question, suggests that while "Christians are obliged to love every human being" the "noble" concept of "the whole human commonwealth as an ethical community of love" is "an impossible ideal."[45] For Volf, "the claim that love's scope is universal does not imply that we do not differentiate in how we ought to love those with whom we have special relations and those with whom we do not."[46] Drawing upon the thought of Augustine and Aquinas, Volf argues that while we are called to give hospitality to the stranger this "does not imply undifferentiated cosmopolitanism that would preclude giving special attention to our own family, ethnic group, nation, or broader culture. Not only is it right to maintain boundaries of discrete group identities.

45. Volf, "Living with the Other," 24.
46. Ibid., 25.

. . . It is also right to devote one's energies so that the group to which we belong would flourish."[47]

For Volf, it is those with whom we have developed "thick" relations—*"proximate others"*—who, on a daily basis, are the others who should be the primary recipients of our care and extension of love. However, while not necessarily his intention, does Volf's advocacy of a differentiation between "thick" and "thin" relations ultimately suggest a two-tiered approach to hospitality, one in which hospitality is extended first to those with whom we have "thick" relations—i.e., biological/cultural relations/fellow-Christians—and then, with the remaining reserves, offered to the "distant" strangers, to those we are "thinly" related to? And if so, does such an ordering, the prioritizing of those to whom we are "thickly" related, over "thinner" relations, really give testimony to the radical nature of God's hospitality? Indeed, does not our entrance into the ecclesia, new birth in Christ, the eating and drinking of the body and blood of Christ, mean that our identity is no longer determined according to biological bloodlines?[48] Is not the gospel a radical call in which the familial demands of kin and relatives are relativized by the greater demand of the kingdom?[49] Paul, rather than establishing a hierarchy or natural order, seems to see the care of fellow-believers ('thick" relations) and others ("thin" relations) as occurring together, instructing the churches of Rome to: "Contribute to the needs of the saints; extend hospitality to strangers" (Rom 12:13). As Terry Veling suggests:

> If our hospitality extends only to the intimate circle of our family and friends, then we are only doing what most people do. We are not extending our lives much further than the conventional ways of the world, whereby we offer friendship to those who we know will offer us friendship in return. Jesus' teaching, however, seeks to offer us a *proposed world that we could inhabit.* . . . The kingdom of God is concerned with friendship and hospitality to those who are not normally "our friends", to those who are not part of our "circle," to those who have no means of returning our hospitality—and this is the true test of what hospitality means. Otherwise, it is simply loving those who love us, which is all too easy, all too human.[50]

---

47. Ibid.

48. John 1:13; 6:52–58.

49. Does Jesus' broadening and widening of his kin (Matt 12:46–50; Mark 3:31–35) hold true for his disciples too?

50. Veling, *Practical Theology,* 46–47. Similarly, Zizioulas suggests that it is the

Nevertheless, even if our experience of God's radical hospitality summons us to love beyond our immediate family and kin, to transcend exclusiveness and offer hospitality to the more *distant* stranger, this still begs the question, *which stranger?*

Throughout this work we have drawn attention to the way in which "distance," as emphasized in the work of Levinas and Derrida, is ultimately problematic. In particular we have noted how the Other of our philosophical interlocutors, distant and separate, transcendent, beyond *being*, unable to be comprehended, is ultimately in danger of becoming an abstraction. As Oliver O'Donovan notes, many Christian theologians themselves appear embarrassed "by the element of proximity in the term 'neighbor' (in Latin, *proximus*)" and instead advocate for a "generalizing interpretation of the love-command." However, parables like the Good Samaritan, O'Donovan contends, "should not be used to support an abstract moral schematization." The parable, O'Donovan rightly points out, is not about deciding from a distance who one's neighbors are, but instead stresses "the element of contingent proximity."[51]

In his *magnum opus Church Dogmatics*, Karl Barth offers some helpful reflections and elucidation on this difficult question of our responsibility to express God's love to "near" and "distant" neighbors. Like Volf and O'Donovan, Barth argues that God's command and the call to responsibility for the Other does not take place in an abstracted vacuum, but rather is always received in a particular context. In contrast to a faceless Other beyond *being*, Barth posits that crucial to a genuine encounter with the Other, is the necessity that we must "look the other in the eye."[52] For Barth: "Being with the other man means encounter with him. Hence humanity is the determination of our being as a being in encounter with the other man."[53]

Resonating with our earlier reflections, for Barth, it is in the process of *seeing* and of being *seen* that the "distinction and particularity" of "man within the cosmos," the distinction of the self "from the one who sees him" becomes evident.[54] For Barth, such *seeing* of the Other is not a one-way process, but rather a dynamic of mutuality. Thus Barth writes:

---

very action of loving a stranger more than one's immediate biological family which provides evidence of the conversion from a "biological" to an ecclesial existence. Zizioulas, *Being as Communion*, 57–58.

51. O'Donovan, *Resurrection and Moral Order*, 240.

52. Barth, *Church Dogmatics* III/2, 250.

53. Ibid., 248.

54. Ibid., 250.

> To see the other thus means directly to let oneself be seen by
> him. If I do not do this, I do not see him. Conversely, as I do
> it, as I let him look me in the eye, I see him. The two together
> constitute the full human significance of the eye and its seeing.
> All seeing is inhuman in which the one who sees hides himself,
> refusing to be seen by the fellow-man whom he sees. The point
> is not unimportant that it is always two men, and therefore a real
> I and Thou, who look themselves in the eye and can thus see one
> another and be seen by one another. [55]

However, in a globalised consumer world saturated with images,
where the daily news broadcasts endless footage of the plight of Others,
an encounter with the Other must be more than visual. Such a constant
stream of staccato images, accompanied with un-emotive 45-second
"news" voice-overs, rather than bringing the Other *closer*, has the opposite
effect. Eventually the images become an undifferentiated blur, a sea of de-
contextualized faces. Against the backdrop of this constant cycle of tragic
human events—played as much to "entertain" as to "inform" and which
remain "news" for a day to be replaced by the next breaking story—we are
in danger of becoming "numbed" to the sea of faces and of slipping into
"compassion fatigue."

It is this problem—the fact that images in an image-saturated world
eventually cease being *seen* and thus lose their impact—which results
in P.R. and marketing companies endlessly seeking new ways to impact
viewers with a *visual* of their product. We grow accustomed therefore to
pictures of starving children with swollen bellies presented with emotive
background music—images employed by "professional" charities as a
marketing tool, *faces* utilized for raising funds for this voiceless and "help-
less" Other.

True encounter of the Other, therefore, requires not merely the engagement of our eyes, but also our aural senses. As Barth states: "Being in
encounter consists in the fact that there is mutual speech and hearing. The
matter sounds simple, and yet it again consists in a complex action: I and
Thou must both speak and hear, and speak with one another and hear one
another."[56] Arthur Sutherland concisely summarizes Barth's important
point here:

> Whereas seeing another human is critical, it is only in speaking
> and hearing that one crosses into the boundary of relationship.

55. Ibid.
56. Barth, *CD III/2*, 252.

> The real problem with encountering a stranger is our imagination: it is why we begin each new encounter with the question, Who are you? Hospitality requires being open to the self-declaration of others, allowing them to say who they are.[57]

Finally, reinforcing what we have already asserted, Barth argues that genuine encounters, built upon this *seeing* and *hearing* of the Other, are then characterized by two further principles: the rendering of mutual aid and a gladness of heart. True hospitality takes place in an encounter with the proximate other in which we see and hear the Other and allow "thick" relations of mutuality and joy to develop.[58]

But what happens in the contemporary world characterized by fracture and isolated living, when those who are affluent and fortunate to live with plenty often live *distant* from the stark and painful realities of the broken, inhospitable world? While not necessarily living behind the walls of "gated communities," much of the church—particularly in the West—is no longer *proximate* to those who are the excluded. How then, does O'Donovan's belief that Christian ethics is characterized by a "contingent nearness," that our neighbor is the one whom we "chanc[e] to be next to . . . in the contingencies of life,"[59] actually operate? Dietrich Bonhoeffer, perhaps of all 20th century theologians, was most aware of this danger of the church becoming disconnected from the harsh inhospitable realities experienced by those classified as Others, scapegoated and excluded from society. For Bonhoeffer, it is the treatment of our most distant neighbor that provides evidence of our spirituality:

> If beyond his neighbour a man does not know this one who is furthest from him, and if he does not know this one who is furthest from him as this neighbour, then he does not serve his neighbour but himself; he takes refuge from the free open space of responsibility in the comforting confinement of the fulfilment of duty. This means that the commandment of love for our neighbour also does not imply a law which restricts our responsibility solely to our neighbor in terms of space, to the man who I encounter socially, professionally or in my family. My neighbour may well be one who is extremely remote from me, and one who is extremely remote from me may well be my neighbour.[60]

57. Sutherland, *I Was a Stranger*, 36.

58. See Barth, *CD III/2*, 260–66.

59. O'Donovan, *Resurrection and Moral Order*, 240.

60. Bonhoeffer, *Letters and Papers*, 259.

Again, Barth offers some helpful reflections on this important point. In contrast to abstracted universal Others, for Barth it is in the particularity of the concrete context and the relationships which compose one's life, that responsibilities to "near and distant neighbours" emerge.[61] While recognizing the factors of language, location-geography, and history used to distinguish and differentiate "near" from "distant" neighbors, Barth refuses to succumb to a tendency within theological ethics of setting up different spheres of ethical behavior. While we receive the command of God in a set context, Barth asserts that "the concept of one's own people is not a fixed but a fluid concept."[62] Echoing our earlier argument, Barth states that the believer, shaped by their relationship with the Triune God is constantly being expanded and widened. For Barth, "the command of God wills that a man should really move out from his beginning and therefore seek a *wider field*."[63] It is, for the Christian, Barth asserts, not "by natural compulsion" but due to an "inner necessity" that one "will transcend the barrier of his own speech and people."[64]

Writing against the grim backdrop of the exposed evils of nationalistic identity, Barth argues that "the one who is really in his own people, among those near to him, is always on the way to those more distant, to other peoples."[65] For Barth: "If His [God's] Word and command are heard and accepted by a man, this man cannot be concerned only with his own people. Beyond this he must be concerned with this greater people. He is again *led out of the narrower into the wider sphere*. Called to obedience among near neighbors, in the same obedience *he is turned to those who are distant*."[66]

Barth acknowledges that this *widening*, this transcending of barriers, the *movement* of *turning* to *the distant other* creates a tension, but believes that the disciple, "obedient to the command of God will always be summoned and ready to endure this tension and to seek to overcome this antithesis."[67] In a manner reminiscent of Derrida's aporetic tension which serves to open us up to the Other, Barth argues that this tension leads to our circle of ethical responsibility being opened and constantly expanded.

61. Barth, *Church Dogmatics* III/4, 288.

62. Ibid., 291.

63. Ibid., 293. Emphasis added.

64. Ibid., 290.

65. Ibid., 294.

66. Ibid., 297. Emphasis added.

67. Ibid., 297–98.

Barth, speaking of the Christian believer, states: "As he holds his near neighbors with the one hand, he reaches out to the distant with the other. And so the concept of his own people is *extended* and *opened out* in this respect too. It is true that he belongs wholly and utterly to his own people. But it is equally true that the horizon by which his people is surrounded and within which it exists as his people is humanity. It is equally true that he himself belongs wholly and utterly to humanity."[68]

Barth's understanding of the terms "near" and "distant" neighbors as "fluid" concepts provides an important clarification of our emphasis on "proximity." It is axiomatic that hospitality does not take place with a faceless other but rather with a stranger who is proximate and who we therefore *see* and *hear*. However, the likelihood of encountering this stranger, our proximity to the other is not merely one of "chance"—one determined by biology, culture (language or history), or, geographic boundaries—but rather is itself dependent on our obedience to God's call. The fact that the identity of the believer is not determined by language, location, or history, but rather that one "is actually led into this sphere" and "belongs to it only provisionally and temporarily," and that the ecclesial and eschatological self "is originally and finally free in relation" to this sphere thus enables us to be called "to the way of a pilgrim."[69] As a pilgrim we are, by the discomforting of the Spirit, *"led out of the narrower into the wider sphere"* and *"turned to those who are distant."*[70]

Hospitality is a practice that requires proximity to the Other, but such proximity involves a conscious, active step of obedience on behalf of the believer. A defining feature of those who have experienced the radical hospitality of the kingdom is the deliberate choice to relocate their lives, to ensure that an encounter with the stranger, the Other, is not an occasional or haphazard event, but rather a frequent and daily occurrence. Such a spirituality of proximity—a defining feature of Liberation Theology, with its recognition of God's "preference for the poor"—is manifested in the practices of "social relocation" or "downward mobility." If, as Ched Myers contends, Jesus' model of ministry and God's work of societal transformation takes place not from the centre of power (Jerusalem) outwards, but rather moves inwards from the margins (Galilee), then the evidence of the ecclesia following in the footsteps of Jesus and responding to the promptings of the discomforting Spirit is its relocation to the periphery, and its

68. Ibid., 298. Emphasis added.
69. Ibid., 302.
70. Ibid., 297. Emphasis added.

proximity therefore to the excluded and forgotten strangers.[71] It is here in the wildernesses of our societies, our own contemporary Galilee and Samaria regions, that a genuine transforming encounter with the Other—that is, Christ and the stranger—can occur, and that a new mode of living which witnesses prophetically against the prevailing discourses and ideologies of our day, begins to emerge. So it is that Jesus, intentionally choosing to take the shorter but more troubled route through Samaria, rather than hurrying through, tarries at wells, and engaging "morally suspect" locals in conversation, seeks to *see* and *hear* the tales of this Other. It is from this deliberate, purposed proximity and the ensuing development of a reciprocal relationship of mutual gift-exchange, that the life-giving water of a new kingdom gushes forth and begins its outward flow.

Cruciform Hospitality

And yet, nevertheless, both human finitude and the reality of human sinfulness mean that relations of mutuality characterized by joyful, abundant and generous, gift-giving are only glimpsed momentarily. Even in the redeemed community of the ecclesia, where human relations are undergoing transformation, the practise of such radical hospitality, and the existence of a new "economy of grace" are not always immediately apparent. Accordingly, New Testament writers do not call for an ethical imitation of the non-competitive gift-giving relations of the Trinity, but rather, recognizing the reality of human finitude and the ravages of sin, call the new community to an *imitation* of the suffering and ultimately self-sacrificial love of Christ.

Jews and Gentiles in the Church in Ephesus are called to "be imitators of God, as beloved children, and live in love, as Christ loved us and gave himself up for us, a fragrant offering and sacrifice to God" (Eph 5:1–2). In calling the believers at Philippi to give up self-interest—and a utilitarian disinterest—for a life of mutual interest, Paul argues that conformity to Christ, exemplified by humility and obedience, ultimately leads to the cross. Indeed, while a new community in which love is exchanged freely may be the ultimate *telos*, this highest good is yet to come in all its fullness.

That the practice of unconditional and universal hospitality is not dependent upon the acceptance of this love-gift or upon a reciprocated response is the central emphasis of Jesus' Sermon on the Mount. Volf, commenting on Jesus' command to his disciples to "be perfect as your heavenly

71. Myers, *Binding the Strong Man*.

Father is perfect," notes that it is not the case "that he was demanding that they emulate the perfection of the eternal divine love." Rather, Volf says:

> The disciples will be the children of their Father in heaven, not so much when they, echoing a divine kind of reciprocity love those who love them (v.46), but when they imitate equally a divine kind of one-sidedness of the God who makes "the sun rise on the evil and on the good, and sends rain on the righteous and on the unrighteous" (v.45) by loving their enemies and praying "for those who persecute" them (v.44). . . . Jesus demanded not so much that we imitate the divine dance of love's freedom and trust, but the divine labor of love's suffering and risk. The love that dances the internal love of the Trinity; the love that suffers is the same love that turned toward a world suffused with enmity. The first is the perfect love of the world to come; the second is that same love engaged in the transformation of the deeply flawed world that is.[72]

To participate in God's generous work of hospitality is to walk the way of the Cross. As Paul states, "to know Christ and the power of his resurrection" requires a "sharing in his sufferings" (Phil 3:10–11). The action of the ecclesia in "being-there-for-others," the cheerful and joyful practise of lavish and excessive hospitality, offered unconditionally, will almost inevitably result in moments of betrayal, loss, humiliation, suffering and possibly death. And yet, such loss is not a masochistic ethic of self-sacrifice, nor a lauding of martyrdom. Rather, one can engage in such giving in the confidence that participation *in* Christ entails our own death, but also ensures our participation in his resurrection victory over death itself.

Ultimately, it is this belief that God *in* Christ has overcome death and hostility once-for-all that provides the basis for the practise of radical hospitality. Jesus' declaration to his disciples remains true for those who await with expectation his return, and the banquet to end all banquets:

> . . . you will have pain, but your pain will turn into joy. When a woman is in labor, she has pain, because her hour has come. But when her child is born, she no longer remembers the anguish because of the joy of having brought a human being into the world. So you have pain now; but I will see you again, and your hearts will rejoice, and no one will take your joy from you. (John 16:20–22)

---

72. Volf, "Trinity Is Our Social Programme," 114.

Being Sustained: Identity-Shaping Practices and Sacraments of the Ecclesia

Throughout this work we have argued that "hospitality" is not in the first instance an ethical activity, but rather, is fundamentally a mode of *being*— a description of the relations of *communion* that exist within the Godhead. As the self enters through faith into this life of *communion* and begins to experience the richness of love of the hospitable God, so it is led, by necessity, to share this hospitality with others.

However, if hospitality is ultimately not something "we do," but rather a practice that stems from "who we are," how does the new "ecclesial self" sustain this way of life in a world of hostility? How in a world where the discourse of terror constantly tells us that the Other is to be feared and in which the market reduces human relations to relations of contractual necessity and obligation, does the Ecclesia continue to remind itself that it gives a different account of human relationality?

The recent work of Christian ethicists such as Stanley Hauerwas and John Howard Yoder has brought back to the attention of the church the central importance that practices play in the formation of Christian character and virtues. In particular, their work has highlighted that the formation of character and virtues is not an individual process, but rather takes place as the self is incorporated into a community and imbibes the narratives and practices that are integral to this community and tradition.[73]

The complex and dynamic relationship between the practices of a community and the narrative/doctrines/beliefs from which these practices stem is observed by Serene Jones, who, drawing on the work of theorists J. L. Austin and Judith Butler, suggests that "human beings become certain types of persons by learning to perform the often unconscious but socially constructed scripts of personhood embedded in the language and cultures in which they live." Such scripts, Jones posits, "are not only performed by us; they also have the constitutive power to perform us."[74] Applying this imagery specifically to the Christian community, Jones suggests one way to conceive of doctrines is as "'dramatic scripts' which Christians perform and by which they are performed."[75]

While Jones' concept of doctrine as a "dramatic script" is useful for reconfiguring an understanding of how doctrine and practices relate to

73. Yoder, *Politics of Jesus*, and Hauerwas, *Peaceable Kingdom*.

74. Jones, "Graced Practices," 60.

75. Ibid., 75.

one another, it is important to note that except in the formal environment of academic theology, believers rarely engage directly with the "propositional statements" of Christian doctrines. Rather, Christian doctrines are themselves communicated through performance and participation in communal practices and sacraments fundamental to the life of the Ecclesia: the reading of the narrative of Scripture, the recitation of the Lord's Prayer, and the celebration of the Eucharist.

The Communal Reading of Scripture

The understanding of Scripture as a "script" which the Christian community *performs* is suggested by a number of writers. In his book *Improvisation: The Drama of Christian Ethics*, Samuel Wells draws on the work of N. T. Wright to suggest that the salvation narrative can be conceived of as a five-act drama: (1) Creation; (2) Israel; (3) Jesus; (4) The Church and (5) Eschaton.[76] Placing particular stress on the Church's performance in Act Four, Wells argues that this performing "requires more than repetition, more even than interpretation" of the text of Scripture which narrates the first three and half acts of the drama. Neither though should the ethical actions of the Church consist of "origination, or creation de novo." Rather, Wells suggests, "the key to abiding faithfulness, is improvisation."[77]

Such *performing-improvisation*, however, is only possible as *the community* gathers to read Scripture and allows this script to reshape its life.[78] As N. T. Wright puts it: "We must allow scripture to teach us how to think straight, because by ourselves we don't, we think bent, we think crooked. . . . the Spirit broods over us as we read this book, to straighten out our bent thinking."[79] Scripture therefore, is best understood not primarily as an *object* which we interpret, comprehend and then perform, but rather as the interrogating *subject* which reads our lives and re-narrates them into

---

76. Wright, "How Can the Bible Be Authoritative?"

77. Wells, *Improvisation*, 65.

78. That Scripture can only be interpreted and embodied in the life of a *community* is stressed by Nicholas Lash, who asserts that "the performance of Scripture *is* the life of the church. It is no more possible for an isolated individual to perform *these* texts than it is for him to perform a Beethoven quartet or a Shakespeare tragedy." Lash, *Theology on the Way to Emmaus*, 43. Emphasis added. Barth makes the same point with the emphatic statement that "any attempt to hear and receive the Word of God in isolation," results in "no real hearing and receiving." Barth, *CD I/2*, 588.

79. Wright, "How Can the Bible Be Authoritative?," 26.

a new script. That is, it is not Scripture that is *read* by the community, but rather, first and foremost, Scripture *that reads us*.

The analogy of Scripture as a dramatic text evocatively conveys the belief that Christian ethical practices are neither grounded in universal principles accessible to individuals through the exercise of reason, nor consists in a strict formalism. Rather, Christian ethical practices are an innovative and risky exercise, which emerge from a *community* as they seek to interpret and participate in God's story of salvation within their own lives and context. This dynamic, of being re-narrated and transformed as ecclesial persons and thus empowered to perform this hospitable script, is evident too in the Christian practice of corporate prayer.

The Lord's Prayer

Our Father in heaven,
hallowed be your name.
Your kingdom come.
Your will be done,
on earth as it is in heaven.
Give us this day our daily bread.
And forgive us our debts,
as we also have forgiven our debtors.
And do not bring us to the time of trial,
but rescue us from the evil one.
    (Matthew 6:9–13)

To engage in the daily recitation of the Lord's Prayer is, for believers, to be reminded afresh of the new community and the distinct narrative to which they are joined. To pray "*Our* Father in heaven, hallowed (holy) is your name" is to recognize that the Father is not *my* God, a God limited by national, cultural, gender or ethnic differences, but that the Wholly Other, transcendent in *otherness*, is *Father to all*. To join in prayer with those one has never met in Iraq, Rwanda, Palestine, Congo, Afghanistan, Colombia and Pakistan, with those who suffer on a daily basis the distress caused by the reality of hostility in the world, is to state that they are not mere faceless and voiceless Others, but are, *in* Christ, brothers and sisters. In appealing that "*Your* kingdom come. *Your* will be done, on earth as it is in heaven," believers both express their deepest desire that the hostility and enmity evident in the world will be overcome by the radical incoming peace of the kingdom, while renouncing the propensity to seek to bring about this reality according to their own time-frame and strategies. They are reminded that the kingdom of peace they long for ultimately begins with the quelling of their own fears, the conversion of their own *hostility*. In praying "Give us *our* daily bread" believers acknowledge that the gifts provided by God are not merely for personal sustenance, but rather, to truly be gifts, must be *passed on* and shared with others in greater need. And yet, this "passing on" of the gift of bread, it is reaffirmed, is only possible through the empowering grace of God. Thus, in asking for "forgiveness from our debts," believers confess the extent to which they continue to be marred by sin—that there remain recalcitrant aspects of their lives which they *struggle* to surrender to God's grace. In such an act of confession it is therefore impressed upon them anew that any attempt to "pass on" God's grace to Others goes hand in hand with a "passing over" of the sins of commission and omission that have been committed against them, that the giving of gifts must be accompanied by a *for-giving* of the hurts suffered at the hands of Others.

Acknowledging that their feeble attempts to "pass on" grace are themselves utterly dependent on both God's initial "passing over"— his overcoming and thus cancelling of a debt economy that leads to bondage and death—and his ongoing graciousness and transformation, believers are led to humbly recognize their reliance as recipients of this grace. Thus, those who have received forgiveness, offer forgiveness and those who have experienced the hospitality of God seek, through the Spirit's empowering, to offer this hospitality onto Others. Finally, the community of praying believers is led to admit the temptation it faces to hoard resources, to seek *distance* and comfort away from the discomforting *gaze* of the Other. Aware of such temptations, whispered by the Accuser through the medium of our televisions, talk-back radio, newspapers, web-blogs and neighborhood gossip, they ask that God by his Spirit will free them from such temptation and instead will lead them down the difficult, but ultimately more life-giving pathway, the path that leads to the stranger.

Late in his life Karl Barth became fond of stating that: "To clasp the hands in prayer is the beginning of an uprising against the disorder of the world." In reciting the Lord's Prayer, believers participate in a practice that opens them once more to God's disordering of their own internal hegemony such that they may therefore participate in his gracious purposes of reordering the world.

Eucharist

Finally, critical to the sustaining of a life of hospitality is participation in the character-forming sacrament of the Eucharist. Theological traditions differ regarding their understanding of the Eucharist. For some, the Eucharist, though inaugurated by Christ, is essentially a human practice, which primarily functions symbolically, as a means to assist the community in "remembering" the story of Christ. Others, harking back to the early church tradition of the "Love-Feast," suggest that the Eucharist is best understood ethically, as a summons to share one's resources and food with others. In sacramental traditions, the Eucharist involves the actual metaphysical presence of the risen Christ, and participation in this sacrament results in ontological transformation of the self as the believer takes the body of Christ into oneself. Following the same dynamic we noted with regard to Scripture and the Lord's Prayer we would contend that the Eucharist does not consist of a mere subjective recollection of Christ's death, the remembrance of an ethical "hero" we seek to honor and then emulate. Instead, the Eucharist is an actual encounter with the Risen Christ, the one who through his death and resurrection has overcome death and hostility. Participation with others in this Love-Feast is dependent therefore on an encounter with the first Gift-Giver, the "origin" of the love shared amongst those around the table. However, as we gather to feast upon the body and blood of Christ, we are called to respond appropriately to these gifts. Our ability to be truly "grateful," to offer "thanks"[80] and to engage in the life-giving cycle of gift reception, thanksgiving and *passing-on*, is dependent on the presence of grace within our lives. Receiving the gift of Christ's body and blood we are confronted once again with the actions or inaction which function as obstacles, blocking the passage of transforming grace. Hence the instructions of Jesus, that to receive God's gift and thus to participate as a vessel of God's divine love requires a reconciliation with others with whom we may be angry (Matt 5:23–24). Likewise, Paul stresses that for the Love-Feast really to be a feast of love requires that those present are "discerning the body" (1 Cor 11:27–34). To participate in God's gifts summons us to *pass-over* the barriers that divide. It is the deconstruction of barricaded lives and the bringing near of the Other who had been *distant*, which allows us to then *pass-on* God's gifts, to participate in the action of mutual gift-giving.

---

80. Eucharist is derived from the Greek word "eukaristos," meaning "grateful" or "thankful."

Thus, as with the reading of Scripture, and the recitation of the Lord's Prayer, participation in the sacrament of the Eucharist is, finally, not about comprehension, but rather about transformation. The presence of Christ in the Eucharist is not something to be seized and held on to but rather is a presence which in eluding our grasp, transforms us. As Cavanaugh suggests, in our participation in the Eucharist it is not we who are *doing the consuming*, but rather, we who are *being consumed*.[81]

Summary

In this chapter we have outlined the shape of the new ecclesial life entered into by those indwelt by the Spirit of Christ. In contrast to either the formalized contractual relations of market-hospitality, or the ethics of self-sacrifice proffered by our philosophical interlocutors, we have contended that the Ecclesia is the site of an alternative—*and the authentic*—form of human life. It is within the Ecclesia that human beings have the opportunity to find their true identity as gift-givers: receiving God's hospitality and empowered to *pass on* such grace, building relationships of mutuality in which gifts of love are exchanged with others. The performance of such gift-giving, in a world still ravaged by hostility, we have suggested, is characterized by five features: (1) the cheerfulness of the giver; (2) the extravagant nature of the gift; (3) the indiscriminate—universal and unconditional—nature of the giving; (4) the proximity of the giver to those who are receiving the gift, and (5) a quiet fortitude and patience in the face of suffering which stem from a confidence that Christ's resurrection means that hostility and inhospitality will not have the last word.

The sustaining of this life of hospitality, lived in the midst of the contemporary globalised world of *endless restlessness*, ongoing antagonism and antipathy, and overwhelming need, is found not in post-modern discourses, nor in the acquisition and consumption of the never-ending novelties of the market. Rather, it is through participation in the centuries-old practices and sacraments of the Ecclesia—Scripture, Prayer, Eucharist—that human beings finds themselves re-narrated into a new story, imbibe the principles of a new economy, and experience an ongoing transformation from hostile selves, fearful of others, to hospitable selves.

---

81. Cavanaugh, *Being Consumed*.

~~~~ *A tête à tête.*

Hosted by the Other

The Journey to Hospitality

(Luke 6:12–16; 9:1–6, 10–17, 51–55; 24:13–35)

JESUS' PLANS TO CREATE A NEW COVENANT PEOPLE WHO THROUGH THEIR lives will witness to the in-breaking hospitality of God's kingdom begin in a rather inauspicious way. His choice of disciples seems somewhat unusual to say the least. Two sets of brothers hailing from Galilee whose "friendly rivalry" from their lives as fishermen spilt over into this new domain as disciples. James and John had particularly fiery tempers and liked to ensure they came out on top. Also, like other Galileans, their fierce regional loyalty was accompanied by distrust, often extending to an outright disdain, of *Others* who did not fit into their plans. Philip, another Galilean from the same town as Simon and Andrew—practical and down to earth—always wanting to know with certainty the "where to" and "what for" (John 14:8), and his friend, Bartholomew. Then there was Matthew, the tax-collector, who understandably kept good distance from the other Simon who made it clear what he thought of this "low-life" collaborator. Blood on the floor would not have been a good look when the "Rabbi" was proclaiming lofty and unrealistic ideals such as "love of one's enemies." There were others jostling for position, seeking to gain favor with the Rabbi. And, there was Judas, who tended to stay aloof of these inner-group dynamics and power politics, concerned either with pragmatic questions: Was there sufficient money in the coffers to fund the ongoing "ministry" of the Rabbi and support crew? Or, with P.R. questions: How was "the ministry" being received by the power-brokers of the day? Altogether, as a rag-tag, motley assemblage, such a travelling troupe promised to be anything but harmonious.

Early in his ministry, Jesus organizes a field-trip, an "experiential-education" module, designed to expose his closest followers to the relations of mutuality integral to life in his kingdom (Luke 9:1–6). The diverse group of disciples are sent to the villages with no resources: bag, bread, money or tunic, their "ministry" and indeed personal sustenance, utterly dependent on the gifts provided by those they seek to minister to. And yet, while the disciples receive the welcome of the villagers, their own reception of these "needy" people is less forthcoming when the crowds later turn up uninvited, jeopardizing their planned private audience with their Rabbi. Indeed, in comparison to the warm welcome they had received from the villages, which had sustained them, allowing them to "bring the good news and cure diseases," the disciples' response to these same crowds is barely veiled hostility: "Send the crowd away, so that they may go into the surrounding villages and countryside, to lodge and get provisions; for we are here in a deserted place" (9:12). It could be suggested that such an instruction is simply an act of pragmatism by the disciples who are beginning to develop the necessary skills required for successful event management. But is this really the case? Could it be, rather, that the disciples, seeking to continue spinning tales of their exploits performed during "*their* mission" are envious of the crowds who now threaten to rob them of time with *their* Rabbi? While the disciples see the hospitality extended to them by the villagers as only right, a de-facto payment for their "teaching and healing" services rendered, here the disciples receive no benefit from the crowds, who rather pose a serious risk, threatening to drain the group's limited resources.

Jesus' audacious proposal that rather than send the crowds away to *purchase* their own provisions the disciples should cater for them, is met with bewilderment by his disciples. Keen to display their common-sense and increasing responsibility, the disciples point out that they have scarce resources—five loaves and two fish, sufficient to feed the thirteen of them. And then realizing that the ever-enigmatic Jesus must be having a laugh at their expense, they join in on the presumed joke, comically stating: ". . . unless we are to go and buy food for all these people!" (9:13). After all, who purchases food for over five thousand "free-loaders," most of whom they barely know? Who hosts, on the spur of the moment, a giant picnic catering for all-comers?

Having for once cottoned onto Jesus' humor, the more at ease disciples—awaiting the Rabbi's instructions now on how they will plan their retreat to share in their own simple fare of bread and fish—are stunned when Jesus proceeds to press the now tiresome joke further. Seating the throngs gathering before them into groups of fifty or so, the increasingly confused disciples find themselves, reluctantly at first but in mounting awe and amazement, participating in a miracle of hospitality. With mouths full and eyes wide open, the disciples find themselves caught up in a new economy, partaking in a foreshadowing of the ultimate banqueting feast.

Such an experience would be expected to alter one's conception of hospitality and gift-giving. Alas, while such incidences—including epiphanic encounters with Moses and Elijah—open the disciples to a new miraculous realm of the kingdom, they, like ourselves, are all too "human" in their brokenness. Competition, not mutuality, still characterizes their relations with one another (9:46–48). Making their way down to Jerusalem for an awaited confrontation with the religious and political elites, the disciples, pausing in the region of Samaria, attempt to find a resting place for their Rabbi. Snubbed by the Samaritan villagers on account of their intended destination, James and John, true to their name and in an exhibition of the fiery temper fuelled by an inner hatred towards the Other, seek to demonstrate their new faith in the miraculous by commanding fire down on their inhospitable hosts. Inauspicious indeed.

Time passes and two disciples, having travelled along with the twelve and others on this journey of learning and discovery, now make their way from the turbulence of Jerusalem to the relative safety of Emmaus. With heavy hearts and confused minds, fearful of the authorities, the two pedestrians are engaged in intense debate and discussion. As they seek to make sense of the tumultuous and ultimately traumatic events of the previous ten days—events which have culminated in the outrageous "idle tale" of "hysterical women" verified by Simon Peter—the two disciples are at first unaware of the presence of the fellow traveler. Interrupted from their discussion, suspicious and fearful, their *faces downcast* both emotionally and physically, vigilantly avoiding eye contact, they are reluctant to engage with this unknown stranger, and do so only when it becomes apparent that the newcomer is oblivious to the events that have transpired in Jerusalem. With a note of incredulity, Cleopas, one of the disciples, sets about filling the naive newcomer in on the events of their roller-coaster journey, revealing who they are and narrating how and why it is that they come to be on the road.

It is at the conclusion of their account, that this stranger then begins the process of re-narrating their story, discovering meaning within the seemingly chaotic chain of events, lifting the shroud of confusion from their veiled minds. They are intrigued at this stranger able to recast what appears to them as a jumbled set of random moments into a larger meta-narrative with meaning and purpose. Despite their fears, the two disciples now urge the stranger to receive their offer of hospitality and join them for an evening of further discussion.

Responding to their invitation in the affirmative, their guest, in actions that recall earlier experiences of hospitality and table fellowship "takes their bread, blesses it, breaks it and offers it back to them."[1] Suddenly the eyes of the disciples are opened. They realize that their traveling companion is in fact the resurrected Jesus, their dinner-guest, the true *Host*. However, their gaze upon Jesus does not bring closure to the moment; the now recognized face of Jesus is not captured or comprehended as a totality. As with other post-resurrection appearances, the *seeing* of the resurrected Jesus leads not to the ending of the story, but rather serves as the beginning of a new narrative. As with countless since, in the reading of Scripture, participation in the Eucharist, and offering of hospitality to the "stranger," the disciples have experienced an encounter with the living Christ. What follows is not inactivity and contemplative navel-gazing, but rather an *immediate* impulse to mission. In the dwindling light of day the disciples retrace their steps, returning to Jerusalem to testify to the dazzling, dawning light of the new post-resurrection world. So it is, with those who encounter the reality of the risen Jesus and experience the radical hospitality of the kingdom which overcomes inner hostility and transforms the self. Summoned out from behind closed doors where they hide from fear, they are empowered to go and live as agents of hospitality, signs of the new economy of the kingdom in the world in which they reside.[2]

1. Luke 9:16 and 22:19.

2. Such imagery draws on Jesus' post-resurrection appearance to the disciples in a locked and darkened room, where they hide "for fear of the Jews" (John 20:19–23). Jesus' entrance, while bringing peace to the disciples, does not lead to a closure to otherness, a stationary stagnancy within the Same. Rather, the breath of the Holy—aka "Disturbing"—Spirit gives rise to a missionary posture as Jesus commands that those who have received the gift of peace to enter into the world and interact with those they fear.

Conclusion

Grounded Hospitality

Community, Ecological Care, and Inter-Faith Relationships

BUILDING RELATIONSHIPS WITH THE STRANGER HAS BECOME INCREAS-
ingly difficult in an age where the dual discourses of the "war on terror"
and "the market" hold sway. The influence of these pervasive discourses
means Others come to be conceived as threats. The stranger is either to be
explicitly feared—a potential "terrorist" coming to "destroy civilization"
and our place in it—or, is simply another abstract commodity, at best,
to be "tolerated," or at worst, competing for limited resources, one to be
struggled against.

In response to this understanding of human relations, essentially
Hobbesian by nature, Emmanuel Levinas' and Jacques Derrida's philosophies of hospitality summon the individual to live not in disregard or fear
of the Other, but rather to recognize that the Other is already within the
self. That is, the self's very existence, constituted by the *call* issuing from
the *face* of the Other, is an existence of "infinite responsibility" *for* the
Other.

The Levinasian and Derridean emphasis on the primacy of the Other
and their placing of ethical subjectivity at the centre of their philosophies
provides a much needed corrective to much of Western philosophical
thought. Likewise, that the central metaphor which guides their ethical
thought is "hospitality" immediately strikes a chord with Christian theology and practice. Nonetheless, despite the richness of their respective
thought ultimately we have argued that the ethical philosophies of Levinas

and Derrida fail to provide a stable foundation upon which to construct an explicit Christian account of hospitality.

Throughout this work we have noted that the term "hospitality" itself, and therefore the practise of such an ethic, are shaped by an underlying ontology—narrative of being—and, by accompanying conceptions of eschatology and teleology. Thus, while Levinas insists that "My task does not consist of constructing ethics; I only try to find its meaning,"[1] the very nature of this meta-ethical project, with its search for meaning, involves—implicitly, at least—engagement with ontological questions. While the Levinasian and Derridean accent on the mystery and the non-classificatory nature of the Other is a positive feature of their thought, the accompanying emphasis on separation and the asymmetrical and unilateral structure they advocate for human relations appears rooted in a belief that violence between the self and the Other is unavoidable. It is the eschewal of any overarching narrative and the failure to explicitly offer an account of the *telos* that motivates human ethical behavior, or to offer a hope that the "hostility" that besets the world will eventually be overcome, which diminishes the achievement of Levinas' and Derrida's ambitious projects. Geoffrey Bennington summarizes our assessment when, referring to Derrida's philosophy, he observes: "Deconstruction . . . quite consistently, gives no grounds for any doctrinal epistemology, ontology or ethics."[2] Indeed, the fact that "deconstruction," while critiquing other theories is considerably more reticent about offering replacement theories or accounts—engaging in the process of "reconstruction"—is a failing that Derrida himself recognizes. Derrida states: "I don't think deconstruction 'offers' anything *as* deconstruction. That is sometimes what I am charged with: saying nothing, not offering any content or any proposition. I have never 'proposed' anything, and that is perhaps the essential poverty of my work. I never offered anything in terms of 'this is what you have to know' or 'this is what you have to do'. So deconstruction is a poor thing from that point of view."[3]

It is this "essential poverty," and therefore the vacuity of terms such as "difference" and the "Other," which means that this post-structuralist "ethic of hospitality" is also, ultimately, incapable of responding to the totalizing, hegemonic and exclusionary discourses of the contemporary world. Within the discourse of global capitalism, *differences* become

---

1. Levinas, *Ethics and Infinity*, 90.
2. Bennington, *Interrupting Derrida*, 16.
3. Derrida, "Hospitality, Justice and Responsibility," 74.

syncretistically and subtlety absorbed and then marketed as new lifestyles to adopt, new products to be consumed. And, as Alistair Kee suggests: "from the perspective of the ideology of exclusion/inclusion the excluded are not the Other from whom we might learn but merely the Lesser at whom we take fright."[4] "Otherness," "difference" and "hospitality" abstracted from any broader narrative account too easily become subsumed and subverted by the prevailing ideologies of the day.[5]

In contrast, the historical Christian faith offers a radically different account of the world than either that proclaimed by contemporary ideological discourses, or given by our French philosophers. According to Christian theology, a life of hospitality ultimately finds it basis not in a summons back to human ethicity, but rather is discovered *as humanity obediently responds in faith to the address of the Divine Other*, putting its hope in the hospitable actions of the Triune God, who, through the Incarnation of the Other and his "once for all" substitutionary sacrifice, has overcome hostility and death. In contrast to the deconstructed self whose relationship with the Other is of a unilateral and non-reciprocal nature, the Christian account testifies to the possibility of a redeemed relationality. As the Spirit—the Disturbing Other—transforms the optics and desires of the self, the Other comes to be seen not as one to be feared nor one to be struggled against. As the self surrenders to the overcoming-embracing love of God found in Christ, the appropriative urge to assimilate and consume the Other is replaced by a desire to enter relations of genuine mutuality.

The emergence of such relationships within a world scarred by histories of hostility and enmity, involves a long journey involving suffering and pain. To undertake such a pilgrimage requires courage and entails a spirituality of ongoing repentance and forgiveness. Still, despite its arduous nature, such a sojourn can be undertaken with confidence for two reasons: Firstly, because one travels the road not alone, but alongside others, and most significantly with a guiding—though often unseen—companion who has trod this path before. And, secondly, because there is the empowering hope that beyond this way of the cross is the promise of resurrection joy.

Unfortunately, the church, all too human, often loses sight of this radically "good news" as its imagination and desires fall prey to the distorting power of other narratives. There have though, even during the

4. Kee, "Blessed Are the Excluded," 362.

5. Ibid., 363.

darkest periods of human history, by God's grace, existed remnant communities, who through their faithful *imitative response*, have continued to give testimony to God's in-breaking hospitality. During the Second World War, Bonhoeffer, lamenting the state of the church in Germany, declared with hope: "The restoration of the church will surely come from a sort of new monasticism which has in common with the old only the uncompromising attitude of a life lived according to the Sermon on the Mount in the following of Christ. I believe it is now time to call people to this."[6]

With the decline of Western Christianity and the emergence of a new post-Christendom context, it is the appearance of such new monastic communities which, as well as keeping Christian faith alive in Western societies, offer perhaps a glimpse—though imprecise and dim—of such an alternative hospitable reality. Christine Pohl, in an appendix to her *Making Room*, highlights eight examples of such communities. Despite their different foci—ministry with the disabled, the poor, homeless, refugees, prisoners or students—their different settings, the distinctive spiritual practices that nourish them, and the different theological traditions upon which they draw, common to each of these communities is the practice of hospitality.[7]

Ultimately, we believe the theology of hospitality we have sketched in this work provides a rich metaphor to shape the ethical life and action of the Church. In particular there is tremendous richness in how a theological notion of hospitality could be applied to two prominent and pressing ethical concerns. The first of these is the contemporary ecological crisis. As noted in passing earlier, Levinas, his attention focused on inter-human relations, seems almost oblivious to the possibility of how his thought may be applied with regard to the non-Human Other. And, while Derrida touches on such questions, he never expands his ethics of

---

6. Bonhoeffer, *Testament to Freedom*, 424.

7. See Pohl, *Making Room*, 188–95. Pohl's list includes communities such as L'Abri, L'Arche, and the Catholic Worker. Other notable communities, which, despite their small size, have arguably played a critical role in the ongoing restoration of the Western church, include Taizé, Iona, and Sojourners. The last two decades has seen a proliferation of what has been termed "neo-monastic movements" in Western countries such as the United States, New Zealand, and Australia. Despite the different *charisms*, contexts, and structures of each of these communities—whether places of silent retreat and prayer, worship, catechism, ecological activism, or solidarity with the poor, whether gathered or dispersed, whether following formal monastic structures or being more organic by nature—the *raison d'être* of each of these communities is similar: a desire to model an alternative way of life in the chaos of late Western modernity.

hospitality explicitly into the field of ecological concerns.[8] However, in an age of anthropogenic global climate change, it is becoming abundantly clear that the plight of the human Other is inextricably related to the condition of the non-Human Other—eco-systems and the planet as a whole. Inter-human and ecological ethics cannot be treated as separate or distinct areas of discussion but must be understood together. What might a Christian theology of hospitality mean not only when the specter of global warming refugees looms large, but also when the very nature of life itself is threatened? What does the "welcoming of the Other" entail if the Other, usually construed as a stranger on the doorstep, is understood also as the threatened species living unbeknownst in the backyard? How might the metaphor of "hospitality" either work alongside, or perhaps, even move beyond metaphors more typically used to frame a Christian ethical response to the created world: metaphors such as dominion, stewardship, or partnership?

A second area of potential ethical application for such theologies of hospitality would be inter-religious relationships. While the twentieth century supposedly heralded the end of religious-motivated conflict, the flames of religious violence, post 9/11, have been reignited. Since 9/11, moderate voices within both Islam and Christianity have been at pains to point out that the conflict is not between "religions." But the reality must be faced that some religious leaders—both Islamic and Christian—their theology shaped by an apocalyptic millenarianism, do see the physical-military struggle as part of the cosmic battle between "good and evil."

In such a context, the practice of hospitality has a critical role in enabling and enhancing the building of relationships of mutual understanding and respect. Historically, inter-religious dialogue has often been an activity engaging theologians, clerics and religious leaders, in venues such as conference centers, religious institutions or universities. But in a world saturated with discourse and rhetoric, is the sharing of yet more words, even in the form of "civil" dialogue, the most appropriate response for cultivating understanding between religious devotees? Does inter-religious dialogue foster the reciprocity essential to the formation of a more just and peaceful "global village"? Some suggest that the starting point for inter-religious exchanges is not *dialogue*, but rather *hospitality*. Pierre-François De Bethune writes:

> Hospitality belongs to the realm of *ethos*, which consists in letting the other in, of ourselves entering the other's space.

8. For discussion on this see ch. 2, n14.

Communication is made by gestures, less explicit than language but also less ambiguous. It means sheltering a stranger or offering food. *It is antecedent to logos and goes beyond it.* It is essentially an experience. Therefore time, and still more warm-hearted attention, must be given to it.[9]

One practical example of such thinking is *The Abraham Path*, an initiative of the Global Negotiation Project at Harvard University, which seeks to build a route of cultural tourism following the footsteps of Abraham / Ibrahim through the countries of the Middle East.[10] It is hoped that everyday pilgrims from Judaism, Islam and Christianity, in retracing the steps of their shared founding Patriarch Abraham, will, in journeying together and being hosted by local families along the route—Muslim, Jewish or Christian—develop a greater understanding and mutual respect for one another. In a radio interview, William Ury, the Director of the Harvard Global Negotiation Project, suggests that the depth of animosity between people sometimes makes "face to face" encounters with the Other too painful or difficult. Instead, Ury notes, the "idea of the Abraham Path Initiative is a side-by side approach." Commenting further on this distinction between a "face to face" and "shoulder to shoulder" approach, Ury states:

Conversations are different when you're sitting across the table from someone than if you're going out for a walk, particularly in a beautiful setting. There's a kind of a quality of side-by-side activity that is more inclusive, that is more casual, is more informal, is less tense. The Abraham Path initiative is a side-by-side activity. I have this feeling and this faith that it will slowly create a space for thousands of conversations that will have all kinds of unexpected turns, that will hold the possibility of creating a new environment that holds the possibility of mutual respect and coexistence based on peace and justice.[11]

Ury's comments remind us that prior to the "face to face" encounter with the Other, so emphasized in Levinasian thought, the practice of hospitality commences by standing in solidarity and walking alongside the Other, "shoulder to shoulder." The example of Christ on the road to Emmaus is instructive. His journey with others begins first in silence, a simple case of accompanying alongside; progresses to respectful listening, and then only later does he begin to speak. It is such sojourning and careful

---

9. De Bethune, *By Faith and Hospitality*, 2–3.

10. See http://www.abrahampath.org/.

11. Ibid.

attentiveness which provides the basis for the "face to face" encounter and participation in table fellowship which follows.

The power of divine hospitality to transcend the exclusionary and distancing boundaries that humanity constructs both physically and psychologically has been the theme of this work. That God's hospitality can overcome seemingly insurmountable barriers is illustrated too in Luke's crucifixion narrative (Luke 23:39–47). Despite the spatial disjunction— three men physically "set apart" from their executors and detractors, "hung up" as objects, serving as deterring examples to others—a brief, but remarkable conversation takes place. The Jewish insurrectionist hanging beside Jesus, naked and broken, his campaign of "liberative terror" ended, inquires as to whether there is room in the divine kingdom for one such as him. Jesus responds: "I tell you the truth, today you will be with me in paradise." A few verses later, with Jesus' passing, a Roman centurion declares: "Surely this was a righteous man." Luke's narrative climaxes with a Jewish insurrectionist—read "terrorist"—and a Roman centurion—read "oppressor"—both recognizing in Christ, the face of divine hospitality.

The practice of hospitality transforms all individuals involved, overcoming fear, indifference and selfishness, creating mutual understanding and respect. More than this though, for Christians, there is the belief that in practising hospitality, in welcoming the stranger, we participate proleptically in an eschatological reality. This is the practise we are invited to perform as we await with longing and expectation the homecoming of the Triumphant Host and the final and eternal banquet where all who have seen the face of Christ—"victims" and "oppressors"—will be welcomed with open arms.

Bibliography

Adams, Rebecca. "Violence, Difference, Sacrifice: An Interview with René Girard." *Violence, Difference, Sacrifice: Conversation on Myth and Culture in Theology and Literature*, a special issue of *Religion and Literature* 25 (1993) 11–33.

Alison, James. *The Joy of Being Wrong: Original Sin through Easter Eyes*. New York: Crossroad, 1998.

Arendt, Hannah. *The Jew as Pariah: Jewish Identity and Politics in the Modern Age*. New York: Grove, 1978.

Attali, Jacques. *Millennium: Winners and Losers in the Coming World Order*. New York: Random House, 1991.

Augustine. *The City of God against the Pagans*. Edited and translated by R. W. Dyson. Cambridge: Cambridge University Press, 1998.

———. *The Confessions*. Translated by Maria Boulding. 2nd ed. Hyde Park, NY: New City, 1997.

———. *The Literal Meaning of Genesis (4.9.16)*. Translated by John Hammond Taylor. New York: Newman, 1982.

Bailey, Kenneth E. "The Shepherd Poems of John 10 and Their Culture." *Irish Biblical Studies* 15 (1993) 2–17.

Barth, Karl. *Church Dogmatics*. Vol. I/2, *The Doctrine of the Word of God*. Translated by G. T. Thomson and Harold Knight. Edited by Geoffrey Bromiley and T. F. Torrance. Edinburgh: T. & T. Clark, 1956.

———. *Church Dogmatics*. Vol. II/1, *The Doctrine of God*. Translated and edited by G. W. Bromiley and T. F. Torrance. Edinburgh: T. & T. Clark, 1957.

———. *Church Dogmatics*. Vol. III/1, *The Doctrine of Creation*. Translated by Harold Knight. Edited by Geoffrey Bromiley and T. F. Torrance. Edinburgh: T. & T. Clark, 1958.

———. *Church Dogmatics*. Vol. III/2, *The Doctrine of Creation*. Translated by Harold Knight et al. Edited by G. W. Bromiley and T. F. Torrance. Edinburgh: T. & T. Clark, 1960.

———. *Church Dogmatics*. III/4, *The Doctrine of Creation*. Edited by G. W. Bromiley and T. F. Torrance. Edinburgh: T. & T. Clark, 1960.

Bauman, Zygmunt. *Life in Fragments: Essays in Postmodern Morality*. Oxford: Blackwell, 1995.

Beasley-Murray, G. R. "Baptism." In *Dictionary of Paul and His Letter*, edited by Ralph P. Martin et al., 60–66. Downers Grove: InterVarsity, 1993.

Bell, Daniel M., Jr. "Forgiveness and the End of Economy." *Studies in Christian Ethics* 20 (2007) 325–44.

Benedict. *The Rule of St. Benedict*. Translated by Timothy Fry. New York: Vintage, 1998.

Bennington, Geoffrey. *Interrupting Derrida*. London: Routledge, 2000.

Bibliography

Benson, Bruce Ellis. *Graven Ideologies: Nietzsche, Derrida & Marion on Modern Idolatry.* Downers Grove: InterVarsity, 2002.

Benveniste, Emile. "Hospitality." In *Indo-European Language and Society,* translated by Elizabeth Palmer, 71–83. London: Faber and Faber, 1973.

Bernasconi, Robert. "What Is the Question to Which 'Substitution' Is the Answer?" In *The Cambridge Companion to Levinas,* edited by Simon Critchley and Robert Bernasconi, 234–51. Cambridge: Cambridge University Press, 2002.

Bernstein, Richard J. "Evil and the Temptation of Theodicy." In *The Cambridge Companion to Levinas,* edited by Simon Critchley and Robert Bernasconi, 252–67. Cambridge: Cambridge University Press, 2002.

———. *The New Constellation: The Ethical-Political Horizons of Modernity/Post-Modernity.* Cambridge: MIT Press, 1991.

Bethune, Pierre-François De. *By Faith and Hospitality: The Monastic Tradition as a Model for Interreligious Dialogue.* Leominster, UK: Gracewing, 2002.

Blanchot, Maurice. *The Writing of Disaster.* Translated by Ann Smock. Lincoln: University of Nebraska Press, 1995.

Boersma, Hans. "Penal Substitution and the Possibility of Unconditional Hospitality." *Scottish Journal of Theology* 57 (2004) 80–94.

———. *Violence, Hospitality and the Cross.* Grand Rapids: Baker Academic, 2004.

Boingeanu, Corneliu. "Personhood in Its Protological and Eschatological Patterns: An Eastern Orthodox View of the Ontology of Personality." *Evangelical Quarterly* 78 (2006) 3–19.

Bonhoeffer, Dietrich. *The Cost of Discipleship.* Translated by R. H. Fuller. London: SCM, 1948.

———. *Letters and Papers from Prison.* Translated by Reginald Fuller et al. Edited by Eberhard Bethge. London: SCM, 1971.

———. *A Testament to Freedom: The Essential Writings of Dietrich Bonhoeffer.* Edited by Geffrey B. Kelly and F. Burton Nelson. San Francisco: HarperOne, 1995.

Borg, Marcus. *Conflict, Holiness and Politics in the Teachings of Jesus.* New York: Mellen, 1984.

Borradori, Giovanna. *Philosophy in a Time of Terror: Dialogues with Jürgen Habermas and Jacques Derrida.* Chicago: University of Chicago Press, 2003.

Bouma-Prediger, Steven, and Brian Walsh. *Beyond Homelessness: Christian Faith in a Culture of Displacement.* Grand Rapids: Eerdmans, 2008.

Boyle, Nicholas. *Who Are We Now?* Edinburgh: T. & T. Clark, 1998.

Bretherton, Luke. *Hospitality as Holiness: Christian Witness amid Moral Diversity.* Aldershot, UK: Ashgate, 2006.

———. "Tolerance, Education and Hospitality: A Theological Proposal." *Studies in Christian Ethics* 17 (2004) 80–103.

Brock, Rita Nakashima. *Journeys by Heart: A Christology of Erotic Power.* New York: Crossroad, 1988.

Brown, Joanne Carlson. "Divine Child Abuse?" *Daughters of Sarah* 18 (1992) 24–28.

Brown, Joanne Carlson, and Rebecca Parker. "For God So Loved the World?" In *Christianity, Patriarchy and Abuse: A Feminist Critique,* edited by Joanne Carlson Brown and Carole R. Bohn, 1–30. New York: Pilgrim, 1989.

Brown, Raymond E. *The Gospel according to John.* 2 vols. Anchor Bible 29–29A. New York: Doubleday, 1966.

Buber, Martin. *I and Thou*. Translated by Ronald Gregor Smith. Edinburgh: T. & T. Clark, 1937.

———. "What Is Man?" In *Between Man and Man*. 2nd rev. ed. London: Routledge, 2002.

Butler, Judith. *Giving an Account of Oneself*. New York: Fordham University Press, 2005.

Caputo, John D. "Before Creation: Derrida's Memory of God." *Mosaic* 39 (2006) 91–102.

———, ed. *Deconstruction in a Nutshell: A Conversation with Jacques Derrida*. New York: Fordham University Press, 1997.

———. *The Prayers and Tears of Jacques Derrida: Religion without Religion*. Bloomington: Indiana University Press, 1997.

Cavanaugh, William T. *Being Consumed: Economics and Christian Desire*. Grand Rapids: Eerdmans, 2008.

Cerf, Vint. "If You Thought the Internet Was Cool, Wait until It Goes Space Age." *Observer*, 17 August 2008, 35.

Chilton, Bruce. *Abraham's Curse: Child Sacrifice in the Legacies of the West*. New York: Doubleday, 2008.

Ciaramelli, Fabio. "Levinas's Ethical Discourse between Individuation and Universality." In *Re-Reading Levinas*, edited by Robert Bernasconi and Simon Critchley, 83–105. Bloomington: Indiana University Press, 1991.

Cixous, Hélène. *Portrait of Jacques Derrida as a Young Jewish Saint*. New York: Colombia University Press, 2004.

Cohen, Richard A. Introduction to *Humanism of the Other*, by Emmanuel Levinas. Translated by Nidra Poller. Urbana: University of Illinois Press, 2003.

Critchley, Simon. Introduction to *The Cambridge Companion to Levinas*, edited by Simon Critchley and Robert Bernasconi, 1–32. Cambridge: Cambridge University Press, 2002.

———. "The Original Traumatism: Levinas and Psychoanalysis." In *Questioning Ethics: Contemporary Debates in Philosophy*, edited by Richard Kearney and Mark Dooley, 230–42. London: Routledge, 1999.

Crossan, John Dominic. *The Historical Jesus: The Life of a Mediterranean Jewish Peasant*. San Francisco: Harper, 1991.

Davidson, Ivor J. "Pondering the Sinlessness of Jesus Christ: Moral Christologies and the Witness of Scripture." *International Journal of Systematic Theology* 10 (2008) 372–98.

Davies, Oliver. *A Theology of Compassion: Metaphysics of Difference and the Renewal of Tradition*. London: SCM, 2001.

Davis, Colin. *Levinas: An Introduction*. Cambridge: Polity, 1996.

Derrida, Jacques. *Adieu to Emmanuel Levinas*. Translated by Pascale-Anne Brault and Michael Naas. Stanford: Stanford University Press, 1999.

———. "The Almost Nothing of the Unpresentable." In *Points . . . Interviews, 1974–1994*, edited by Elisabeth Weber, 78–88. Stanford: Stanford University Press, 1995.

———. "Circumfession: Fifty-Nine Periods and Periphrases." In *Jacques Derrida*, by Geoffrey Bennington and Jacques Derrida. Chicago: University of Chicago Press, 1993.

———. "Debat: Une Hospitalite sans condition." In *Manifeste pour l'hospitalite, aux Minguettes*, edited by Mohammed Seffahi, 133–42. Grigny: Paroles d'aube, 1999.

———. "Deconstruction and the Other: An Interview with Derrida." In *Dialogues with Contemporary Continental Thinkers: The Phenomenological Heritage*, edited by Richard Kearney, 107–26. Manchester: Manchester University Press, 1984.

———. "Dialanguages." In *Points . . . Interviews, 1974–1994*, edited by Elisabeth Weber, 132–55. Stanford: Stanford University Press, 1995.

———. "Différance." In *Margins of Philosophy*, 1–27. Chicago: University of Chicago Press, 1982.

———. "Discussion with Richard Kearney." In *God, the Gift, and Postmodernism*, edited by John D. Caputo and Michael J. Scanlon, 130–36. Bloomington: Indiana University Press, 1999.

———. "The Ends of Man." In *Margins of Philosophy*, 109–36. Chicago: University of Chicago Press, 1982.

———. *The Gift of Death*. Translated by David Wills. Chicago: University of Chicago Press, 1995.

———. *Given Time: I. Counterfeit Money*. Translated by Peggy Kamuf. Chicago: University of Chicago Press, 1992.

———. "*Honoris Causa*: This Is *Also* Extremely Funny." In *Points . . . Interviews, 1974–1994*, edited by Elisabeth Weber, 399–421. Stanford: Stanford University Press, 1995.

———. "Hospitality, Justice and Responsibility: A Dialogue with Jacques Derrida." In *Questioning Ethics: Contemporary Debates in Philosophy*, edited by Richard Kearny and Mark Dooley, 65–83. London: Routledge, 1999.

———. "Hostipitality." In *Acts of Religion*, edited by Gil Anidjar, 356–420. London: Routledge, 2002.

———. "Khôra." In *On the Name*, edited by Thomas Dutoit, 87–127. Stanford: Stanford University Press, 1995.

———. "A 'Madness' Must Watch Over Thinking." In *Points . . . Interviews, 1974–1994*, edited by Elisabeth Weber, 339–64. Stanford: Stanford University Press, 1995.

———. *Margins of Philosophy*. Translated by Alan Bass. Chicago: University of Chicago Press, 1982.

———. *Memoirs of the Blind: The Self-Portrait and Other Ruins*. Translated by Pascale-Anne Brault and Michael Naas. Chicago: University of Chicago Press, 1993.

———. *Monolingualism of the Other or the Prosthesis of Origin*. Translated by Patrick Mensah. Stanford: Stanford University Press, 1998.

———. *Of Grammatology*. Translated by Gayatri Chakravorty Spivak. 11th ed. Baltimore: John Hopkins University Press, 1992.

———. *On Cosmopolitanism and Forgiveness*. Translated by Mark Dooley. Edited by Simon Critchley and Richard Kearney. London: Routledge, 2001.

———. *The Other Heading: Reflections on Today's Europe*. Translated by Pascale-Anne Brault and Michael B. Naas. Bloomington: Indiana University Press, 1992.

———. *The Politics of Friendship*. Translated by George Collins. New York: Verso, 1997.

———. *Specters of Marx: The State of Debt, the World of Mourning, and the New International*. Translated by Peggy Kamuf. New York: Routledge, 1994.

———. "Structure, Sign and Play." In *Writing and Difference*, 278–93. Chicago: University of Chicago Press, 1978.

———. "The Time of a Thesis: Punctuations." In *Philosophy in France Today*, edited by Alan Montefiore, 34–50. Cambridge: Cambridge University Press, 1983.

———. "Violence and Metaphysics." In *Writing and Difference*, 79–153. Chicago: University of Chicago Press, 1978.

———. *Writing and Difference.* Translated by Alan Bass. Chicago: University of Chicago Press, 1978.

Derrida, Jacques, and Anne Dufourmantelle. *Of Hospitality.* Translated by Rachel Bowlby. Stanford: Stanford University Press, 2000.

Derrida, Jacques, and Maurizio Ferraris. *A Taste for the Secret.* Translated by Giacomo Donis. Edited by Giacomo Donis and David Webb. Cambridge: Polity, 2001.

Derrida, Jacques, and Elisabeth Roudinesco. "Unforeseeable Freedom." In *For What Tomorrow . . . A Dialogue*, 47–61. Stanford: Stanford University Press, 2004.

———. "Violence against Animals." In *For What Tomorrow . . . A Dialogue*, 62–76. Stanford: Stanford University Press, 2004.

Douglas, Mary. *Leviticus as Literature.* Oxford: Clarendon, 1999.

———. *Purity and Danger: An Analysis of Concepts of Pollution and Taboo.* Middlesex, UK: Penguin, 1970.

Drehle, David von. "A New Line in the Sand." *Time*, 7 July 2008, South Pacific edition, 26–33.

Dunnill, John. "Communicative Bodies and Economies of Grace: The Role of Sacrifice in the Christian Understanding of the Body." *Journal of Religion* 83 (2003) 79–93.

Fergusson, David. *Church, State and Civil Society.* Cambridge: Cambridge University Press, 2004.

Fisk, Robert. *The Great War for Civilization: The Conquest of the Middle East.* London: Fourth Estate, 2005.

Flanagan, Richard. *The Unknown Terrorist.* Sydney: Picador, 2006.

Ford, David F. *Self and Salvation: Being Transformed.* Cambridge: Cambridge University Press, 1999.

Friedman, Thomas L. *The Lexus and the Olive Tree.* New York: Anchor, 2000.

Frost, Michael. "Becoming the Poor." Video, 3:55. http://www.theworkofthepeople.com/becoming-the-poor.

Girard, René. *The Scapegoat.* Translated by Yvonne Freccero. Baltimore: Johns Hopkins University Press, 1986.

———. *Things Hidden since the Foundation of the World.* Translated by Stephen Bann and Michael Metteer. Stanford: Stanford University Press, 1987.

———. *Violence and the Sacred.* Translated by Patrick Gregory. Baltimore: Johns Hopkins University Press, 1977.

Gittins, Anthony J. *A Presence That Disturbs: A Call to Radical Discipleship.* Liguori, Missouri: Liguori/Triumph, 2002.

Green, Ronald M. "Enough Is Enough: *Fear and Trembling* Is *Not* about Ethics." *Journal of Religious Ethics* 21 (1993) 191–209.

Gunton, Colin E. *The Actuality of the Atonement: A Study of Metaphor, Rationality and the Christian Tradition.* London: T. & T. Clark, 1988.

———. *Christ and Creation.* Carlisle, UK: Paternoster, 1992.

———. *The One, the Three and the Many: God, Creation and the Culture of Modernity.* Cambridge: Cambridge University Press, 1993.

———. *The Promise of Trinitarian Theology.* 2nd ed. Edinburgh: T. & T. Clark, 1997.

Habel, Norman. *The Land Is Mine: Six Biblical Land Ideologies.* Minneapolis: Fortress, 1995.

Bibliography

Haenchen, Ernst. *John: A Commentary on the Gospel of John.* Translated and edited by Robert W. Funk. Vol. 1. Hermeneia. Philadelphia: Fortress, 1984.

Hari, Johann. "How We Fuelled the Deadliest War in the World—and It's Starting Again." *Huffington Post,* 29 October 2008. http://www.huffingtonpost.com/johann-hari/how-we-fuellled-the-deadl_b_139096.html.

Hart, David Bentley. *The Beauty of the Infinite: The Aesthetics of Christian Truth.* Grand Rapids: Eerdmans, 2004.

Hauerwas, Stanley. *The Peaceable Kingdom.* Notre Dame: University of Notre Dame Press, 1983.

———. *Sanctify Them in the Truth* Nashville: Abingdon, 1998.

Hays, Richard. "Ecclesiology and Ethics in 1 Corinthians." *Ex Auditu* 10 (1994) 31–43.

Hiebert, Paul. "The Category 'Christian' in the Mission Task." *International Review of Mission* 72 (1983) 421–27.

Horner, Robyn. *Rethinking God as Gift: Marion, Derrida and the Limits of Phenomenology.* New York: Fordham University Press, 2001.

Hugo, Victor. *Les Misérables.* Vol. 1. Ware, UK: Wordsworth, 1994.

Human Rights Watch. "'The Island of Happiness': Exploitation of Migrant Workers on Saadiyat Island, Abu Dhabi." May 2009. http://www.hrw.org/sites/default/files/reports/uae0509web_4.pdf.

Hütter, Reinhard. "Hospitality and Truth: The Disclosure of Reality in Worship and Doctrine." In *Bound to Be Free: Evangelical Catholic Engagements in Ecclesiology, Ethics and Ecumenism,* 56–77. Grand Rapids: Eerdmans, 2004.

Irigaray, Luce. "Questions to Emmanuel Levinas: On the Divinity of Love." In *Re-reading Levinas,* edited by Robert Bernasconi and Simon Critchley, 109–18. Bloomington: Indiana University Press, 1991.

Janicaud, Dominique. *Phenomenology and the "Theological Turn": The French Debate.* New York: Fordham University Press, 2000.

Johnson, Luke T. *The Writings of the New Testament: An Interpretation.* Philadelphia: Fortress, 1986.

Jones, Serene. "Graced Practices: Excellence and Freedom in the Christian Life." In *Practicing Theology: Beliefs and Practices in Christian Life,* edited by Miroslav Volf and Dorothy C. Bass, 51–77. Grand Rapids: Eerdmans, 2002.

Kant, Immanuel. *Foundations of the Metaphysics of Morals and What Is Enlightenment?* Translated by Lewis White Beck. Indianapolis: Bobbs-Merrill, 1959.

———. *To Perpetual Peace: A Philosophical Sketch (1795).* Translated by Ted Humphrey. Indianapolis: Hackett, 2003.

Katz, Claire Elise. "The Voice of God and the Face of the Other: Levinas, Kierkegaard, and Abraham." *Journal of Textual Reasoning* 10 (2001). http://jtr.lib.virginia.edu/archive/volume10/Katz.html.

Kearney, Richard, and Mara Rainwater, eds. *The Continental Philosophy Reader.* London: Routledge, 1996.

Kee, Alistair. "Blessed Are the Excluded." In *Public Theology for the 21st Century: Essays in Honour of Duncan B. Forrester,* edited by William F. Storrar and Andrew R. Morton, 351–64. London: T. & T. Clark, 2004.

Keller, Catherine. *The Face of the Deep: A Theology of Becoming.* London: Routledge, 2003.

Kierkegaard, Søren. *Fear and Trembling.* Translated by Walter Lowrie. Princeton: Princeton University Press, 1941.

Kilby, Karen. "Perichoresis and Projection: Problems with Social Doctrines of the Trinity." *New Blackfriars* 81 (2000) 432–45.

Krakauer, John. *Into the Wild*. London: Pan, 2007.

Lash, Nicholas. *Theology on the Way to Emmaus*. London: SCM, 1986.

Levinas, Emmanuel. *Difficult Freedom: Essays on Judaism*. Translated by Sean Hand. Baltimore: John Hopkins University Press, 1990.

———. *Ethics and Infinity: Conversations with Philippe Nemo*. Translated by Richard A. Cohen. Pittsburgh: Duquesne University Press, 1985.

———. "Ethics of the Infinite: An Interview with Emmanuel Levinas." In *Dialogues with Contemporary Continental Thinkers*, edited by Richard Kearney, 49–70. Manchester: Manchester University Press, 1984.

———. *Humanism of the Other*. Translated by Nidra Poller. Urbana: University of Illinois Press, 2003.

———. *In the Time of Nations*. Translated by Michael B. Smith. London: Athlone, 1994.

———. *Of God Who Comes to Mind*. Translated by Bettina Bergo. Stanford: Stanford University Press, 1998.

———. *Otherwise than Being or Beyond Essence*. Translated by Alphonso Lingis. Dordrecht, Netherlands: Kluwer Academic, 1991. Reprint.

———. *Outside the Subject*. Translated by Michael B. Smith. Stanford: Stanford University Press, 1993.

———. *Proper Names*. Translated by Michael B. Smith. London: Athlone, 1996.

———. *Totality and Infinity: An Essay in Exteriority*. Translated by Alphonso Lingis. Pittsburgh: Duquesne University Press, 1969.

Levinas, Emmanuel, and Richard Kearney. "Dialogue with Emmanuel Levinas." In *Face to Face with Levinas*, edited by Richard Cohen, 13–33. Albany: State University of New York Press, 1986.

Lewis, C. S. "Is Theology Poetry?" In *They Asked for a Paper*, 150–65. London: Bles, 1962.

———. "The Weight of Glory." In *Screwtape Proposes a Toast and Other Pieces*, 94–110. London: Collins-Fontana, 1965.

Llewelyn, John. "Am I Obsessed by Bobby? (Humanism of the Other Animal)." In *Re-reading Levinas*, edited by Robert Bernasconi and Simon Critchley, 234–45. Bloomington: Indiana University Press, 1991.

———. *Emmanuel Levinas: The Genealogy of Ethics*. London: Routledge, 1995.

MacIntyre, Alasdair. *After Virtue: A Study in Moral Theory*. 2nd ed. London: Duckworth, 1994.

Marion, Jean-Luc. *Being Given: Toward a Phenomenology of Givenness*. Translated by Jeffrey L. Kosky. Stanford: Stanford University Press, 2002.

———. *Excess: Studies in Saturated Phenomenon*. Translated by Robyn Horner and Vincent Berraud. New York: Fordham University Press, 2002.

———. *God Without Being*. Translated by Thomas A. Carlson. Chicago: University of Chicago Press, 1991.

———. "In the Name." In *God, the Gift, and Postmodernism*, edited by John D. Caputo and Michael J. Scanlon, 20–53. Bloomington: Indiana University Press, 1999.

Marks, Herbert. "Biblical Naming and Poetic Etymology." *Journal of Biblical Literature* 114 (1995) 21–42.

Bibliography

Marshall, Christopher D. "Atonement, Violence and the Will of God: A Sympathetic Response to J. Danny Weaver's *The Nonviolent Atonement*." *Mennonite Quarterly Review* 77 (2003) 69–92.

———. *Beyond Retribution: A New Testament Vision for Justice, Crime and Punishment*. Auckland: Lime Grove, 2001.

Mauss, Marcel. *The Gift: The Form and Reason for Exchange in Archaic Societies*. Translated by W. D. Halls. London: Routledge, 1990.

McFadyen, Alistair I. *The Call to Personhood: A Christian Theory of the Individual in Social Relationships*. Cambridge: Cambridge University Press, 1990.

Melchert, Norman. *The Great Conversation: A Historical Introduction to Philosophy*. 5th ed. Vol. 1. Oxford: Oxford University Press, 2006.

Mensch, James. "Abraham and Isaac: A Question of Theodicy." In *Hiddenness and Alterity: Philosophical and Literary Sightings of the Unseen*, 175–97. Pittsburgh: Duquesne University Press, 2005.

Milbank, John. "Can a Gift Be Given? Prolegomena to a Future Trinitarian Metaphysic." *Modern Theology* 11 (1995) 119–61.

———. "The Soul of Reciprocity, Part One: Reciprocity Refused." *Modern Theology* 17 (2001) 335–91.

———. "The Soul of Reciprocity, Part Two: Reciprocity Granted." *Modern Theology* 17 (2001) 485–507.

———. *Theology and Social Theory: Beyond Secular Reason*. Oxford: Blackwell, 1993.

———. *The Word Made Strange: Theology, Language, Culture*. Cambridge: Blackwell, 1997.

Milne, Bruce. *The Message of John*. Leicester, UK: InterVarsity, 1993.

MoLoney, Anastasia. "Vigilante Heaven." *New Internationalist* 376 (2005) 22–24. http://newint.org/features/2005/03/01/death-squads/.

Moltmann, Jürgen. *The Crucified God: The Cross of Christ as the Foundation and Criticism of Christian Theology*. London: SCM, 1974.

———. *Theology and Joy*. Translated by Richard Ulrich. London: SCM, 1973.

Moorehead, Caroline. *Human Cargo: A Journey among Refugees*. London: Chatto & Windus, 2005.

Moran, Dominic. "Decisions, Decisions: Derrida on Kierkegaard and Abraham." *Telos* 123 (2002) 107–30.

Myers, Ched. *Binding the Strong Man: A Political Reading of Mark's Story of Jesus*. 2nd ed. Maryknoll: Orbis, 2008.

Newman, Elizabeth. *Untamed Hospitality: Welcoming God and Other Strangers*. Grand Rapids: Brazos, 2007.

Nouwen, Henri J. M. *Reaching Out: The Three Movements of the Spiritual Life*. Glasgow: Collins, 1976.

Nutu, Ela. *Incarnate Word, Inscribed Flesh: John's Prologue and the Postmodern*. Sheffield: Sheffield Phoenix, 2007.

O'Donovan, Oliver. *Resurrection and Moral Order: An Outline for Evangelical Ethics*. Leicester, UK: InterVarsity, 1986.

Ogletree, Thomas W. *Hospitality to the Stranger: Dimensions of Moral Understanding*. Philadelphia: Fortress, 1985.

Olthuis, James H. "Crossing the Threshold: Sojourning Together in the Wild Spaces of Love." In *The Hermeneutics of Charity: Interpretation, Selfhood, and Postmodern*

Faith, edited by James K. A. Smith and Henry Isaac Venema, 23–40. Grand Rapids: Brazos, 2004.

———. "Face-to-Face: Ethical Asymmetry or the Symmetry of Mutuality?" In *The Hermeneutics of Charity: Interpretation, Selfhood, and Postmodern Faith*, edited by James K. A. Smith and Henry Isaac Venema, 135–56. Grand Rapids: Brazos, 2004.

Peters, Ted. *God as Trinity: Relationality and Temporality in Divine Life*. Louisville: Westminster John Knox, 1993.

Phillips, Peter. "The Cross of Christ, Sacrifice and Sacred Violence." *New Blackfriars* 8 (2000) 256–64.

Pickstock, Catherine. *After Writing: On the Liturgical Consummation of Philosophy*. Oxford: Blackwell, 1998.

Pohl, Christine D. *Making Room: Recovering Hospitality as a Christian Tradition*. Grand Rapids: Eerdmans, 1999.

Purcell, Michael. *Levinas and Theology*. Cambridge: Cambridge University Press, 2006.

Putnam, Robert D. *Bowling Alone: The Collapse and Revival of American Community*. New York: Simon & Schuster, 2000.

Rawls, John. *A Theory of Justice*. Rev. ed. Oxford: Oxford University Press, 1999.

Reynolds, Jack. "The Other of Derridean Deconstruction: Levinas, Phenomenology and the Question of Responsibility." *Minerva—An Internet Journal of Philosophy* 5 (2001). http://www.minerva.mic.ul.ie/vol5/derrida.html.

Ricoeur, Paul. *Oneself as Another*. Translated by Kathleen Blamey. Chicago: University of Chicago Press, 1992.

Robbins, Lionel. *An Essay on the Nature and Significance of Economic Science*. London: Macmillan, 1952.

Robinette, Brian. "A Gift to Theology? Jean-Luc Marion's 'Saturated Phenomenon' in Christological Perspective." *Heythrop Journal* 48 (2007) 86–108.

Rorty, Richard. "Habermas and Lyotard on Postmodernity." In *Essays on Heidegger and Others: Philosophical Papers*, 164–77. Cambridge: Cambridge University Press, 1991.

Rosello, Mireille. *Postcolonial Hospitality: The Immigrant as Guest*. Stanford: Stanford University Press, 2001.

Rubenstein, Mary-Jane. "Relationality: The Gift after Ontotheology." *Telos* 123 (2002) 65–80.

Ruether, Rosemary Radford. *Sexism and God-Talk: Toward a Feminist Theology*. London: SCM, 1983.

Sarna, Nahum M. *Genesis*. JPS Torah Commentary. Philadelphia: Jewish Publication Society, 1989.

Schnackenburg, Rudolf. *The Gospel according to St. John*. Translated by Kevin Smyth. Vol. 1., *Introduction and Commentary on Chapters 1–4*. London: Burns & Oates, 1968.

Schwartz, Regina. *The Curse of Cain: The Violent Legacy of Monotheism*. Chicago: University of Chicago Press, 1997.

Smith, James K. A. "The Call as Gift: The Subject's Donation in Marion and Levinas." In *The Hermeneutics of Charity: Interpretation, Selfhood, and Postmodern Faith*, edited by James K. A. Smith and Henry Isaac Venema, 217–27. Grand Rapids: Brazos, 2004.

———. "*In Memoriam*: Jacques Derrida (1930–2004)." *ChristianityToday.com*, 1 October 2004. http://www.christianitytoday.com/ct/2004/octoberweb-only/10-18-24.0.html.

———. *Jacques Derrida: Live Theory*. New York: Continuum, 2005.

Sommer, Mark. "From Turmoil to Tourism: Following the Path of Abraham." Radio broadcast, 55:00. 1 January 2006. A World of Possibilities: The World of Islam series. Produced by Mainstream Media Project. http://www.prx.org/pieces/15454-from-turmoil-to-tourism-following-the-path-of-abr.

Sutherland, Arthur. *I Was a Stranger: A Christian Theology of Hospitality*. Nashville: Abingdon, 2006.

Swartley, Willard M. "Discipleship and Imitation of Jesus/Suffering Servant: The Mimesis of New Creation." In *Violence Renounced: René Girard, Biblical Studies and Peacemaking*, edited by Willlard M. Swartley, 218–45. Telford, PA: Pandora, 2000.

Tanner, Kathryn. *Economy of Grace*. Minneapolis: Fortress, 2005.

———. *Jesus, Humanity and the Trinity: A Brief Systematic Theology*. Edinburgh: T. & T. Clark, 2001.

———. "Kingdom Come: The Trinity and Politics." *Princeton Seminary Bulletin* 28 (2007) 129–45.

Taylor, Mark C. *Erring: A Postmodern A/theology*. Chicago: University of Chicago Press, 1984.

Thiessen, Karen Heidebrecht. "Jesus and Women in the Gospel of John." *Direction: A Mennonite Brethren Forum* 19 (1990) 52–64.

Torrance, Alan J. *Persons in Communion: Trinitarian Description and Human Participation*. Edinburgh: T. & T. Clark, 1996.

Torrance, James B. "Covenant or Contract? A Study of the Theological Background of Worship in Seventeenth-Century Scotland." *Scottish Journal of Theology* 23 (1970) 51–76.

Torrance, T. F. *The Christian Doctrine of God: One Being, Three Persons*. Edinburgh: T. & T. Clark, 1996.

———. *The Trinitarian Faith: The Evangelical Theology of the Ancient Catholic Church*. Edinburgh: T. & T. Clark, 1988.

Trible, Phyllis. "Depatriarchalizing in Biblical Interpretation." *Journal of the American Academy of Religion* 41 (1973) 30–48.

Turner, M. M. B. "Holy Spirit." In *Dictionary of Jesus and the Gospels*, edited by Joel B. Green and Scot McKnight, 341–51. Downers Grove: InterVarsity, 1992.

UNICEF. *Progress of Nations 2000*. New York: UNICEF, 2000. http://www.unicef.org/publications/index_5628.html.

United Nations, Department of Economic and Social Affairs, Population Division. *Trends in International Migrant Stock: The 2008 Revision*. July 2009. http://www.un.org/esa/population/migration/UN_MigStock_2008.pdf.

United Nations Development Programme. *Human Development Report 1999*. New York: Oxford University Press, 1999. http://hdr.undp.org/sites/default/files/reports/260/hdr_1999_en_nostats.pdf.

Valevicius, Andrius. *From the Other to the Totally Other: The Religious Philosophy of Emmanuel Levinas*. New York: Lang, 1988.

Vanier, Jean. *Community and Growth*. 2nd ed. Sydney: St. Paul, 1980.

Veling, Terry A. *Practical Theology: "On Earth as It Is in Heaven."* Maryknoll: Orbis, 2005.

Volf, Miroslav. *After Our Likeness: The Church as the Image of the Trinity.* Grand Rapids: Eerdmans, 1998.

———. *Exclusion and Embrace: A Theological Exploration of Identity, Otherness, and Reconciliation.* Nashville: Abingdon, 1996.

———. *Free of Charge: Giving and Forgiving in a Culture Stripped of Grace.* Grand Rapids: Zondervan, 2006.

———. "Living with the Other." *Journal of Ecumenical Studies* 39 (2002) 8–25.

———. "Theology for a Way of Life." In *Practicing Theology: Beliefs and Practices in Christian Life*, edited by Miroslav Volf and Dorothy C. Bass, 245–63. Grand Rapids: Eerdmans, 2002.

———. "The Trinity Is Our Social Programme: The Doctrine of the Trinity and the Shape of Social Engagement." In *The Doctrine of God and Theological Ethics*, edited by Alan J. Torrance and Michael Banner, 105–24. London: T. & T. Clark, 2006.

Volf, Miroslav, and Judith M. Gundry-Volf. *A Spacious Heart: Essays on Identity and Belonging.* Harrisburg, PA: Trinity, 1997.

Von Rad, Gerhard. *Genesis: A Commentary.* Translated by John H. Marks. 2nd rev. ed. London: SCM, 1963.

Waldenfels, Bernhard. "Levinas and the Face of the Other." In *The Cambridge Companion to Levinas*, edited by Simon Critchley and Robert Bernasconi, 63–81. Cambridge: Cambridge University Press, 2002.

Ware, Timothy. *The Orthodox Church.* Rev. ed. London: Penguin, 1987.

Weaver, J. Denny. *The Nonviolent Atonement.* Grand Rapids: Eerdmans, 2001.

Webster, John. Review of *Self and Salvation*, by David F. Ford. *Scottish Journal of Theology* 54 (2001) 548–59.

Wells, Samuel. *Improvisation: The Drama of Christian Ethics.* Grand Rapids: Brazos, 2004.

Westerhoff, Caroline A. *Good Fences: The Boundaries of Hospitality.* Harrisburg, PA: Morehouse, 2004.

Westphal, Merold. Review *Of God Who Comes to Mind*, by Emmanuel Levinas. *Modern Theology* 15 (1999) 522–24.

Whitacre, Rodney A. *John.* IVP New Testament Commentary. Downers Grove: InterVarsity, 1999.

Wilks, John. "The Trinitarian Ontology of John Zizioulas." *Vox Evangelica* 25 (1995) 63–88.

Williams, Rowan. *On Christian Theology.* Oxford: Blackwell, 2000.

Wood, David. *The Deconstruction of Time.* Edited by John Sallis. Atlantic Highlands, NJ: Humanities, 1989.

———. "Much Obliged." *Philosophy Today* 41 (1997) 135–40.

Wright, Addison G. "The Widow's Mite: Praise or Lament?—A Matter of Context." *Catholic Biblical Quarterly* 44 (1982) 256–65.

Wright, N. T. "How Can the Bible Be Authoritative?" *Vox Evangelica* 21 (1991) 7–32.

———. *Jesus and the Victory of God: Christian Origins and the Question of God.* London: SPCK, 1996.

Wright, Tamra, et al. "The Paradox of Morality: An Interview with Emmanuel Levinas." In *The Provocation of Levinas: Rethinking the Other*, edited by Robert Bernasconi and David Wood, 168–80. London: Routledge, 1988.

Wyschogrod, Edith. *Emmanuel Levinas: The Problem of Ethical Metaphysics.* The Hague: Nijhoff, 1974.

———. "Language and Alterity in the Thought of Levinas." In *The Cambridge Companion to Levinas,* edited by Simon Critchley and Robert Bernasconi, 188–205. Cambridge: Cambridge University Press, 2002.

Yannaras, Christos. *The Freedom of Morality.* Translated by Elizabeth Briere. Crestwood, NY: St. Vladimir's Seminary Press, 1984.

Yoder, John Howard. *The Politics of Jesus.* Grand Rapids: Eerdmans, 1972.

Zimmermann, Nigel K. "Karol Wojtyla and Emmanuel Levinas on the Embodied Self: The Forming of the Other as Moral Self-Disclosure." *Heythrop Journal* 50 (2009) 982–95.

Zizioulas, John D. *Being as Communion: Studies in Personhood and the Church.* Crestwood, NY: St. Vladimir's Seminary Press, 1985.

———. *Communion and Otherness: Further Studies in Personhood and the Church.* Edited by Paul McPartlan. London: T. & T. Clark, 2006.

Made in the USA
Columbia, SC
25 July 2019